Developing Web Components with Svelte

Building a Library of Reusable UI Components

Second Edition

Alex Libby

Apress®

Developing Web Components with Svelte: Building a Library of Reusable UI Components, Second Edition

Alex Libby
Belper, Derbyshire, UK

ISBN-13 (pbk): 979-8-8688-1179-1   ISBN-13 (electronic): 979-8-8688-1180-7
https://doi.org/10.1007/979-8-8688-1180-7

Managing Director, Apress Media LLC: Welmoed Spahr
Acquisitions Editor: James Robinson-Prior
Development Editor: James Markham
Coordinating Editor: Gryffin Winkler

Cover designed by eStudioCalamar

Cover image by Freepik.com

Distributed to the book trade worldwide by Apress Media, LLC, 1 New York Plaza, New York, NY 10004, U.S.A. Phone 1-800-SPRINGER, fax (201) 348-4505, e-mail orders-ny@springer-sbm.com, or visit www.springeronline.com. Apress Media, LLC is a California LLC and the sole member (owner) is Springer Science + Business Media Finance Inc (SSBM Finance Inc). SSBM Finance Inc is a **Delaware** corporation.

For information on translations, please e-mail booktranslations@springernature.com; for reprint, paperback, or audio rights, please e-mail bookpermissions@springernature.com.

Apress titles may be purchased in bulk for academic, corporate, or promotional use. eBook versions and licenses are also available for most titles. For more information, reference our Print and eBook Bulk Sales web page at http://www.apress.com/bulk-sales.

Any source code or other supplementary material referenced by the author in this book is available to readers on GitHub (https://github.com/Apress). For more detailed information, please visit https://www.apress.com/gp/services/source-code.

If disposing of this product, please recycle the paper

This is dedicated to my family, with thanks for their love and support while writing this book.

Table of Contents

About the Author

Alex Libby is a front-end engineer and seasoned book author who hails from England. His passion for all things open source dates back to the days of his degree studies, where he first came across web development and has been hooked ever since. His daily work involves extensive use of React, Node.js, JavaScript, HTML, and CSS. Alex enjoys tinkering with different open source libraries to see how they work. He has spent a stint maintaining the jQuery Tools library and enjoys writing about open source technologies, principally for front-end UI development.

About the Technical Reviewer

Vadim Atamanenko is an experienced software engineer with over 25 years of experience, a senior member of the IEEE and Harvard Square associations, and an active participant in the scientific community. He is the author of numerous scientific articles, an expert in international hackathons, a lecturer in software development courses, and currently serves as the Head of the Development Department at Freedom Life Insurance Company. Vadim also shares his knowledge and expertise through more than 40 articles published in online publications in two languages (English and Russian). He is always open to meeting new people and exchanging knowledge.

Acknowledgments

Writing a book can be a long but rewarding process; it is not possible to complete it without the help of other people. I would like to offer a huge vote of thanks to my editors, in particular, Nirmal Selvaraj and James Robinson-Prior; my thanks also to Vadim Atamanenko as my technical reviewer, James Markham for his help during the process, and others at Apress for getting this book into print. All have made writing this book a painless and enjoyable process, even with the edits!

My thanks also to my family for being understanding and supporting me while writing. I frequently spend a lot of late nights writing alone or pass up times when I should be with them, so their words of encouragement and support have been a real help in getting past those bumps in the road and producing the finished book that you now hold in your hands.

Introduction

Developing Web Components with Svelte, Second Edition is for people who want to learn how to quickly create web components that are efficient and fast using the upcoming Svelte framework and associated tools.

This project-oriented book simplifies the setting up of a Svelte web component library as a starting point before beginning to explore the benefits of using Svelte to create components not only usable in this framework but equally reusable in others such as React, Vue, and Angular. We can use this as a basis for developing an offer that we can customize to our needs, across multiple frameworks. It will equip you with a starting toolset that you can use to create future component libraries, incorporate the processes into your workflow, and that will allow you to take your components to the next level.

Throughout this book, I'll take you on a journey through creating the base library, before adding a variety of components such as a select box, tabs, and the typical tooltip components. We will also touch on subjects such as writing documentation, testing components, and deploying into production – showing you how easy it is to develop simple components that we can augment later quickly. With the minimum of fuss and plenty of practical exercises, we'll focus on topics such as building the functionality, styling, testing in a self-contained environment, and more – right through to producing the final result viewable from any browser!

Developing Web Components with Svelte, Second Edition uses nothing more than standard JavaScript, CSS, and HTML, three of the most powerful tools available for developers: you can enhance, extend, and configure your components as requirements dictate. With Svelte, the art of possible is only limited by the extent of your imagination and the power of JavaScript, HTML, and Node.js.

Changes in This Edition

Below are some of the changes made for this edition of *Developing Web Components with Svelte*:

- Updated Storybook to version 8

- Updated Svelte to version 4

- Refactored all Storybook stories to use a newer format, switching from default Svelte to JavaScript

- Fixed issues in the RadioButton component

- Included a new section on accessibility

- Included a new Animation chapter and components: Alarm, Switch, and ProgressBar

- Updated installation of Svelte project to use Vite as a replacement: this bypasses workarounds used when creating the original library project

- Refreshed color scheme to new shade and named library GarnetUI (to avoid confusion)

- Added coverage testing

- Added a new Avatar component as conversion from React to Svelte

- Updated documentation to use a new format as part of the update to Storybook 8

- Switched to using Vitest from Svelte Testing Library
- Removed the SideBar component (as this didn't work well in Storybook)
- Added a new Switch component

CHAPTER 1

Getting Started

Let's suppose for a moment that you've spent any time developing with frameworks such as React. In that case, I'm sure you will have come across the principle of creating web components. We can drop these self-contained, reusable packages of code into any number of projects, with only minor tweaks needed to configure the package for use in your project. Sound familiar?

What if you found yourself creating multiple components and were beginning to reuse them across multiple projects? We could use them individually, but that wouldn't be the most effective way – instead, why not create a component library?

Creating such a library opens some real possibilities – we could build our library around standard components that everyone uses or focus on a select few that follow a theme, such as forms. At this point, you're probably assuming that we'd do something in React, right?

Wrong. Anyone who knows me knows that I like to keep things simple – while there is nothing technically wrong with React (it's a great framework), I want to do something different.

We will build such a component library for this book, but the framework I've elected to use is a relatively new kid on the block – Svelte. It, however, won't just be **another** library, but one based around web components! Why, I hear you ask?

© Alex Libby 2025
A. Libby, *Developing Web Components with Svelte*,
https://doi.org/10.1007/979-8-8688-1180-7_1

There are many reasons for doing this, but performance is the most important one – Svelte's architecture is different from most frameworks, making it superfast than many of its rivals and one that suits web component architecture perfectly. It means we can create something in Svelte (easy to pick up) and use it in React, Angular, Vue, and so on. Any framework that uses JavaScript (and potentially npm packages) can effectively use this library. Throughout this book, we'll explore how to write web components using Svelte, bring them together in a unified library, and explore the steps required to release them to the world at large with minimal effort.

In time-honored tradition, we must start somewhere – there's no better place than to start with a look at what we will create through this book, set some boundaries, and get some of the tools and resources ready for use. Let's first answer this question before we do so (and get anyone up to speed who hasn't used web components).

What Are Web Components?

To answer this question, we must go back ten years to the Fronteers Conference in 2011, where web components were first introduced to developers.

There are many ways to describe what a web component is, but I like the definition given by Riccardo Canella in his article on the Medium website, where he states that

> ...Web components are a set of web platform APIs that allow you to create new custom, reusable, encapsulated HTML tags to use in web pages and web apps.

This definition is just a tiny part of what they are – in addition, it's essential to know that they

- Are based on web standards and will work across modern browsers

- Can be used with any JavaScript-based framework

Wow – that's powerful stuff! Gone are the days when we had to use a React component in a React-based site or, likewise, for Angular. Just imagine: we could build a component in Svelte and then use it in different frameworks – as long as they are based on JavaScript.

There is one question, though, that I bet some of you are asking: Why choose Svelte? It's a valid question, as Svelte is not as well known as other frameworks such as React.

However, there are three reasons for choosing this framework:

- It's a fair bet that many of you use React in some capacity; we could develop a web component in React, but we would be missing out on one key factor: interoperability. We need to build the component using a different framework, such as Svelte.

- Svelte's architecture pushes compilation into the build process, preventing the need for a runtime library when operating in a browser (unlike its competitors such as React). It means the end code is superfast – it doesn't have the overhead of that library, plus compiled code is as close as you will get to pure HTML, CSS, and JavaScript.

- Svelte's developers decided not to reinvent the wheel –
  if JavaScript already has a perfectly adequate solution,
  then Svelte uses this instead of trying to add a custom
  equivalent!

- Svelte is designed to include markup and styling for a
  component in one file, not multiple. Each component
  is self-contained, making it more portable and suited to
  a web component design.

- This lightweight architecture also means that any
  core dependencies will be minimal compared to
  frameworks such as React. Any that we need will be just
  those required to operate the framework – it does not
  include any extra dependencies for operations such as
  manipulating date or time.

Okay – enough talk: let's crack on with something a little more
practical! Before we get into the nuts and bolts of building our library, let's
first have a quick peek at a small example I've put together to see how a
Svelte-based web component works in more detail.

For this book, we'll create a folder called `garnet` for our library. I will
refer to this as the "project folder" – please use this folder unless
otherwise indicated in the text.

Taking First Steps

For the first demo, I've reworked an example by Simon O. available
from GitHub – you can see the original version at `https://github.com/`
`FroyoNom/Svelte-Weather-Forecast`. I've simplified my version to only
display the current weather, hard-code the location to New York (Apress'
office!), and use the `luxon` date library instead to provide the current date.

You may get a request from the browser asking for your location in this demo – please click Allow. We need this for the demo to operate correctly.

Okay – let's crack on with the demo.

RUNNING A DEMO COMPONENT

To run the weather component demo, follow these steps:

1. First, we need to get a key from OpenWeatherMap.org – head over to `https://home.openweathermap.org/users/sign_up`, and sign up with the correct details (it's a free service, although I would recommend using a free email address such as Gmail). Make sure you store the key safely, as we will need it later in this exercise.

2. Next, go ahead and download the archive file from the code download accompanying this book – extract the contents to a new folder called `weather-app`, not your project folder.

3. Once extracted, open the `.env` file at the root of the folder you created in step 2, then add your API key from step 1, as indicated in the file.

4. Fire up a Node.js terminal session, then change the working folder to that separate folder from the previous step.

5. At the prompt, enter `npm install` to install the demo, and press Enter.

6. Once done, enter `npm run dev` at the prompt, and press Enter to run the application. We should see a weather component displayed on the page if all is well, as shown in Figure 1-1.

Figure 1-1. The OpenWeatherMap component demo

I designed that demo to be a quick and easy start, although it, in reality, hides a lot of code under the covers. At face value, it would be difficult to tell if we had written this using Svelte – don't worry, it has!

To prove this, crack open a copy of the `weather-app` folder from the code download, then look at the contents in your text editor. Don't worry if you don't understand it all – getting a feel for how we structure a Svelte component at this stage is more important. We'll go through it in more detail when creating components in the next chapter. Let's review the code from that last demo before continuing with the rest of this chapter.

Breaking Apart the Code

At first glance, you might be slightly bewildered by some of the code in the example – what does it all do? We use quite a bit of code, but we only need to be concerned with what's in the src folder at this stage.

We went through the usual steps of downloading, extracting, and firing up the demo in localhost, using standard Node commands to get the demo running.

What makes our demo tick, though, is the code within the `src` folder. Other files and folders are present, but we will return to these later in the book. The `src` folder is where we store all the core component code – ours has `lib` and `assets` folders, `vite-env.d.ts`, and `App.svelte`. The `lib` folder holds the code for each component – this is where we'll store our code as we progress through this book.

Although Svelte has two files that act as a starting page for a Svelte site (`main.js`, in the `\src` folder, and the `index.html` file at root), we will primarily use the former. The plan for our library is to display each component using Markdown files in a Storybook installation and use the `index.html` file in a secondary capacity to demonstrate how we might reference each component outside of a Svelte environment. Don't worry too much about the specifics of how we will do this – we will go through everything in detail throughout this book. For now, it's important to know where we will store our components and that we have two ways to display them in our environment.

We will use other files and folders throughout this book, some of which you will recognize, such as `package.json`. Others may not be so familiar; we will go through examples throughout this book.

Okay – let's move on: now that we've created a demo component, it's time we got stuck into the star attraction for this book: our component library!

Throughout this book, we'll create the basis for our component library and flesh it out with a selection of components. There is plenty we could choose from – indeed, space constraints mean we can't add them all! The key is that we'll learn how to structure our library, add components, test them, and generally make sure we have something worthwhile toward the end of the book.

Let's start first with the background to this project so we can set the scene and understand what's coming up later in the book.

Background to the Project

So, where do we begin? Let me introduce you to what we will be creating: the Garnet UI library.

This UI library will contain a mix of components – all of these you will find in use on many websites, particularly ecommerce ones! The great thing about creating a component library is that you can pick and choose which components to add; if people don't like one or are not using it, we can deprecate it from the library. Hopefully, that won't be the case with the ones I've chosen – I've listed them in Table 1-1.

Table 1-1. *List of Components for Our Garnet UI Library*

Category	Components
Basic Components	Input box and variations, such as email or password fields
	Checkbox
	RadioButton
	Slider
Action Components	SelectBox
	Accordion
	Spinner
Navigation Components	Breadcrumbs
	SideBar (and Hamburger)
	Tabs
Notification Components	Dialog boxes (such as error, info, warn)
	Alert
	Tooltip
Grid Components	Grid (Row and Column)
Animation Components	Collapsible DropDown
	Animated ProgressBar
	Switch

If you're wondering about the name – it came from an interest I have in precious stones and a trip to a gemstone museum in Prague a few years ago. They had an incredible array of garnets on display (which happen to be the national gemstone for the Czech Republic) – garnet red is also one of my favorite colors, plus it's a nice short name to boot!

Okay – let's crack on: now that we've decided what we will include in our library, let's turn our attention to strategy. What approach will we take? It's time to decide on some of the tools we will use and our approach for each component.

Our Approach and Strategy

As with any project, it's crucial to have a strategy – we need to decide where (and how) to take the project. Otherwise, it could quickly become a disorganized mess!

We could take this project in many different directions; for now, we will focus on simplicity (mainly as space constraints mean creating something feature-rich and complex in the space of a book would be difficult). With this in mind, I've outlined the approach we will take for this project:

- We'll create a minimum viable product or MVP approach – this will be enough to get something started and published, but we can add to it later.

- I've elected to use GitHub and GitHub Pages for hosting, primarily because I already have several repositories, so using GitHub will help keep things simple. Feel free to use an alternative such as BitBucket or GitLab – both operate similarly to GitHub.

- An essential theme for this project will be to keep
  things simple, at least for now – I would love to create
  something complex and full of features, but I won't
  be able to do it justice in this book. For us, it's more
  important to get the groundwork in place and running
  first; it will mean that some features we might want are
  not present initially (such as using vanilla JavaScript
  rather than TypeScript or excluding some properties
  for a component). Once the basis is operational, we can
  develop and refine the library later.

- For each component, we'll work on developing code
  first. Once done, we'll style it before hooking it into an
  instance of Storybook as our demonstration tool. Tests
  for each component will come later, once we have built
  all the components, in Chapter 8.

- For this library, I've elected to use the Cypress testing
  suite as a personal choice – there are others out there,
  such as testing-library or Jest, which work equally well.
  You may have a testing tool you already use, so feel free
  to use that instead; the critical point is testing our new
  components, not which tool to use!

Okay – I think that's enough for now: let's move on to our next task. We
need to determine what we need in terms of accounts, tools, and the like.
As a developer, you may already have some of these tools installed; feel
free to use them or use alternatives if you prefer! That aside, let's look at the
list in more detail.

Determining Our Needs

Before getting stuck into setting up Svelte and building our library, we need to determine which tools we will use for our project. In a sense, we need to do a little housekeeping – I loathe housekeeping, but hey, needs must, as they say!

This list will cover everything needed: I will assume that you will use the tools outlined in the list for this book. If you already have something installed, feel free to skip the requirement or use an alternative solution.

Leaving that aside, let's cover which tools we need to have, alongside the usual requirements such as Internet access and a decent text editor:

- The first requirement is Node.js (and npm) – we will use this to structure our Svelte project and turn code into components. Please download and install the version appropriate for your platform; default settings will suffice for this project.

- We also need an account at GitHub and a valid email address – we use the latter to validate your account. Once registered, we will use it to set up two repositories – one for the code and another for documentation.

- To publish the component on npm, we will also need an account – you can sign up for one at `https://www.npmjs.com/signup` if you don't already have one.

- A project folder on your PC or laptop – for this book, I will assume you are using one called `garnet`, which is at the root of your C: drive. If you want to use something different, please adjust it to suit as you work through each exercise.

11

This list should be enough to get us started – anything else we can download, or I will give you directions at the appropriate time. Let's begin with the bit I know you're waiting for: installing Svelte and setting up our library.

Setting Up the Project

The first task in building our library is to install Svelte – assuming you have Node.js installed, we can use npm to download and install the framework. Let's look at the steps involved in more detail as part of the next exercise.

INSTALLING SVELTE

To get the basis for our library set up, follow these steps:

1. First, crack open a Node.js terminal session, then change to the root of your C: drive.

2. At the prompt, go ahead and enter `npm create vite@ latest garnetui -- --template svelte`, then press Enter.

3. You may see this question (or something similar) – when prompted, press y to respond:

```
Need to install the following packages:
  create-vite@5.2.3
Ok to proceed? (y)
```

4.   Svelte will now install. After a few moments, it will prompt us to run these commands; go ahead and enter each, pressing Enter after each one:

```
cd garnetui
npm install
npm run dev
```

5.   When prompted, fire up your browser and navigate to `http://localhost:5173` – if all is well, we should see the demo site running in our browser, as shown in Figure 1-2.

Figure 1-2. *Our Svelte demo site running*

6.   Browse to the `garnetui` folder in your file manager – if all is well, we should see something akin to the extract shown in Figure 1-3.

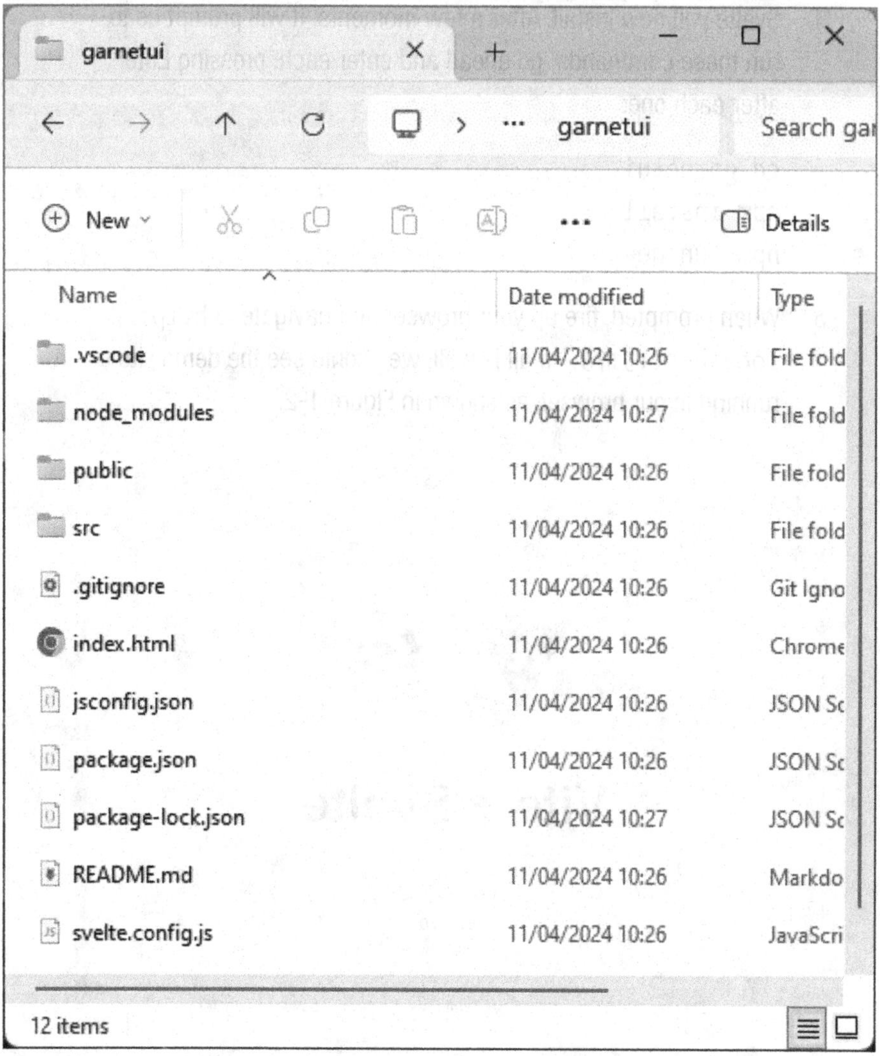

Figure 1-3. *The initial file listing for our component library*

Excellent – we now have a basis for building our component library! Although installing Svelte is straightforward, it's worth exploring what we achieved in the last demo. With that in mind, let's take a moment to review the changes we made in more detail.

Understanding What Happened

One of the great things about using Svelte is how easy it is to set up a starting site. We do everything using npm, a tool many developers already use in their projects, so many commands will look familiar. The only oddity is that while we created a Svelte site, we downloaded Vite – what is all that about?

Vite is the bundling tool Svelte uses to package code ready for deployment. We ran the `npm create` command to create what is effectively a Vite site, but we used a template to format it as a Svelte site. It's worth noting that as part of running this command, we had to download Vite – this is a one-off; it will not prompt us again if we create more Svelte sites.

Once the download was completed, we changed into the `garnet` folder and ran a typical `npm install` command to set up dependencies. With that done, we fired up the Svelte development server before browsing the results in our browser. We still have a long way to go, but this last step helps confirm we have a solid basis in place, ready to build our project!

Okay – let's move on to our next task. We will, of course, be building components throughout this book, but how will we display them? We need the means to show them off to potential users to see how they look and assess if they will suit their requirements.

The best way to do this is to use a tool called Storybook – it's available for download from `https://storybook.js.org/` and works with various frameworks, including Svelte. Let's set up an instance as part of our next demo.

Integrating a Playground

If you've spent any time developing code – particularly with frameworks such as React – you may well have come across Storybook.

For the uninitiated, it's an excellent tool for showcasing any components we developers write – the tool supports a wide range of frameworks, including Svelte. We'll use it in our project to showcase the components we create for our library – let's dive in and explore how to set it up as part of our next exercise.

SETTING UP STORYBOOK

To set up Storybook for our Svelte project, follow these steps:

1. First, crack open a Node.js terminal session, then change the working folder to our project area.

2. At the prompt, enter `npx sb init --builder @storybook/builder-vite` and press Enter to install Storybook.

3. If prompted, press y to proceed (we're using npx to download and install Storybook, so it needs confirmation to proceed with the download).

4. Once installed, Storybook will preconfigure support automatically; if successful, it will automatically display a blank Storybook page in your browser, as shown in Figure 1-4.

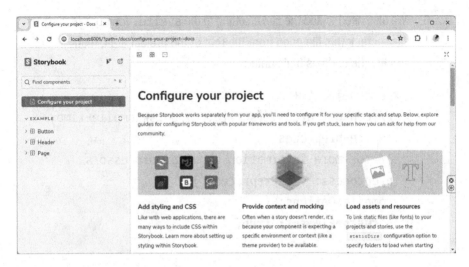

Figure 1-4. *Storybook successfully launched*

If Storybook fails to detect Svelte, choose yes and use the arrow keys to go down to `svelte`, then press Enter to select. Storybook will manually add support for Svelte.

5. There is a change we must make – this is to tell Svelte that we're creating custom web components. Crack open `vite.config.js` at the root of our project folder, then update the code within as highlighted:

```
export default defineConfig({
  plugins: [svelte()],
  compilerOptions: {
    customElement: true
  }
})
```

6. We also need to add the same setting to the `svelte.config.js` file – crack this file open from the root of the project area, then modify the code as highlighted:

```
export default {
  // Consult https://svelte.dev/docs#compile-time-
  svelte-preprocess
  // for more information about preprocessors
  preprocess: vitePreprocess(),
  compilerOptions: {
    customElement: true,
  },

};
```

7. At this point, we can also remove the `\src\stories` and `\src\assets` folders. This folder is the Storybook examples folder, which we don't need for our project.

Great – we now have Storybook in place, ready for us to start adding components! It is a perfect medium to show off the components we create throughout this book; while installing Storybook is a one-liner, we need to ensure it installs the proper support for your project.

With that in mind, let's dive in and explore the changes we made in the last exercise to see how Storybook fits into the bigger picture of our component library.

Understanding What Happened

So, what did we achieve in the last demo?

We started by running the `npx sb init` command to download and set up Storybook; this set up both the application and support for Svelte automatically. While Storybook supports a wide range of frameworks,

18

the developers have focused on automating detection for the chosen framework as part of the installation.

The key to making that automation work lies in detecting the presence of the correct configuration file – in our case, `vite.config.js`. To make sure it works, it's best to let Storybook install itself into a folder at the root level – if you browse the file structure, you will see it has created a folder called `.storybook`. If we hadn't, the automated step could have failed, and we might have ended up installing Storybook manually into the wrong folder or not at all!

To finish the setup, we removed the demo stories and assets that come with Storybook. We don't need these files for the final library, so removing them keeps the setup tidy. We then rounded out the demo by running the command to launch Storybook so we could confirm it launched without issue.

Summary

We can see creating components and a library as something of a rollercoaster. There will be highs and lows, successes and challenges to deal with as we develop what will become our final library. Over these last few pages, we've started to look at our project's background and get ourselves ready to create the component library – let's take a moment to review what we have learned before beginning the real development work.

We started with a quick demo of a Svelte component that I had adapted to get a feel for typical code and how one would run. We then moved on to discussing the background of our project before defining the approach and strategy we would take, along with what we would need.

Next, we set up the initial framework ready for use before finishing with integrating an instance of Storybook and ready to display our components.

We can see creating a website as something of a rollercoaster – there will be highs and lows, successes and challenges to deal with as we begin to develop what will become our final solution. Over these last few pages, we've started to look at our project's background and get ourselves ready to create the site – let's take a moment to review what we have learned before beginning the real development work.

Excellent – we have our initial structure in place, with confirmed requirements: it's time we began the real development! We'll start with something simple first: creating the basic components, which we will do in the next chapter.

CHAPTER 2

Creating Basic Components

With our initial project set up, it's time to start creating and adding components!

For this (and the next few chapters), we will build some sample components ready for inclusion in our library. We could have chosen to include any one of dozens of different components, but to keep things simple, I've decided to pick four to start with: InputBox, Checkbox, RadioButton, and Slider.

For each component, I've made a few assumptions in terms of how we will develop these components:

- Use HTML5 tags where possible.

- Aim to use an MVP approach: features will be missing, but that will come later.

- Take the approach of developing components, then adding styles, and finally linking into Storybook.

- Add variants where possible and start documentation (which we can improve over time).

Keeping this approach in mind, let's start with the first addition to our library, which is creating the Input field component.

© Alex Libby 2025
A. Libby, *Developing Web Components with Svelte*,
https://doi.org/10.1007/979-8-8688-1180-7_2

Creating the Input Component

We will start with something simple for our first component – the ubiquitous input field! You will, of course, see this versatile component anywhere: it might be as a text box on one website but configured to accept only email addresses or telephone numbers on other sites.

We'll keep things simple and start implementing a plain text field for now, but we'll discuss more ideas later when we hook the component into Storybook.

BUILDING THE INPUT COMPONENT

To build our Input component, follow these steps:

1. First, go ahead and create a new folder called `\components` under the `\src\lib` folder.

2. Next, crack open a new file in your text editor, then add this code – there is a good chunk, so we'll add it section by section, starting with a Svelte directive to convert it into a web component:

```
<svelte:options customElement="garnet-input" />
```

3. Leave the next line blank, then add this script block – this sets up some imports and export declarations, along with an `on:input` event handler:

```
<script>
   export let label = "Label:";
   export let placeholder = "default placeholder";
```

```
    export let disabled = false;
    export let inputName = "";
    export let fieldID = "";
    export let value = undefined;
    const dispatch = createEventDispatcher();
    const onInput =(e)=>{
      dispatch('input', { text: e.target.value});
    }
</script>
```

4. Once added, skip a line, then add in this markup – this will form the basis of our component:

```
<div class="garnet-input">
  {#if label}
    <label for={fieldID}>
      {label}
    </label>
  {/if}
  <input
    type="text"
    id={fieldID}
    name={inputName}
    {placeholder}
    {disabled}
    bind:value
    on:input={onInput}
  >
</div>
```

5.   Miss a line after the closing `</div>` tag, then add this styling code:

```
<style>
  .garnet-input { display: flex; flex-direction: row;
    font-family: Arial, Helvetica, sans-serif;
  }
  input[type="text"] { width: 200px; border-
  radius: 4px; border-color: #733635; height: 30px;
  outline: none; }
  label { padding-right: 10px; display: flex; align-
  self: center; }
  input:disabled {
    cursor: not-allowed;
  }
</style>
```

6.   Save the file as `Input.svelte` in the Input folder, and close all open files.

We now have an Input component in place – most of it will look familiar as it is (in the main) standard HTML markup. However, there are a few exciting features in this code we should cover, so before we get stuck into testing our new component, let's look at the code in more detail.

Breaking the Code Apart

For this exercise, our first task was to create the initial folder structure, which will form the basis for our library – this will also help maintain the separation of assets, if needed, at a later date.

Next, we switched to creating the core component and added a
`<svelte:options...>` directive that turns our component into a web
component. It may only be a one-liner, but it is critical to making
everything work and allow us to create our component in Svelte but use
it in frameworks such as React. At the same time, we also created several
exports for variables such as placeholder or `onInput`. This export keyword
makes each value available elsewhere, which will be ideal for testing each
component later in Storybook.

In the declarations at the top of `Input.svelte`, you will see that we've
provided some values – Svelte will use these by default if no values are
passed into the component when calling it in code.

The final task for this exercise was to add the markup that will form the
basis for the Input component – we based it on typical markup for a text
input field but adapted it to reference each exported field. There are two
exceptions: `on:input` and the `bind:value` spread operator.

The former (`on:input`) is Svelte's equivalent of a standard JavaScript
onInput change handler. It works the same way as plain JavaScript, even if
the syntax looks slightly different!

It's worth noting that you don't always need to put the callback for the
`on:input` as we have done here; using `on:input={on:input}`
with an appropriate event handler will work just as well.

Okay – let's move on: next up, we need to test our component. We will
use the Storybook instance we set up in the previous chapter, and it's a
perfect way to test the original component and add variants – let's dive in
and look in more detail.

Hooking the Component into Storybook

As tools go, Storybook is an immensely versatile piece of kit. It supports various frameworks, such as React or Angular, and can also accept content in several formats (e.g., JavaScript or Markdown).

We should be aware of one thing, though, which is our use of Svelte. In previous versions of Storybook (before version 8), support was not quite as mature as for other frameworks – this has radically improved in the current version. That said, we'll be using JavaScript-formatted story files. We could have gone with the Svelte equivalent, which uses Markdown, but JavaScript offers more choices.

We will still use Markdown, but only in the documentation files that link to our Storybook installation.

With that all in mind, let's dive in and look at how we will set up the Storybook installation for our Input component as part of the next exercise.

ADDING TO STORYBOOK

To set up the component in the Storybook instance, follow these steps:

1. First, crack open a new file in your text editor – save it as Input.stories.js in the Input folder from the previous exercise.

2. Next, go ahead and add this code – we'll break it into sections, starting with three import statements:

```
import Input from "./Input.svelte";
import { action } from "@storybook/addon-actions";
import { fn } from "@storybook/test";
```

3. To render any component in Storybook, we need to specify a
    template. We could use different versions for each component,
    but for now, we'll use this one to keep things simple:

```
export default {
  title: "Garnet UI Library/Basic Components/Input",
  component: Input,
  argTypes: {
    disabled: { control: "boolean" },
    oninput: { action: "changed" },
    placeholder: "",
  },
  on: { input: fn().mockName("on-input") },
};
```

4. With a template in place, we can now display our component.
    Go ahead and add this Story block:

```
export const Default = (args) => ({
  Component: Input,
  props: {
    ...args,
    label: "Text:",
    placeholder: "Enter your text here",
    props: args,
    on: { input: fn().mockName("on-input") },
  },
});
```

5. We have one more part to add before viewing the results –
    documentation. Go ahead and extract a copy of Docs.mdx from
    the code download and drop it into the Input folder.

6. It contains some rudimentary documentation in Markdown format – we'll talk more about this when we review the code.

7. Save and close the file. Next, switch to your Node.js terminal session, then set the working folder to our garnet project area.

8. At the prompt, enter npm run storybook and hit Enter – if all is well, we should see Storybook launch and display in our browser at http://localhost:6006/. Click the Input link on the left to display the Default variant we just created, as shown in Figure 2-1.

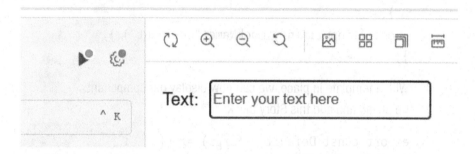

Figure 2-1. *Displaying the Input component in Storybook*

Just a heads up – you will notice that although I've specified http://localhost:6006 as the URL, it does redirect when loading. This is perfectly normal; using the short form in the text is easier!

9. Now click the Docs link on the left, under Input – if all is well, we should see an extract of the documentation appear, as in Figure 2-2.

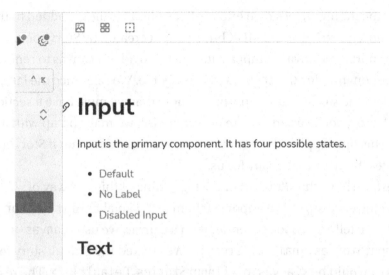

Figure 2-2. *An extract of documentation for the Input component*

Excellent – things are starting to take shape now! We now have the first of many components set up in Storybook: it might be a simple one, but that doesn't matter. The critical point is that we have a sound basis for building and developing our components.

In the meantime, this would be an excellent opportunity to review our code changes. We've already talked about the core component, but we've covered some valuable features in the Storybook implementation, so let's take some time to review the code in more detail.

Understanding What Happened

Although we added a simple Input component to our library in the last exercise, the simplicity hides a mix of technologies – we used Svelte for the core component, JavaScript to add our story to Storybook, and Markdown for our documentation! It's a potent mix, but it seems to work very well. We could have chosen to use Markdown for our story (thanks in no small part to Storybook's versatility), but as mentioned just now, JavaScript offers us more choices.

For the moment, let's dive into the Docs file. This file we added in the last demo isn't strictly pure MDX but a variant created by Storybook. In it, we import the Canvas component, which provides a canvas to render our component, plus the Input.stories.js file. We reference the latter for each of the stories – it's important to note that we must have a section for each Storybook variant we create; otherwise, we may end up with an error. (This only applies if we manually create the stories, not if Storybook generates them automatically for us.)

Next, we have the <Meta of=...> tag – think of this as a way of referencing each story. We imported them using an alias of InputStories, so when we tell Storybook to render it on a canvas, we use <Canvas of={InputStories.{name of story}>. We created the Default story for now, so it would be <Canvas of={InputStories.Default} />. The rest of the code is standard Markdown – we have the [...](...) as named anchor links to each subsection and use the standard format for headings, such as ## Input.

Okay – we're almost finished with this component, but there is one more task we should explore: How can we add a variant for our component?

Adding Variants

It is something you will hear about when creating component libraries such as ours, and it highlights the importance of good planning: variants. So what are they?

They are just variations on a theme – we can use elements such as Input fields for plain text, email addresses, or even choosing colors! The trick here is understanding what each element can support and ensuring we have sufficient properties to support that variation. For example, if we wanted not to display a label by default and add email support to our component, we might create something like this in Storybook:

```
export const NoLabel = (args) => ({
  Component: Input,
  props: {
    ...args,
    label: "",
    props: args,
    on: { input: fn().mockName("on-input") },
  },
});
```

Let's put that into practice and add it to our setup now as part of our next demo – we'll also add a second variant to disable the component.

DEMO – ADDING VARIANTS FOR INPUT

To add the new variants, follow these steps:

1. First, crack open `input.stories.js`, then scroll to the bottom of the page.

2. Leave a line blank, then add the following code – this will remove the label from our component:

```
export const NoLabel = (args) => ({
  Component: Input,
  props: {
    ...args,
    label: "",
    props: args,
    on: { input: fn().mockName("on-input") },
  },
});
```

31

3. Miss a line, then add this code to set a disabled property if needed:

```
export const Disabled = (args) => ({
  Component: Input,
  props: {
    ...args,
    placeholder: "disabled field",
    label: "Text",
    disabled: true,
  },
});
```

4. Save the file and close it – next, go ahead and open the original Input.svelte file: we need to add a slight tweak to our styling.

5. At the bottom of the file before the closing </style> tag, add this style declaration:

```
input:disabled {
  cursor: not-allowed;
}
```

6. Save and close that file. Crack open the Docs.mdx file under the Input folder – we need to add some extra entries for our new variants. Miss a line, then add this markup:

```
## NoLabel
```

```
This is to set or hide the label for the input field
component
```

```
<Canvas of={InputStories.NoLabel} />
```

DisabledInput

This disables the component

`<Canvas of={InputStories.Disabled} />`

7. Save the file and close it. Switch to your Node.js terminal session, then set the working folder to our garnet project area.

8. At the prompt, enter `npm run storybook` and hit Enter – if all is well, we should see Storybook launch and display in our browser at `http://localhost:6006/`.

9. Click the Input entry on the left, under `Basic Components` – you should now see two new entries: `No Label` and `Disabled`.

10. If you click No Label, you will see our Input component rendered without a label, as shown in Figure 2-3.

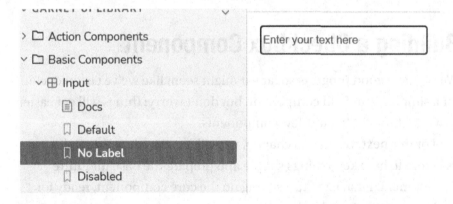

Figure 2-3. *The new Input component displayed in Storybook*

11. The Disabled entry will show the same Input component, but this time, you will not be able to enter any text – it will also show a `not-allowed` cursor (the "no-entry" logo).

As you can see, it's straightforward to add new variants – Storybook allows us to use different formats to create our variants, but the critical point here is that we're just passing properties to our component, so it knows how to render on-screen.

Before we carry on, there is one gotcha that we need to be aware of – you will notice that I've not added a variant to deal with a format such as email. It would be an obvious choice – input boxes are designed to handle formats such as dates, email, and so on. However, we can't add it to our iteration, at least not yet: we set two-way binding in the component (bind:value), and Svelte gets very upset if you try to make the type field of the input box dynamic! That isn't to say we can't do it – it needs changes, which we would have to add as a new iteration of our component.

Okay, it's time to move on. Let's focus on creating our next component, the humble checkbox. It's a doyen of forms and pages all over the Internet; it's straightforward to construct something as a starting point for future development.

Building a Checkbox Component

We've made good progress so far – it might seem like we've covered a lot for a simple Input field component, but don't worry: things will get easier as we go through the next few components.

For this next tool in this chapter, we will use the same principles as before to help keep things simple and prepare the base for future development. First, let's start setting up the core component, ready for deployment into Storybook.

BUILDING THE CHECKBOX COMPONENT

Adding a checkbox component is easy – we can use techniques similar to the input component we created earlier in this chapter. To do so, follow these steps:

1. First, create a folder called Checkbox under the \src\lib\ components folder.

2. Next, crack open your text editor and create a new file called Checkbox.svelte. Add the following code to this file, beginning with the <script> block to import a Svelte function, define some exported variables, and create a handleChange event handler:

```
<svelte:options customElement="garnet-checkbox" />

<script>
  import { createEventDispatcher } from 'svelte';

  export let checked = false;
  export let label = "Checkbox";
  export let disabled = false;
  const dispatch = createEventDispatcher();

  function handleChange(event) {
    const { checked } = event.target;
    dispatch('change', { checked });
}</script>
```

3. We can now add in the markup that will form the basis of our component – for this, add this code below the <script> block, missing a line first:

```
<div class="garnet-checkbox">
  <input
```

35

```
      type="checkbox"
      bind:checked={checked}
      id="name"
      {disabled}
      on:change={handleChange}
    />
    <label for="name">
      {label}
    </label>
  </div>
```

4. There is one last step for us to complete, which is to add some
    styling. Leave a line blank after the closing </div> tag, then
    add this block of code:

```
<style>
  .garnet-checkbox {
    display: flex;
    align-items: center;
    font-family: Arial, Helvetica, sans-serif;
  }

  input[type="checkbox"] {
    -webkit-appearance: none;
    appearance: none;
    margin: 0;
    font: inherit;
    color: currentColor;
    width: 18px;
    height: 18px;
    border: 2px solid currentColor;
    border-radius: 2px;
```

```
    transform: translateY(-1px);
    display: grid;
    place-content: center;
  }

  input[type="checkbox"]::before {
    content: "";
    width: 10px;
    height: 10px;
    clip-path: polygon(14% 44%, 0 65%, 50% 100%, 100%
    16%, 80% 0%, 43% 62%);
    transform: scale(0);
    transform-origin: bottom left;
    transition: 120ms transform ease-in-out;
    box-shadow: inset 16px 16px #733635;
  }

  input[type="checkbox"]:checked::before {
    transform: scale(1);
  }

  input[type="checkbox"]:disabled {
    color: #959495;
    cursor: not-allowed;
    opacity: 0.4;
  }

  label {
    margin-left: 5px;
    user-select: none;
  }
</style>
```

5. Save the file and close it – the component is now in place.

We now have a component in place, ready to test – granted, it's not a complex one, but the key here is to focus on creating the basis for something we can develop over time. In the meantime, let's pause for a moment to review the code we added in the last demo – you will see some similarities to the previous component, but it's worth reiterating through them as practice!

Exploring the Code Changes

The first task was to create a folder for our new component – inside this, we added Checkbox.svelte, which contains the code for our component.

We first import the createEventDispatcher function from Svelte, to take care of managing events. We followed this by defining several variables, including checked and label, which we make available for consumption in code, such as in Storybook. At the same time, we also add a default handleChange event handler – this we can call externally (such as from Storybook) to dispatch a change event to the checkbox element.

We then added the HTML markup for the component before finishing with adding styles to give our component its final look and feel. Although our code uses the same format as the previous component, there are two things I want to highlight: the order of properties and the use of on:change.

I'm a great believer in keeping consistency when it comes to coding – not only is using a proper naming convention worthwhile, but keeping the same order of values is equally important. It keeps things tidier and makes it easier to trace issues if we pass random values between components! With this in mind, I tend to pass values through first and leave functions to last.

You will notice that we've only included a select number of props for this component. Some people might ask how we deal with those props we don't know about and therefore need to pass to the component – typically, we could use the ...$$props operator, which will serve this purpose.

However, it's not recommended, as Svelte can't optimize the code properly if we pass props that it doesn't know about. There may be occasions where we must use it, but these should be rare, and it's better to amend the component to include these extra props as part of the makeup of the component.

Okay – let's move on: it's time to test our component using the Storybook instance we set up in the previous chapter. We'll use similar techniques as before, which helps make it quicker to add – let's dive in and explore the steps required in more detail.

Adding Variations in Storybook

From the first component, we've already seen that setting up an instance in Storybook is relatively straightforward. Once we get past choosing which formats to use when creating the first component, we can reuse most of its code for subsequent additions to the library. To see what I mean, check out the next exercise, where we add the newly created Checkbox component to Storybook.

ADDING VARIATIONS

To add variations for our Checkbox component, follow these steps:

1. First, crack open a new file in your text editor, then add this code – as before, we will go through it in blocks, starting with the declarations:

```
import Checkbox from "./Checkbox.svelte";
import CheckboxDecorator from "./CheckboxDecorator.svelte";

let statusMessage = "";
```

2. To render the component as a new instance in Storybook, we
    need to create a function that acts as a template. Leave the
    next line blank, then add this function:

```
export default {
  title: "Garnet UI Library/Basic Components/Checkbox",
  component: Checkbox,
  decorators: [() => CheckboxDecorator],
  argTypes: {
    checked: { control: "boolean" },
    label: { control: "text" },
    oninput: { action: "changed" },
  },
};
```

3. We can now render the Checkbox component – we will add it
    as a Default instance, with no additional parameters, save for
    a checked property, and an on:change event:

```
export const Default = () => ({
  Component: Checkbox,
  props: {
    checked: true,
    label: "This is a test",
  },
  on: {
    change: (event) => {
      event.detail.checked == true
        ? (statusMessage = "checked")
        : (statusMessage = "unchecked");
      document.getElementById("message").innerHTML =
        `Status: Checkbox is ${statusMessage}`;
    },
```

```
    },
});
```

4. Save the file as `Checkbox.stories.js` in the Checkbox folder.

5. We have two further steps to complete before previewing the results – we need to add the `Docs.mdx` file, referenced in step 4. Extract a copy of this file from the code download, then drop it in the Checkbox folder.

6. Next, we need to add a decorator to our component – for this, go ahead and create a new file called `CheckboxDecorator.svelte`, and add this code:

```
<div>
    <slot />
</div>
<div id="message">Status: Checkbox is checked</div>

<style>
    div { margin-top: 10px; }

    #message { font-family: Arial, Helvetica,
    sans-serif; }
</style>
```

7. Save and close all open files. Next, switch to your Node.js terminal session, then set the working folder to our garnet project area.

8. At the prompt, enter `npm run storybook` and hit Enter – if all is well, we should see Storybook display in our browser at `http://localhost:6006/`. Click the Checkbox link on the left to display the Default variant we just created, as shown in Figure 2-4 (overleaf).

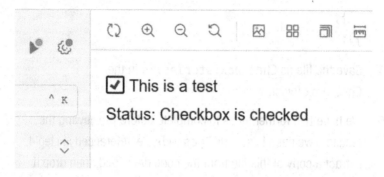

Figure 2-4. Displaying the new Checkbox component in Storybook

9. We've added one variant into Storybook for this component, but what others could we add? For now, a disabled variant would be a good start – as a starting point, we can replicate the Default story and then set `disabled` to `true`. As long as we give the story a new name, then it will render in Storybook.

The code download contains the expanded version if you need any inspiration!

We've now added our second component; we've almost finished the Basic Components section for our library! There is one more we will add shortly, but before doing so, let's first break for a moment to review the code we added in the last demo in more detail.

Breaking the Code Apart

So, what did we achieve in the last demo? We began by adding some imports to the Storybook file for the component itself, followed by declaring a variable to display a message (more in a moment). We then added a default template to render our component; this contained properties such as the title, the component, and argTypes (think of these as props) that we wanted to use to display it on-screen.

With the template in place, we then added the story. As with other components, this takes the form of a function – inside it, we define the component we want to use, plus the prop values we want to pass, and an on:change event handler.

We then rounded out the demo by adding the Docs.mdx documentation file from the code download and created a CheckboxDecorator.svelte file before executing the command to build and run Storybook with the latest updates for our components.

Now – let's revisit that message variable: Why do we need it? It's a good question: it ties in with the decorator file we created for this demo. Let me explain what is going on here.

We have our component in Checkbox.svelte – this will work as expected. The decorator file is purely for Storybook: we use it to add extra markup that we need to render the component correctly. In our case, we added a <slot> element (as a placeholder for the component) alongside our check message (to confirm if the component displays the expected result). We update the contents of this message in the on:change handler within Storybook to show whether the checkbox is checked or unchecked when we click the component.

Okay – let's move on: we're done with Checkbox, so it's time to start on the next component: RadioButton. Radio buttons and checkboxes use the same core element at heart – an input – but the markup we need to use in Svelte is somewhat different! We can still use a native input element, so let's take a look at how we create a set of radio buttons as a component for our library.

Adding a RadioButton Component

Creating a radio button component is a little more complicated than checkboxes, as we have to iterate through several child elements, rather than just a single one, as we might do with a checkbox component. (We often use radio buttons when we need to choose a single option from several, whereas we may only need to confirm acceptance with a single checkbox.)

With this in mind, let's take a look at the markup we need as part of our next demo – we'll focus on the critical part, which is the markup and Svelte script required to create our demo.

ADDING A RADIOBUTTON COMPONENT

To set up our component, let's walk through the steps required:

1. First, create a folder called RadioButton under the \src\lib\ components folder.

2. Next, crack open your text editor and create a new file called RadioButton.svelte. Add the following code to this file, beginning with the Svelte tag to transform our component into a web component, followed by the <script> block, and defining some exported variables:

```
<svelte:options customElement="garnet-radiobutton" />
<script>
  export let selectOptions = [
    {
      value: "Test slot 1",
      label: "Test slot 1"
    },
```

```
    {
      value: "Test slot 2",
      label: "Test slot 2"
    },
    {
      value: "Test slot 3",
      label: "Test slot 3"
    }
  ];

  export let legend = "Legend";
  export let disabled = false;
  export let userSelected = selectOptions[0].value;

  const slugify = (str = "") =>
    str.toLowerCase().replace(/ /g, "-").
    replace(/\./g, "");
</script>
```

3. Next, miss a line, then add this markup – this will form the basis of our component:

```
<fieldset id="garnet" {disabled}>
  <div class="legend" id={`label-
  ${legend}`}>{legend}</div>
  {#each selectOptions as { value, label }}
    <input
      class="sr-only"
      type="radio"
      id={slugify(label)}
      on:change
      bind:group={userSelected}
      value={value} />
```

```
        <label for={slugify(label)}> {label} </label>
        {/each}
    </fieldset>

    <style>
        ...ADD STYLING HERE...
    </style>
```

4. To finish off the component, we need to add some styling –
    there is quite a bit to add, so for reasons of space, go ahead
    and copy the styling from the code download accompanying
    this book, then add it as indicated in the previous step.

5. Save and close the file. We're almost done – the last
    step is to extract a copy of Docs.mdx from the code
    download accompanying this book. Drop this file into the
    RadioButton folder.

Excellent – we now have a RadioButton component! As you can see
from the code, there are some similarities (such as the type, value tags,
and label). However, radio buttons require more code to implement, as
we have to iterate through each button we need to render in our projects.

Now that we have our component, let's move on and take a look at how
it will appear when we set it up in Storybook.

ADDING IT TO STORYBOOK

To initialize the component in Storybook, follow these steps:

1. First, crack open a new file in your text editor, then add this
    code – as before, we will go through it in blocks, starting with
    the imports and a declaration for the data we'll use:

```
import RadioButton from "./RadioButton.svelte";
import { action } from "@storybook/addon-actions";
import { fn } from "@storybook/test";
let selectOptions = [
  {
    value: "Armstrong-Siddeley",
    label: "Armstrong-Siddeley",
  },
  {
    value: "Jaguar Mark II",
    label: "Jaguar Mark II",
  },
  {
    value: "Ford Zephyr",
    label: "Ford Zephyr",
  },
];
```

2. Next, we need to add our story template – for this, leave a line,
    then add this export:

```
export default {
  title: "Garnet UI Library/Basic Components/
  RadioButton",
  component: RadioButton,
  argTypes: {
    options: selectOptions,
    disabled: { control: "boolean" },
    onchange: { action: "changed" },
  },
  on: { change: fn().mockName("on-change") },
};
```

3. We can now add our variations – we'll add two: the first one is
    the Default variant, which renders the radio buttons without any
    changes:

```
export const Default = (args) => ({
  Component: RadioButton,
  props: {
    ...args,
    selectOptions,
  },
  on: { change: action("on-change") },
});
```

4. For our second, we'll add a variant that disables the component
    if we set a disabled property to true:

```
export const Disabled = (args) => ({
  Component: RadioButton,
  props: {
    ...args,
    selectOptions,
    disabled: true,
  },
  on: { change: action("on-change") },
});
```

5. Save the file as `RadioButton.stories.js`, then close it. We
    need two more files, which are the `Docs.mdx` documentation
    and a RadioButtonDecorator.svelte file – we can get them from
    the code download accompanying this book. Drop the file into
    the `RadioButton` folder.

6. Switch to your Node.js terminal session, then make sure the
    working folder is set to our garnet project area.

7. At the prompt, enter npm run storybook and hit Enter – if
    all is well, we should see Storybook display in our browser at
    http://localhost:6006/. Click the Checkbox link on the
    left to display the Default variant we just created, as shown in
    Figure 2-5.

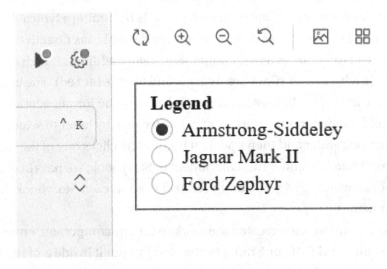

Figure 2-5. *Adding a RadioButton component*

If all goes well, we should now have a working radio button
component. In our example, you can see an interesting choice of data: all
three being of classic cars (one of my favorite things), with examples dating
as far back as 1920! Leaving that aside, we've covered some interesting
concepts in creating and rendering the component, so let's take a moment
to explore the code in more detail.

Exploring the Changes Made

Creating a radio button component has been a challenge, particularly around rendering it in Storybook – building the markup was easy, but getting it to trigger and render the correct choice was something else! That said, we now have something that works, at least as an MVP!

For this component, we've followed what is becoming a typical format for our library – we started by adding the `svelte:options` directive to tell Svelte to treat this as a web component, before adding a bunch of exports (such as `selectOptions`, `legend`, and `userSelected`). The critical ones here are `selectOptions` and `userSelected` – the former acts as placeholder data for our component, while we use the latter to select the top entry on render and then update it if someone clicks one of the radio buttons. When we render this component in Storybook, we pass in our target data, which is why you don't see Test slot 1, etc., in Storybook, but our car names.

Moving on, we then created the markup for our component – most of this is standard HTML for a radio button set; I've put it inside a `<fieldset>` element for now, but we could set a variant not to render this fieldset if we wanted. The critical parts of this markup are the #each block, `on:change` tag, and `bind:group={userSelected}`.

The #each block we use here is a Svelte function, similar to a map command in React – we iterate through each data block and add the values and labels to new instances of inputs, so it renders a radio button for each data element. Inside the markup, we have `on:change` and `bind:group` – the former works just like an onChange event in React. We don't pass it a custom event handler, though, as we want Svelte to pass it through to the native element; think of this as an abstract layer over the top of a standard `<input>` element! The `bind:group` provides two-way data binding, so if a radio button is selected, we can get the name of it in userSelected.

Switching to the Storybook setup, we first import our component, followed by the action and function plugins from Storybook. We then provide our data (this allows us not to have to store our real data in the component). We then created our default template for each story, which specifies the component name, and the `argtypes` to expect. In here, we set options for data, followed by control switches in Storybook for the `disabled` property and `onchange` event handler. In each of the stories, we specify the component we want to use (i.e., RadioButton), followed by passing in the default arguments and only changing those we need, such as data (`selectOptions` or `disabled`).

Phew – it's a little complex, but it does show how we can start to use more options when using Storybook! At this stage, we saved and closed everything before relaunching Storybook to preview the results in our browser.

Okay – let's crack on: for this chapter's fourth and final component, we will explore creating a Slider component. It's not one you're likely to see as often as the others, particularly on ecommerce sites, but it is still an equally important tool to have in the toolbox. Let's dive in and take a closer look at how we might set up such a component.

Constructing the Slider Component

If we're tasked with constructing a Slider component, it's easy to think we might have to build something from the ground up. It's a valid supposition; we can control what features to add and how to construct them. It will result in a lot more code, though, when most browsers already natively support the HTML range element – let's see what happens when we use it to create our next component.

BUILDING THE SLIDER COMPONENT

To build the final component for this chapter, follow these steps:

1. First, create a new folder called `Slider` under the `\src\`
    `lib\components` folder at the same level as the previous two
    components.

2. Next, crack open your text editor, then add this code – we'll do
    this in blocks, starting with importing the style sheet and setting
    some exported declarations:

    ```
    <svelte:options customElement="garnet-slider" />

    <script>
      export let id = "sliderChoice";
      export let min = 0;
      export let max = 100;
      export let step = 1;
      export let val = 50;
      export let disabled = false;
      export let ticks = false;
      export let label = "Please select a value:";
    </script>
    ```

3. With the declarations in place, we can now add the markup
    used to render our component. The first half deals with the
    slider itself:

    ```
    <div class="garnet-slider">
      <div class="range-slider">
        <label for={id}>{label}</label>
        <input
          type="range"
    ```

```
    id={id}
    {min}
    {max}
    {step}
    name={id}
    bind:value={val}
    {disabled}
  />
```

4. This part shows the ticks and selected value underneath the slider, which we will use in a variant:

```
    {#if ticks}
      <div class="sliderticks">
        <span>0</span>
        <span>25</span>
        <span>50</span>
        <span>75</span>
        <span>100</span>
      </div>
    {/if}
  </div>
  <div class="selectedValue">Value: {val}</div>
</div>
```

5. There is one last change we need to make, which is to add some styling. Leave a line blank after the closing </div> tag, then add this code:

I've reproduced the styles here, but in compressed format for space – they are listed in full in the code download for easy copying!

```
<style>
  .garnet-slider { display: flex; align-items:
  center;    font-family: Arial, Helvetica,
  sans-serif; }

  input[type="range"] { -webkit-appearance: none;
  appearance: none; width: 100%; cursor:
  pointer;    outline: none; border-radius: 15px;
  height: 6px;    background: #ccc; margin: 20px
  0 0 0; }

  input[type="range"]::-webkit-slider-thumb { -webkit-
  appearance: none; appearance: none; height: 15px;
  width: 15px; background-color: #733635;    border-
  radius: 50%; border: none; transition: .2s ease-
  in-out; }

  input[type="range"]::-moz-range-thumb { height: 15px;
  width: 15px; background-color: #733635;    border-
  radius: 50%; border: none; transition: .2s ease-
  in-out; }

  input[type="range"]::-webkit-slider-thumb:hover {
    box-shadow: 0 0 0 10px rgba(115, 54, 53 .1)
  }

  input[type="range"]:active::-webkit-slider-thumb {
    box-shadow: 0 0 0 13px rgba(115, 54, 53 .2)
  }

  input[type="range"]:focus::-webkit-slider-thumb {
    box-shadow: 0 0 0 13px rgba(115, 54, 53 .2)
  }
```

```
input[type="range"]::-moz-range-thumb:hover {
  box-shadow: 0 0 0 10px rgba(115, 54, 53 .1)
}

input[type="range"]:active::-moz-range-thumb {
  box-shadow: 0 0 0 13px rgba(115, 54, 53 .2)
}

input[type="range"]:focus::-moz-range-thumb {
  box-shadow: 0 0 0 13px rgba(115, 54, 53 .2)
}

.sliderticks { display: flex; justify-content: space-
between; padding: 0 7px; }

.sliderticks span { display: flex; justify-content:
center; width: 1px; height: 10px; background: d3d3d3;
line-height: 40px; }

.selectedValue { padding: 20px 0 0 15px ; }

/* Disabled styles */
input[type=range]:disabled { opacity: 0.4; }

input[type=range]:disabled::-moz-range-track,
input[type=range]:disabled::-webkit-slider-thumb,
input[type=range]:disabled::-moz-range-thumb {
  background: rgb(115, 54, 53);
}
</style>
```

6. Save the file as `slider.svelte`, then close all open files.

55

Cool – our slider component is now in place. We need to add it to our Storybook instance to see it operate. Fortunately, this is easy to do – we can use similar code to that used for the previous two components; let's look at what's required for the next exercise.

Adding the Component to Storybook

Adding in the new Slider component is straightforward – we can use the same structure as previous components, making it super easy to slot into our Storybook setup. Let's focus on getting the basics in place as part of the next exercise.

SETTING UP THE SLIDER IN STORYBOOK

With the component now in place, we can now add the component and documentation to Storybook:

1. First, create a new file called `Slider.stories.mdx`, at the root of the Slider folder.

2. Next, go ahead and add this code – we'll break it down section by section, beginning with the relevant imports:

    ```
    import Slider from './Slider.svelte';
    import SliderDocs from './SliderDocs.mdx';
    ```

3. To render the component as a new instance in Storybook, we need to create a function that acts as a template. Leave the next line blank, then add this function:

    ```
    export default {
        title: "Garnet UI Library/Basic Components/Slider",
        component: Slider,
        label: "Example Slider",
    ```

```
  argTypes: {
    val: 1,
    min: 0,
    max: 100,
    step: 10,
    ticks: false,
  },
};
```

4. With the template in place, we can now add the Story code to render our new Slider component:

```
export const Default = {
  args: {
    label: "Text:",
  },
};
```

5. Let's add a couple of variants – take a copy of the code from step 4, then miss a line and paste it into the file. Change the Story name to Step, then replace label: "Text" with step: 25 and ticks: true, as shown below:

```
export const Step = {
  args: {
    step: 25,
    ticks: true,
  },
};
```

6. Repeat the same process, but this time swap the `args` values for `disabled: true`, as shown below:

```
export const Disabled = {
  args: {
    disabled: true,
  },
};
```

7. Save and close the file. We have one more step to complete before previewing the results – we need to add the `Docs.mdx` file, referenced in step 4. Extract a copy of this file from the code download, then drop it in the `Slider` folder.

8. Once done, switch to your Node.js terminal session, then make sure the working folder is set to our garnet project area.

9. At the prompt, enter npm run storybook and hit Enter – if all is well, we should see Storybook fire up in our browser at `http://localhost:6006/`. Click the Slider link on the left, then Step, to display the Step variant we created, as shown in Figure 2-6.

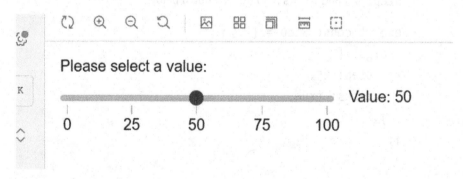

Figure 2-6. *Displaying the Slider component in Storybook*

Great – we've created the first set of components for our library! Things are shaping up well; we have a solid basis for developing the code at a later date. In the next chapter, we will focus on adding the next batch of components, but for now, let's round out this chapter with a final look at the changes made in the last exercise.

Exploring the Code

Adding components to our Storybook instance should be a little more familiar now – the key is preparing the code for the first, which we can reuse in subsequent components.

Keeping that thought in mind, we started by creating the `Slider.stories.js` file for Storybook, into which we first imported our Slider component. We then added a default template, which sets the `title`, specifies the `component`, and assigns several props values for our component.

Next, we set up our initial story block, which we labeled `Default`. Here, we set up a basic instance of the Slider component; we then added two more variants, one to show what happens when we use the `step` option and another when the slider is `disabled`.

We then switched to creating a variant – we talked about how this should be straightforward, given our desire to use consistent code, and that this should make adding variants easier. We then rounded out the demo by adding a prepared `Docs.mdx` documentation file before firing up Storybook and previewing the results in a browser.

Summary

In Chapter 1, I mentioned that creating components and a library can be a rollercoaster. As we develop our final library, there will be highs and lows, successes, and challenges to overcome. Over these last few pages, we've started that journey to add in our component – let's take a moment to review what we learned in this chapter.

The focus throughout this chapter was creating the code for each component – we started by constructing the code for a typical input field before hooking it into our Storybook instance and adding in some variants to showcase how we can make our components more useful.

We then created our second and third components, the Checkbox and RadioButton. Both followed the same format, but we touched on how both components may share similar markup (using the input element); the latter requires more markup to handle each radio button we want to display.

The fourth and final component we covered for this chapter was the Slider – we worked through creating the core component. Adding it to Storybook was more straightforward, though, as this is one of those components where we have to provide values for it to operate, not just because we want to change how it works; it's something to bear in mind when creating tools for our toolbox.

Okay – let's move on: it's time for some action. You might have to pardon the pun, as it wasn't the best lead-in to what we will cover in the next chapter. Suffice it to say, we will focus on components that show a little action in some way (yes – there's the link). Intrigued? Stay with me, and I will reveal it all in the next chapter.

CHAPTER 3

Building Action Components

Lights, camera, action...

Okay – we're not about to create the next movie blockbuster! Instead, it's the turn of the next batch of components we will be building, which all have some form of action (if you pardon the pun).

In the previous chapter, we started by creating some simple components based on standard HTML5 elements, which we could refine into more complex versions as the library matures over time. Our next batch of components is a little more involved and shows a moving part in (most) respects – hence the reference to the title of this chapter!

Over the following few pages, we will, in turn, create SelectBox, Spinner, and Accordion components – let's begin with the SelectBox.

Creating the SelectBox Component

The typical select box type component is one you will find everywhere online. It, of course, is perfect for choosing options on ecommerce websites, such as the size of shoes, the quantity of a particular item, or whether we want standard or expedited delivery. To construct this component, I've elected to use the standard HTML `<select>` element; let's make a start on building it as part of the next exercise.

© Alex Libby 2025
A. Libby, *Developing Web Components with Svelte*,
https://doi.org/10.1007/979-8-8688-1180-7_3

BUILDING THE SELECTBOX COMPONENT

To build our SelectBox component, follow these steps:

1. First, create a new folder called `SelectBox` at the root of the `\src\lib\components` folder.

2. Next, crack open a new file and add this code – we'll start with adding a tag to turn our code into a web component and creating a few variables for export:

```
<svelte:options tag="garnet-selectbox" />

<script>
  export let selectOoptions = [];
  export let displayText = a => a.value;
  export let index = 1;
  export let disabled = false;
  export let selected = {};
  export let label = "Test dropdown:"

  const dispatch = createEventDispatcher()

  $: selected = selectOptions.find((o) => o.id
=== index);
```

3. Miss a line, then add in this little function and the closing script tag:

```
  function handleChange() {
    dispatch('change', { text: selected });
  }
</script>
```

4. We can now add the markup for our component – much of this standard HTML markup, but it does include some Svelte tags:

```
<div class="garnet-selectbox">
  <label for="garnet-selectbox">{label}</label>
  <select bind:value={index} on:change={handleChange}
  name="garnet-selectbox">
    {#each selectOptions as option, i}
      <option value={i + 1} {disabled}>
        {displayText(option)}
      </option>
    {/each}
  </select>
</div>
```

5. Next, we need to add some styling. Leave a line blank, then add this code:

```
<style>
  .garnet-selectbox {
    display: flex;
    align-items: center;
    font-family: Arial, Helvetica, sans-serif;
  }

  label { padding-right: 10px; }

  select {
    padding: 5px 100px 5px 5px;
    font-size: 16px;
    border: 1px solid #733635;
    height: 34px;
    border-radius: 10px;
  }
```

```
option:disabled {
    cursor: not-allowed;
}
</style>
```

6. Save the file as `SelectBox.svelte`, then close the file.

We now have our component in place, although you will notice that we've not yet tested it – we will do that once we hook the component into our Storybook instance. For now, let's take some time to review the code in more detail. There are some exciting features present that are helpful!

Understanding What Happened

So far, we've added four components to our library – hopefully, by now, you will start to see some similarities in the steps we take, which will help speed up the process of getting out an initial version of a component!

The SelectBox component we created in the last exercise is no different – we created a component folder before setting up the file for our component. We then exported several variables required for operating our SelectBox component in this file. We also added a `$:` or reactive statement block to assign whatever value we select in the `selectOptions` array to the selected variable.

Reactive statements are a vital function of Svelte – Svelte executes these before any component updates. It allows us to intercept any value within the statement block and store it whenever it is updated.

Next up, we added the markup for our component – most of this is standard HTML for select boxes, but there are a couple of points of note. We first bind the contents of `value` to the `<select>` element; data typically flows from parent to child in Svelte, but this allows it to flow both ways (and update on any change). We then have a Svelte {#each}...{/each} block, which iterates through the <option...> tag to display the values from our options array that we will pass into the component. The displayText function extracts the relevant value from the options array. The SelectBox component knows which display value to show and what to set as the value property for that entry.

Last but by no means least, we also added a set of style rules for our component – these use our theme color plus set a few attributes so that our component at least renders correctly on the page.

Okay, let's crack on: we have our component in place and some rudimentary styling. It's time to test our code, so let's fire up Storybook and set up an entry for our component.

Adding the Component to Storybook

Right – where were we? Ah, yes...adding our component to Storybook.

One of the benefits of careful planning is that we can reuse existing code – to date, we've created three components, which all use the same format when hooking them into Storybook.

It might seem a little repetitious, but don't forget: reusability means we can be a lot more agile! I will come back to this when we review the changes made shortly, but for now, let's work through setting up our new component in Storybook as part of the next demo.

```
LINKING INTO STORYBOOK
```

Adding the component into Storybook is straightforward – we will reuse the existing code format from previous examples, with only minor changes needed. To see what I mean, let's set up the SelectBox component we created just now using these steps:

1. First, go ahead and create a new file, then add this code – as before, we have a reasonable chunk to add. Let's start with the initial `<script>` block to import the component and documentation, along with some functions from Storybook:

```
import SelectBox from "./SelectBox.svelte";
import SelectBoxDecorator from "./SelectBoxDecorator.
svelte";
```

2. With the initial configuration in place, we can now focus on our component – as before, we first need to add a default story to act as our template for all future stories. Skip a line, then add this block in – it's similar to previous examples, with only a minor change of component:

```
let optionValues = [
    { id: 1, value: "aaa" },
    { id: 2, value: "bbb" },
    { id: 3, value: "ccc" },
    { id: 4, value: "ddd" },
];

export default {
    title: "Garnet UI Library/Action Components/
    SelectBox",
    component: SelectBox,
    decorators: [() => SelectBoxDecorator],
```

```
    argTypes: {
      checked: { control: "boolean" },
      label: { control: "value" },
      oninput: { action: "changed" },
      selectOptions: optionValues,
    },
  };
```

3. We can now render our component – for this, we will create a
    Default function, so go ahead and add this block:

```
export const Default = () => ({

  Component: SelectBox,
  props: {
    selectOptions: [optionValues,
    label: "",
  },
  on: {
    change: (event) => {
      document.getElementById("message4").innerHTML =
        `SelectBox value is ${JSON.stringify(event.
        detail.text.value)}`;
    },
  },
});
```

4. Let's also add a second story – this one will disable the
    component:

```
export const WithLabel = () => ({
  Component: SelectBox,
  props: {
    selectOptions: optionValues,
    ],
```

```
        label: "This is a test",
      },
      on: {
        change: (event) => {
          document.getElementById("message4").innerHTML =
            `SelectBox value is ${JSON.stringify(event.
            detail.text.value)}`;
        },
      },
    });
```

5. We can add a third story – this one will disable the component when rendered:

```
export const Disabled = {
  component: SelectBox,
  args: {
    selectOptions: optionValues,
    ],
    disabled: true,
  },
};
```

6. Save the file as SelectBox.stories.js, then close the file.

7. You will see from the code that we've specified SelectBoxDecorator.svelte, but have not yet created it! Go ahead and open a new file in your editor, then add this markup and styling:

```
<div>
  <slot />
</div>
<div id="message4">SelectBox value is (not selected)</div>
```

```
<style>
  div { margin-top: 10px; }

  #message4 { font-family: Arial, Helvetica, sans-serif; }
</style>
```

8. Save the file as `SelectBoxDecorator.svelte` in the
    SelectBox folder, then close it. We have everything in place, so
    let's test it! Switch to a Node.js terminal session, then set the
    working folder to our project area.

9. At the prompt, enter `npm run storybook` and hit Enter – if
    all is well, we should see Storybook launch and display in our
    browser at `http://localhost:6006/`. Click the Default
    link under SelectBox on the left to display the variant we just
    created, as shown in Figure 3-1.

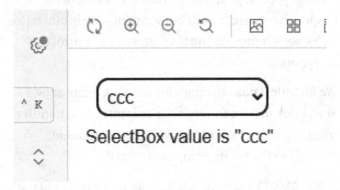

Figure 3-1. *The SelectBox component on display in Storybook*

And voila! Our new component is rendering in Storybook – we used a
Storybook decorator to prove that when selecting an entry in the drop-
down, we can capture and display it on-screen. It's an interesting effect
that runs independently of our component. Let's dig into the code to see
how it and other key features work, before we continue creating the next
component in this chapter.

Exploring the Code in Detail

To hook our SelectBox component, we began by creating our Storybook page. We imported our component and a Storybook decorator file we will use (more on this in a moment).

We then moved on to the critical part – our template. It's primarily the same as previous components; after all, there is no need (at this time) to make it any more complicated! In this template, we include a few properties:

- The title of the component (which acts as the navigation when Storybook is running).

- The name of the component and a reference to the decorator file.

- An `argTypes` object, which contains details of properties we use for our component – in this instance, we've set a bunch of entries that we can control in Storybook.

- We include a pass-through for `oninput` – this allows Storybook to pass through the `oninput` event handler triggered when interacting with the component, through to the Svelte component itself.

- A `selectOptions` object, which includes test data that we use to render the component in Storybook.

We then added a Story block for Default, into which we passed our `selectOptions` array as a prop, along with setting the label property to an empty string as a starting point and an instance of the `selectOptions` array as data for rendering the component. We repeated this step to add a second story – this time, we marked it as `WithLabel` and added some text to the label parameter within our component. Ideally, we'd probably set the label property as empty by default so that we can provide text if needed. It's something we can look at changing in a future iteration.

We finish by adding a third story, which this time has a disabled property set to `true` so that we can disable the SelectBox component when appropriate.

To round things off, we saved and closed all files before launching Storybook and previewing the results in our browser. Before we change tack and explore our next component, I want to cover a few points of note:

- You will have noticed that we used the HTML5 native element as a basis for our components. It does present a question: Is this the best approach? I don't think there is a right or wrong answer; it will depend on the browsers you want (or have) to support. I hope they will be recent (within the last 2–3 years), so the issue of supporting HTML5 should not even be something we need to worry about. The great thing about our MVP approach is that we could decide to convert to a custom, ground-up component; only time will tell!

- You will see that we added a `SelectBoxDecorator.svelte` file – this is a nifty technique to use! Put simply, we can add extra markup around a component when rendering it in Storybook, which we need but don't want to include in the component itself. Here, we're using it to render the contents of the selected value exported from the component itself.

For more details, please refer to the main Storybook website at `https://storybook.js.org/docs/writing-stories/decorators`

- The original version of this component (back in the first edition of this book) had an icon displayed in the drop-down. I added this as a bonus, based on a hack I discovered on the StackOverflow website. I've tried to replicate it but struggled, so I have removed it (at least for now). Touch wood – if I can get it working, it may reappear in a future edition!

Let's move on – we're making great progress, with our second component now in place and working. It's for us to look at the next one in this bunch. It's one where we could get into a spin if we're not careful (oops – sorry about the pun!). Yes, our next one is a spinner – essential if you need to render lots of data on the page that might take a while to load...

Creating the Spinner Component

I'm sure you will have seen data returned on some websites that takes a while to display, right?

We could display that data, but a better UX experience is to render a loading element (or spinner) while we retrieve that data. Fortunately, it's easy enough to create the basis for something we can develop later – let's look at the code required to construct our component.

BUILDING THE SPINNER

To set up our spinner component, follow these steps:

1. First, create a new folder called `Spinner` inside the `\src\ lib\components` folder of our project area – this is where we will store the code for our component.

2. Next, crack open a new file and add this code – we'll go
   through it block by block, starting with some declarations we
   export when using the component:

```
<script>
  export let color = "#733635";
  export let duration = "0.75s";
  export let size = "60";
  export let variant = "";
  export let unit = 'px';
  export let pause = false;

  let durationUnit = duration.match(/[a-zA-Z]/)?.
  [0] ?? 's';
  let durationNum = duration.replace(/[a-zA-Z]/, '');
  const range = (size, startAt = 0) =>

  [...Array(size).keys()].map((i) => i + startAt);
</script>
```

3. Next, we need to add the markup for our component, so leave a
   line blank and add this code:

```
<div class="garnet-spinner">
  <!-- Circle spinner -->
  <div>
    <div
      class="circle"
      style="--size: {size}px; --color: {color};
      --duration: {duration}"
    />
  </div>
</div>
```

4. To finish off the basic component, we need to add some styling – go ahead and leave a line blank, then add these rules:

```
.garnet-spinner {
  display: flex;
}

/* circle spinner */
.circle {
  height: var(--size);
  width: var(--size);

  border-color: var(--color) transparent var(--color) var(--color);
  border-width: calc(var(--size) / 12);
  border-style: solid;
  border-radius: 50%;
  animation: var(--duration) linear 0s infinite normal none running rotateCircle;
}

@keyframes rotateCircle {
  0% {
    transform: rotate(0);
  }
  100% {
    transform: rotate(360deg);
  }
}
</style>
```

5. Save the file as `Spinner.svelte` in the Spinner folder, then close it.

We now have our Spinner component in place – although a large part of it is standard HTML and CSS, it does include a few exciting techniques of note. Let's pause for a moment and review the code to understand how it all hangs together in more detail.

Understanding What Happened

We began by creating our Spinner component folder, into which we started to assemble the core component code – the first task was to add a bunch of exports for properties we will use later, such as color, duration, variant, and size. These have default string values applied, but two will change; more on this in a moment.

Next, we then added the markup for our component. This uses the CSS variable function `var()` to turn string-formatted values (`size`, `color`, and `duration`) into variables in the format `var(--XX)`. The XX is the variable's name; in this case, we use all three exported variables to style our spinner – for example, color would appear in the markup as `var(--color)`.

The remaining CSS code is standard, so it should be reasonably self-explanatory – we use a custom `@keyframe` called `rotateCircle` to animate our spinner. The only property of interest, though, is `border`, where we specify three properties – we can effectively treat these as three parts of the circle. Change one, and we change a third of the wheel, which can lead to some interesting effects!

We then finished by adding the markup – spinners typically don't need anything more than an empty `<div>` element; if we style it correctly, it will show as our intended spinner in a browser.

Adding the Component to Storybook

We have the code in place for our component, so it's time to add it to our Storybook instance. The process is largely the same as the previous components, so the code will look a little more familiar now. Let's dive in and take a look at it in more detail.

HOOKING THE COMPONENT INTO STORYBOOK

Adding our Spinner into Storybook is straightforward as we're able to reuse much of the same code as before – to see what I mean, follow these steps:

1. First, go ahead and create a new file, then add this code – as before, we have a reasonable chunk to add. Let's start with the initial import block to import the component and documentation, along with some functions from Storybook:

```
import Spinner from './Spinner.svelte';
```

2. Next, we need to create our template and initial configuration. As before, it adds a title, sets the name of the component we want to use in the navigation, tells Storybook which component we are using, and defines the type of arguments we want to pass to instances of the component in Storybook:

```
export default {
  title: "Garnet UI Library/Action Components/Spinner",
  component: Spinner,
  argTypes: {
    color: "#733635",
    duration: "0.75s",
    size: "40",
    variant: "circle",
  },
```

```
    parameters: {
      docs: {
        story: {
          height: "100px",
        },
      },
    },
  };
```

3. We can now render our component. For this, we create a story
    and pass the properties required to configure our spinner
    component. In this instance, we'll set the default values, which
    will show as a Circle spinner – go ahead and add this block:

```
export const Circle = {
  args: {
    color: "#733635",
    duration: "0.75s",
    size: "40",
    variant: "circle",
  },
};
```

4. Save the file as `Spinner.stories.mdx` in the `\src\lib\`
    `components\Spinner` folder, then close the file.

5. We also need to add a documentation file – for this, go ahead
    and download a copy of `Docs.mdx` from the code download,
    then drop it into the `\src\lib\storybook` folder.

6. We have everything in place, so let's test it! Switch to a Node.
    js terminal session, then set the working folder to our cobalt
    project area.

7. At the prompt, enter npm run storybook and hit Enter – if
    all is well, we should see Storybook launch and display in our
    browser at http://localhost:6006/. Click the Default link
    under Spinner on the left to display the variant we just created,
    as shown in Figure 3-2.

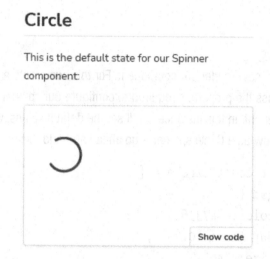

Circle

This is the default state for our Spinner
component:

Show code

Figure 3-2. *Displaying the Spinner component in Storybook*

Excellent – the Spinner is now in and working: it's a shame that we
can't see it spin in print, so, hopefully, it works as expected for you on-
screen! In this instance, we created a circular spinner as our default; we
can add variants, although there is a little twist.

Remember how we added a disabled property as a variant with
SelectBox? We disable the component, but it still looks like the same
SelectBox. If we add a variant with Spinner, it will look different from our
original spinner – to see what I mean, we will add a variant shortly, and I'll
take you through how we can pick other examples available elsewhere and
replicate their effect into our component.

Before we do that, let's quickly review the code changes we made in the last demo in more detail. Much of what we added will start to look familiar (remember that point from earlier about reusability!), but it's still worth looking to recap what we added in the demo.

Breaking Apart the Code

Adding our Spinner component to Storybook should now be a relatively familiar process – as before, we start by creating our Storybook page and importing the component.

We then added a default function as our template. This specifies which settings to use for each variant in the absence of any that we do not set as part of a specific variant (or story). In this case, we set the title of our component's story, which component to use (Spinner), and the various default settings to use under argTypes. At the same time, we also added a parameters block, which contained a height of 100px. Without it, the Spinner component could look as if it had been cut off in some instances! This height value changes the height of the canvas in Storybook only to make it easier to view – it does not affect the component itself.

With our default template in place, we then turned our attention to setting our default instance of the Spinner component. It is a simple object in which we set args and pass in the properties we want to use, such as color, size, and duration.

To finish off, we extracted a copy of the Docs.mdx file, which will act as the documentation for our component. We'll explore how to set up our documentation in more detail in Chapter 8, but for now, all we need to know is that it will display instances of each variant of our components, plus any ancillary information we want to display. To prove it all works, we launched Storybook to preview the results in a browser.

Creating Variants

In that last demo, we set up the Spinner component to operate in Storybook. The process should be relatively familiar, as we've tried to keep it similar for all components. However, remember how I stated that if we added a variant for Spinner, it would likely be very different from something added for SelectBox?

Spinner is one of those components where we probably wouldn't enable or disable a component, such as we did for SelectBox. Instead, we focus on timing, color, size, and duration, resulting in a different look and feel! It might sound a little confusing, but trust me – the following exercise will make it much more apparent, so let's dive in and take a look.

"CHANGING THE LOOK"

I've titled this next exercise slightly differently than the others, but with good reason. Although we will create a variant, it looks so different from the original that it could be a separate component in its own right! That aside, here's what we need to do to add that new variant to our demo:

1. First, crack open Spinner.svelte, then add this line before the closing </script> tag:

    ```
    const range = (size, startAt = 0) =>
      [...Array(size).keys()].map(i => i + startAt);
    ```

2. Scroll down to the markup block – we need to tweak the existing code. First, find this line: <div class="garnet">, then amend the original <div class = "circle"...> block to look like this – changes are marked in bold:

    ```
    <!-- Circle spinner -->
    {#if variant == "circle"}
      <div>
    ```

```
<div
  class="circle"
  style="--size: {size}px; --color: {color};
  --duration: {duration}"
/>
</div>
{/if}
```

3. Leave a line blank after that closing {/if} tag, then add this code for our variant:

```
<!-- Jumper spinner -->
{#if variant =="jumper"}
  <div style="--size: {size}px; --color: {color};
  --duration: {duration};">
    {#each range(3, 1) as version}
      <div
        class="jumper"
        style="animation-delay: {(1 / 3) *
        (version - 1)}s;"
      />
    {/each}
  </div>
{/if}
```

4. Next, we need to add the CSS for our variant – go ahead and add this below the rotate block:

```
.jumper {
  height: var(--size);
  width: var(--size);
  border-radius: 100%;
  animation-fill-mode: both;
  position: absolute;
```

```
    opacity: 0;
    background-color: var(--color);
    animation: bounce var(--duration) linear infinite;
}
@keyframes bounce {
    0% { opacity: 0; transform: scale(0); }
    5% { opacity: 1; }
    100% { opacity: 0; transform: scale(1); }
}
```

5. In the `.circle` style rule declaration, go to the end of the block, then change the word `rotate` to `rotateCircle`.

6. Scroll down to the line starting `@keyframes rotate...`, then change the word rotate for `rotateCircle`.

7. Save and close all files. Fortunately, the changes required for Storybook are not so complex! For this, crack open Spinner. stories.js, then scroll to the bottom of the page and add this block:

```
export const Jumper = {
  args: {
    color: "#733635",
    duration: "1s",
    size: "60",
    variant: "jumper",
  },
};
```

8. We have everything in place, so let's test it! Switch to a Node.js terminal session, then set the working folder to our project area.

9. At the prompt, enter `npm run storybook` and hit Enter – if all is well, we should see Storybook launch and display in our browser at `http://localhost:6006/`.

10. Click the Jumper link under Spinner on the left to display the variant we just created in "mid-jump," as shown in Figure 3-3.

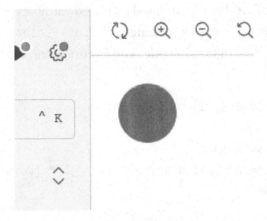

Figure 3-3. *Displaying the Spinner variant*

Wow – our Spinner looks different now! This is the beauty of this component: even though the core markup is largely the same, varying the properties we pass in can render something completely different.

Breaking Apart the Code

We began with adding an exported variable called variant, which we will use to specify which variant to run when calling our component. We also added a new const for range – we use this in the new effect to create a splash effect as part of our animation. At the same time, we renamed the original `rotate` @keyframes block to `rotateCircle` – this wasn't essential, but it helps provide a better separation of concerns once we add the @keyframes block for our new variant.

We then switched to adding the CSS styles required for the variant – this came in two parts, starting with creating the basis for the spinner, followed by that new @keyframes block to animate it. Next came the markup – first, we wrapped the original markup in a Svelte {#if}... {/else} block before adding the new markup for our variant.

83

Take a closer look at the markup for our variant: there are a couple of interesting points of note. We use CSS variables throughout, such as --size or --color. We also defined exported variables at the top of the file in the same name, so a statement such as --color: {color} becomes --color: #733635 in code. The feature of interest, though, is the #each block:

```
{#each range(3, 1) as version}
  <div
    class="jumper"
    style="animation-delay: {(1 / 3) * (version - 1)
    + "px"};"
  />
{/each}
```

Here, we use a standard Svelte {#each...as} block, similar to React but with slightly different syntax. But, the real magic happens in the animation-delay style. Our block iterates through three instances of the div (range(3,1) equates to 3, 2, 1); the calculation provides a gradual step effect, similar to jumping into a puddle of water, hence the animation's name!

Expanding the Options Available

So far, we've created two spinners and set them to display in Storybook – what if we wanted to create more? There are dozens of examples available on the Internet, many of which we should be able to replicate in our library, using similar properties to the ones we use for the existing examples.

To prove how we might do this, I picked one from the svelte-loading-spinners package, created by Eric Schumertl (and available from https://schum123.github.io/svelte-loading-spinners/). It's called Jellyfish (yes, that is indeed its name!) – with a bit of work, I was able to come up with this:

```
<!-- Jellyfish spinner -->
{#if variant == "jellyfish"}
  <div style="--size: 60px; --color: {color}; --motionOne:
  -12px; --motionTwo: 15px; --motionThree: -12px;
  --duration: 2.5s;">
    {#each range(6, 0) as version}
      <div
        class="ring"
        class:pause-animation={pause}
        style="animation-delay: {version * (+durationNum / 25)}
        {durationUnit}; width: {version * (+size / 6) + unit};
        height: {(version * (+size / 6)) / 2 + unit};"
      />
    {/each}
  </div>
{/if}
```

You can see how it all fits together in the version I've added to Spinner.svelte in the accompanying code download. Compare that with the original at https://github.com/Schum123/svelte-loading-spinners/blob/master/src/lib/Jellyfish.svelte, and you will see most of the code can lift over with little modification needed.

Okay – let's continue: next up, let's look at creating our next component, the Accordion.

Creating the Accordion Component

Let me ask you a question.

Hands up, how often have you been on a website where the author (or company) has added a ton of information but given no thought about its display? You take one look and think, "Ugh – time to vote with my feet…" as they say!

That example might sound a little extreme, but I've been on thousands of sites over the years where I still see designers display lots of information with little regard to how they lay it out on the page. One way to fix that could be to use an instance of what we will develop next: an accordion.

These are great for storing lots of information – such as product specs, reviews, and the like – in a compact manner, and we can select which tab to display for further details. Accordions are not challenging to create, although they require more code than we've done so far. Let's dive in and look at creating one as our next component to see what I mean.

BUILDING THE ACCORDION COMPONENT

To set up our accordion component, follow these steps:

1. First, create a new folder called `Accordion` inside the `\src\lib\components` folder within our project area – this is where we will store the code for our component.

2. We need some sample data for this component to work – go ahead and extract a copy of `accordiondata.json` from the accompanying code download and drop it into the Accordion folder.

3. Next, crack open a new file and add this code – we'll go through it block by block, starting with some declarations we export for use within the component:

```
<svelte:options customElement="garnet-accordion" />
<script>
  import AccordionItem from "./AccordionItem.svelte";
  export let data = [];
</script>
```

4. We need to add the markup that will form our component – for
    this, leave a blank line, then add this code:

```
<div class="garnet-accordion">
  {#each data as entry}
    <AccordionItem title={entry.title}>
      <p>{entry.text}</p>
    </AccordionItem>
  {/each}
</div>
```

5. Next, miss a line, then add this block – it will provide some
    basic styling for our Accordion container:

```
<style>
  .garnet-accordion {
    display: flex;
    flex-direction: column;
    width: 450px;
  }
</style>
```

6. Save the file as Accordion.svelte, then close the file.

7. You will notice a reference to AccordionItem in that code – we
    now need to create that component. For this, go ahead and
    crack open a new file, then add this code:

```
<svelte:options customElement="garnet-accordionitem" />

<script>
  import { slide } from "svelte/transition";
  import accordionData from "./accordiondata.json";
  export const data = accordionData;
```

```
    export let title = "";
    let isOpen = false;

    const toggle = () => isOpen = !isOpen
</script>
```

8. Last but by no means least, we need to add the markup for our component – this first block defines the button used to open and close each list item:

```
<button on:click={toggle} aria-expanded={isOpen}>
    <svg
        width="20"
        height="20"
        fill="none"
        stroke-linecap="round"
        stroke-linejoin="round"
        stroke-width="2"
        viewBox="0 0 24 24"
        stroke="currentColor">
            <path d="M9 5l7 7-7 7"></path>
    </svg>
    {entry[0]}
</button>
```

9. This second part triggers an animation if the user opens the drawer:

```
{#if isOpen}
    <ul transition:slide={{ duration: 300 }}
    class="garnet">
        <slot></slot>
    </ul>
{/if}
```

10. We need to add some styling – for this, miss a line after the closing {/if}, then add this code:

```
<style>
  .garnet { display: flex; font-family: Arial,
  Helvetica, sans-serif; }
  svg { transition: transform 0.2s ease-in; }

  [aria-expanded="true"] svg { transform:
  rotate(0.25turn); }

  button.accordionItem { display: flex; align-items:
  center; background-color: #733635; color: #ffffff;
  border: none; }

  button[aria-expanded="false"].accordionItem {
  margin-bottom: 2px; }

  button.accordionItem:hover { background-color:
  #733635; }

  ul { border: 1px solid #d19c9b; margin: 0;
  margin-bottom: 2px; padding: 5px 10px 10px 20px; }
</style>
```

11. Save the file as AccordionItem.svelte in the AccordionItem folder, then close it.

Great – we can knock another component off the list of tasks to create our library! This one is a little special, though, as it is a composite component or one made up of more than one subcomponent (all of the others are single component based).

This structure change presents one interesting point – how do we pass data down and ensure any that should stay local to their parent do stay local? Before we move on to the next and final component for this chapter, now's a perfect opportunity to review the code to see how our component hangs together in more detail.

Understanding What Happened

So far, all the components we've added have had one thing in common. They are effectively unitary components, or, for those of you familiar with it, atomic components (if you follow the Atomic Design principles created by Brad Frost, about which he has posted on his website at https://bradfrost.com/blog/post/atomic-web-design/). Our accordion component is the odd one out, as this is a molecule – we combined several elements to form our component.

To understand the difference, let's break down the steps we took: we started with the requisite folder creation (as before) before creating Accordion.svelte – this contained an import to the AccordionItem atom (or subcomponent), along with an empty object for data within the child component, AccordionItem:

```
<script>
  import AccordionItem from './AccordionItem.svelte'
  export let data = [];
</script>
```

At present, we're relying on making our data available via a JSON file. As we can use Web Components in any framework, we must pass values in string format; other formats are not accepted.

Moving on, we set up the markup for each item within the Accordion. We iterate through the data block using a Svelte #each function while at the same time destructuring each item as an instance of entry. This we pass into the AccordionItem component as a value for the title prop.

When we explore the AccordionItem component, things get more interesting – here, we have two imports, one for the slide transition effect and another for the style sheet. We then export entry (which we use to pass down the values to each instance of AccordionItem) and title (the heading for each bar in the Accordion) before defining a scoped variable isOpen for use within the Accordion component.

Next up, we then moved on to creating the markup for the button that acts as the trigger for each accordion item. It contains an SVG image of the chevron icon wrapped inside a button, followed by a Svelte {#if}...{/if} block to iterate through each entry and display it in the body of the Accordion item.

You will notice that we define data twice in this demo, but in slightly different formats (once in Accordion, but again in AccordionItem), even though data isn't imported until we get to AccordionItem!

I must admit this is a little odd, but it is needed to ensure we can pass in a title for each accordion drawer and the correct contents for that drawer. While it works for now, I would look to refactor this in a future iteration so that Accordion becomes more of a container and we keep data in AccordionItem.

An interesting part of this component lies in the use of the <slot> tag in AccordionItem – this allows us to pass in any data we wish (and, to an extent, structure too). I've wrapped each accordion drawer in a transition to make for a smoother effect, but the result will be up to you!

Adding the Component to Storybook

We have the code in place for our Accordion, so let's add it to our Storybook instance without further ado. The process for doing this is pretty much the same as the previous components, so, hopefully, the code will start to look more familiar by now – let's jump in and explore what's required in more detail.

LINKING INTO STORYBOOK

Setting up the Accordion to work in Storybook should be straightforward as we will use the same code process as other components. We only need to make small changes to our code to reflect using a new component – to see what I mean, follow these steps:

1. First, go ahead and create a new file in the same way as we've done before, then add this code – we'll start with the initial `<script>` block to import the component and documentation, along with some functions from Storybook:

```
import Accordion from "./Accordion.svelte";
```

2. With the initial configuration in place, we can set up the Accordion – we first need to insert the template, with only minor changes of component name required:

```
export default {
  title: "Garnet UI Library/Action Components/
  Accordion",
  component: Accordion,
  argTypes: {
    isOpen: false,
    data: [],
  },
  parameters: {
    docs: {
      story: { height: "500px", },
    },
  },
};
```

3. We can now render our component. We will use the same
    format as before and pass the properties required to configure
    our accordion component into it. Go ahead and add this block:

```
export const Default = {
  Component: Accordion,
  args: {
    isOpen: false,
    data: [
      {
        title: "Heading 1",
        text: "aorem ipsum dolor sit amet, consectetur
        adipiscing elit. Sed malesuada, nulla sed lacinia
        accumsan, ligula arcu interdum urna, eget rhoncus
        sapien orci scelerisque metus.",
      },
      {
        title: "Heading 2",
        text: "In bibendum commodo orci nec semper.
        Nam magna mauris, ornare eu semper sit amet,
        vehicula sed metus",
      },
      {
        title: "Heading 3",
        text: "Mauris tortor mi, scelerisque nec metus
        nec, finibus euismod lacus. Maecenas non
        porttitor arcu",
      },
    ],
  },
};
```

4.   Save the file as `Accordion.stories.js` in the `\src\lib\`
     `components/Accordion` folder, then close the file.

5.   As with previous components, we need to extract a copy of
     `Docs.mdx` from the code download and then drop it into the
     `Accordion` folder. The markdown in this file will add a page
     ready for us to insert documentation for our component.

6.   Switch to a Node.js terminal session, then set the working
     folder to our cobalt project area.

7.   At the prompt, enter `npm run storybook` and hit Enter – if
     all is well, we should see Storybook launch and display in our
     browser at `http://localhost:6006/`. Click the Default link
     under Spinner on the left to display the variant we created, as
     shown in Figure 3-4.

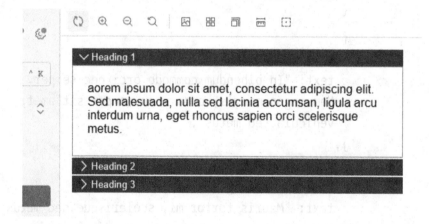

Figure 3-4. *The Accordion component on display in Storybook*

We're starting to cook now to coin that phrase! We've created the code
for all three components for this chapter and added them to our Storybook
instance. Before moving on to the next chapter and exploring our next
batch of features, let's review the changes made in the last demo to see
how our Accordion component hooks into Storybook.

Reviewing the Code

Adding an Accordion component to Storybook should now be a relatively familiar process – as before, we start with creating our Storybook page and then importing the component.

We then added a `default` function that acts as our default template (hence the name!), with properties to display the component page in the correct order. It includes setting the navigation structure in Storybook and a `docs:` height property. We first used this in the Spinner component – it controls the space available in the iframe element that Storybook uses to render the component. Without it, you wouldn't see all the accordion displayed properly – it will look cut off!

We then moved on to the critical part – displaying the Default instance of our component. Here, we passed the `open` and `data` properties to control when the accordion is open and the data to display. To finish off, we extracted a copy of the `Docs.mdx` file, which will act as documentation for the component, before launching Storybook to preview the results in our browser.

Before we wrap up this chapter, I want to cover one small but important point about this component: the use of the JSON data file. We defined `accordiondata.json` as our data source; while this works OK, it's not ideal, as it introduces a dependency into our component. It would be better in a future iteration to see if we can remove this dependency – we may still need to use JSON data, but I think there is scope to make the component more flexible when importing data.

Summary

And that's a wrap...!

Yes, indeed – we've added all three Action components to our library; each has its respective page in our Storybook instance. It means we've reached the halfway point of constructing features for our library, with only two more categories to add later in the book. Before we get on building the next category of components, let's take a moment to review what we have learned in this chapter.

As we saw in the previous chapter, we focus on adding each component to our library and setting it up in Storybook. We started with the SelectBox component before swiftly moving on to creating the Spinner component. It was a little more involved as we explored adding a new variant – we learned that even though we use the same markup, changes in styling effectively meant we had the equivalent of a new component.

We explored setting up an accordion component for the third and final component in this chapter. It was a little more complex, as we had to create two components: the main Accordion as the parent container and AccordionItem for displaying each item in the accordion component.

Okay, let's crack with creating the next batch: next up is our navigation-based component group. We'll look at creating components such as a navigation bar and buttons, a menu and tabs, and more – intrigued? Stay with me, and I promise to navigate you through everything in the next chapter if you pardon that terrible pun!

CHAPTER 4

Building Navigation Components

I may not have gone where I intended to go, but I think I have ended up where I needed to be.

That quote by the author Douglas Adams, from his 1988 detective novel, *The Long Dark Tea-Time of the Soul*, may have had a somewhat humorous edge, but I think it's an apt phrase to describe the theme for this chapter – they are all about navigation.

Good navigation is essential for any site – we can produce a mix of components (such as the ones we've built so far) for different pages, but if we can't navigate to them, we might as well pack up and go home!

Over the following few pages, we will build three components – a set of Tabs, a Breadcrumb trail, and a Chip component (so we can quickly browse to filtered collections of items). We will use similar methods throughout to help keep consistency and make it easier to develop; let's start with the Breadcrumbs component.

© Alex Libby 2025
A. Libby, *Developing Web Components with Svelte*,
https://doi.org/10.1007/979-8-8688-1180-7_4

Creating the Breadcrumbs Component

Hands up – how often have you had to navigate around a large website with less-than-ideal navigation? I'm sure you will have done it at least once...

We would typically navigate using links or menu options, but we might also use breadcrumbs. This latter navigation scheme shows where we are on a site, making it easier to go back and forth without remembering which menu option to choose or which link to click. Breadcrumbs (or breadcrumb trails) have only been around for around 20 years, but the term comes from the Hansel and Gretel tale, where two children leave a breadcrumb trail to find their way home. It seems somewhat ironic that a feature synonymous with larger websites dates back to the early 19th century!

But I digress. We will create a simple Breadcrumbs component for our first navigation component. We'll base it around a standard HTML unordered list, with some styling and the option to use a custom image or text for the divider. Let's dive in and look at how to create it in more detail.

For the custom image, I've used icons from the Iconify library (https://icon-sets.iconify.design/). This tool allows us to choose hundreds of icons from multiple sources by specifying the icon's family and name!

BUILDING THE BREADCRUMB TRAIL COMPONENT

To build our Breadcrumbs component, follow these steps:

1. First, create a new folder called Breadcrumbs at the root of the
    `\src\lib\components` folder.

2. Next, crack open a new file and add this code – we'll start with
    importing the style sheet, creating a few variables for export,
    and adding some default data from a JSON file:

```svelte
<svelte:options customElement="garnet-breadcrumbs" />
<script>
  export let divider = "/";
  export let iconFamily = "";
  export let iconName = "";
  export let breadcrumbItems = [];

  import Icon from '@iconify/svelte';
</script>
```

3. We can now add the markup for our component – much of this
    standard HTML markup, but it does include some Svelte tags.
    The first takes care of checking to see if we display a custom
    image or plain text as a divider:

```svelte
<div class="garnet-breadcrumbs">
  <ul class="breadcrumb">
  {#each breadcrumbItems as breadcrumbIitem, i}
    <li>
      <!-- Breadcrumb divider -->
      {#if i !==0}
        {#if !iconFamily && !iconName}
          <span>{divider}</span>
```

```
      {:else}
        <!-- Use icons from https://icon-sets.
        iconify.design/ -->
        <Icon icon={`${iconFamily}:${iconName}`} />
      {/if}
    {/if}
```

4. The second part of this block iterates through each item to determine if it is the link or end tag:

```
      <!-- Render each breadcrumb -->
      {#if i === breadcrumbItems.length - 1}
        {breadcrumbIitem.text}
      {:else}
        <a href={(breadcrumbIitem.href)} data-
        testid="breadcrumbLink">
          { breadcrumbIitem.text}
        </a>
      {/if}
    </li>
  {/each}
  </ul>
</div>
```

5. Next, miss a line after the closing `</div>`, and add these style rules:

```
<style>
  .garnet-breadcrumbs {
    display: flex;
    font-family: Arial, Helvetica, sans-serif;
  }
  ul.breadcrumb {
    padding: 10px 16px;
```

```
      list-style: none;
      background-color: #eee;
    }
    ul.breadcrumb li {
      display: inline;
      font-size: 18px;
      vertical-align: text-bottom;
    }
    ul.breadcrumb li a {
      color: #733635;
      text-decoration: none;
      vertical-align: text-bottom;
    }
    ul.breadcrumb li a:hover {
      color: #d19c9b;
      text-decoration: underline;
    }
    ul.breadcrumb li span {
      display: inline;
      padding: 8px;
    }
  </style>
```

6. Save the file as `Breadcrumbs.svelte`, then close any open files.

Excellent – we have our component in place. The next task is to try it to make sure it works; as before, we'll work through adding it to our Storybook instance. Before we get to that, let's take a moment to review the code changes made – most of it should be self-explanatory, but some interesting Svelte techniques within the code are worth exploring in more detail.

Understanding What Happened

At first glance, you might feel a little confused with the double conditional block in this component – it does feel like we've gone a little overboard in using them! The reality is that we need to perform these nested checks – the key to making this component work lies in the #each block we use inside the garnet <div> element.

We started by creating our component folder before adding the core component file. In this file, we have the now-familiar customElement tag, followed by defining some exported variables (divider, name of the icon family, and the icon itself, as well as an empty object for our data – more on this in a moment). At the same time, we also import the iconify/svelte library, which we will use later when rendering the icon in Storybook.

Let's switch back to the data for a moment. Although I've created an object for our data, I've set it to as an exported variable: this allows us to supply the data in instances like Storybook so that we can keep a clear separation between it and our component.

The real magic happens in the #each block that comes next – we iterate through the object, first checking to see if we need to display a divider. If the position of i (the index) is zero, we don't show one; otherwise, we display either a text or image-based divider, depending on what we set in the image or divider properties.

Once we've confirmed what to display, we then iterate through the object – we show a text label if the index matches the position of the last item or a link for all other entries. We end up with links for each entry in the chain, except for the last item, which indicates our chosen page. To round off the task, we added some basic styling, ready for us to test when adding the component to Storybook.

Adding the Component to Storybook

I know I've mentioned this before, but one of the benefits of careful planning is making code consistent and reusable. Keeping this level of reusability is perfect for making development more rapid; after all, why reinvent the wheel when it's unnecessary? On that note, let's continue with our Breadcrumbs component and set it up to work in our Storybook instance.

ADDING TO STORYBOOK

To get our Breadcrumbs component working in Storybook, follow these steps:

1. First, go ahead and create a new file, then add this code — as before, we have a reasonable chunk to add. Let's start with the initial `<script>` declaration block to import the component and assign some example data to a variable:

```
import Breadcrumbs from "./Breadcrumbs.svelte";

let levels = [
  { href: "/", text: "Dashboard" },
  { href: "/reports", text: "Annual reports" },
  { href: "/reports/2019", text: "2019" },
];
```

2. With the initial configuration in place, we can now focus on our component — as before, we first need to add a template. Skip a line, then add this block in — it's similar to previous examples, with only a minor change of component and `argTypes`:

```
export default {
  title: "Garnet UI Library/Navigation Components/
  Breadcrumbs",
  component: Breadcrumbs,
```

```
  argTypes: {
    BreadcrumbItems: levels,
    image: { control: "boolean" },
  },
};
```

3. We can now render our component – for this, we will create a
    story function similar to earlier components. Go ahead and add
    this block:

```
export const Default = (args) => ({
  Component: Breadcrumbs,
  props: {
    ...args,
    breadcrumbItems: [
      { href: "/", text: "Dashboard" },
      { href: "/reports", text: "Annual reports" },
      { href: "/reports/2024", text: "2024" },
    ],
  },
});
```

4. Let's also add a second story – this one will show a custom
    image instead of a text-based character, which we set as our
    default divider in the component:

```
export const CustomImage = (args) => ({
  Component: Breadcrumbs,
  props: {
    ...args,
    iconFamily: "material-symbols",
    iconName: "arrow-right-alt",
    breadcrumbItems: [
      { href: "/", text: "Dashboard" },
```

```
        { href: "/reports", text: "Annual reports" },
        { href: "/reports/2024", text: "2024" },
      ],
    },
});
```

5. Although we set a / as our default divider, it doesn't mean
    we're limited to using just this – what if we wanted to use other
    characters? No problem: here's our third story, which this time
    uses a double arrow as our divider (highlighted in bold):

```
export const TextDivider = (args) => ({
    Component: Breadcrumbs,
    props: {
        ...args,
        divider: ">>",
        breadcrumbItems: [
            { href: "/", text: "Dashboard" },
            { href: "/reports", text: "Annual reports" },
            { href: "/reports/2024", text: "2024" },
        ],
    },
});
```

6. Save the file as `Breadcrumbs.stories.js` in the
    `Breadcrumbs` component folder, then close the file.

7. We have one last file to add – our documentation. For this,
    extract a copy of `Docs.mdx` and drop it into the `Breadcrumbs`
    folder in our project area.

8. We have everything in place, so let's test it! Switch to a Node.
    js terminal session, then set the working folder to our garnet
    project area.

9. At the prompt, enter npm run storybook and hit Enter – if all is well, we should see Storybook launch and display in our browser at http://localhost:6006/. Click the Default link under Breadcrumbs on the left to display the variant we just created, as shown in Figure 4-1.

Figure 4-1. *Displaying the Breadcrumbs component with a standard divider*

10. Click the Custom image link on the left – this variant swaps out the double slash and replaces it with a custom arrow icon (Figure 4-2).

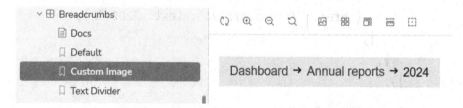

Figure 4-2. *Displaying the Breadcrumb variant with a custom image*

It never ceases to amaze me how a standard element that has been around for decades is something we can turn into a useful feature with little more than a couple of functions and some styling!

List elements are incredibly versatile; Svelte's light touch means we can create all manner of components with minimal extra code. This concept was no different for the Breadcrumbs component we've just made – let's take a moment to review the code in more detail before cracking on with our next navigation component.

Exploring the Code in Detail

Much of this component follows a similar pattern to the others we've already created – we started with the now-familiar customElement tag before adding a block of test data, which we assign to the levels object.

We then set out our default template, in which we specify our title (which we will use to create the navigation in Storybook). We also add the name of our component (here, Breadcrumbs) and the argTypes, which define the prop types we want to use.

Next up, we added two function blocks that act as our stories – the first is Default, which defines the data to use. In the second story, I've added iconFamily and iconName – remember how I referred to them when creating the component? Adding them gives a new edge to our component – rather than manually pulling in custom images, we set family and icon names; the Iconify package we import does the heavy lifting! We might want to specify something specific to us, like an in-house icon, but that can come in a future update.

Okay – let's move on: our next component is one you will likely find at the bottom of online posts, articles, and the like. I'm talking about the humble chip – not the one you might get in a takeaway fish and chips meal on a Friday night, but the one we use to categorize items online, such as posts. These may be small, but they play a crucial part in navigating to filtered collections of content – let's dive in and look at how we might create such a component for our library.

Building a Chip Component

Any site naturally needs content of some form – after all, an empty site wouldn't be very useful to anyone! This content will vary – it might be posts about a subject such as photography or collections of products for sale (such as honey – love the stuff!).

Whatever the content, we need a way to quickly see items of a related type of content, such as all pots of honey for sale or articles for a particular kind of camera. One way we might do this is by using chips – we can pass in a link to a collection of items so that the reader can quickly access that content without difficulty. It's a valuable component to have in our library, so let's dive in and look at how we might create one in more detail.

CREATING A CHIP COMPONENT

To build our chip component, follow these steps:

1. First, go ahead and create a new folder called `Chip` under `\src\lib\components`.

2. Next, crack open a new file and add this code – we'll start with the now-familiar `svelte:options` directive, followed by importing our icon and a function from Svelte:

```
<svelte:options customElement="garnet-chip" />
<script>
   import DeleteIcon from './DeleteIcon.svelte';
   import { createEventDispatcher } from 'svelte';
```

3. Miss a line, then add these exported variables – we'll use these in the component itself, but also when we add our "story" in Storybook:

```
   export let active = true;
   export let close = false;
```

108

```
export let chipContent = "";
export let selected = false;
export let outline = false;
```

4. We need to add a small function to handle the close button –
   we set this to simply pass through the event to the onClose
   equivalent in the element:

```
const dispatch = createEventDispatcher();
function onClose(e) {
  active = false;
  dispatch('close', e);
}
```

5. This next property will take care of switching between one of
   two styles we will use – filled and outline. We'll return to this
   shortly when we add our component to Storybook.

```
$: outline = outline;
</script>
```

6. Next, it's time for the markup – it's not a large component, so
   go ahead and copy the code below into your document:

```
<div class="garnet-chip">
  {#if active}
    <!-- svelte-ignore a11y-no-static-element-
    interactions -->
    <!-- svelte-ignore a11y-click-events-have-key-
    events -->
    <div
      class="chip"
      class:selected
      class:outline
      on:click>
```

```
            <span>{chipContent}</span>
            {#if close}
              <span class="close" on:click={onClose}>
                <DeleteIcon />
              </span>
            {/if}
          </div>
      {/if}
    </div>
```

7. To finish off this part, we need to add some styling – there is a
   nice chunk to add, so we'll begin with the container .garnet
   style rule:

```
<style>
  .garnet-chip {
    display: flex;
    font-family: Arial, Helvetica, sans-serif;
  }
```

8. This next rule contains most of the styles for the chip itself:

```
  .chip {
    color: #733635;
    align-items: center;
    cursor: default;
    display: inline-flex;
    line-height: 20px;
    max-width: 100%;
    outline: none;
    overflow: hidden;
    padding: 0 12px;
    position: relative;
    text-decoration: none;
```

```
vertical-align: middle;
white-space: nowrap;
border-radius: 25px;
padding: 10px;
background-color: #d3d3d3;
}
```

9. The remaining styles take care of the close button and setting an outline style variant (we will use this in Storybook):

```
.close { cursor: pointer; margin-left: 6px; margin-
right: -6px; display: flex; }
.close:focus, .close:hover, .close:active {
    opacity: 0.72;
}
.outline { background-color: #ffffff; border: 1px
solid #d3d3d3; }
</style>
```

10. At this point, we can save and close all open files – we will test our component in the next exercise, which will be up shortly.

Perfect – we now have a working Chip component! We can now pull it into Storybook and test that it works as expected. This next stage should be relatively familiar by now, so before we crack on with adding the new component to Storybook, let's quickly cover off the changes we made for our Chip component in more detail.

Exploring the Code Changes

As with all components in this book, we use a similar pattern – we start with the now-familiar customElement tag before adding two imports, one for an icon and another for the createEventDispatcher function from Svelte.

Next, we created some variables (active, close, chipContent, selected, and outline), which we set to be exportable – we'll use them all later when we add our component to Storybook. At the same time, we then added a placeholder onClose function. It allows us to set an onClose event handler when we use the component and pass it directly to the component itself. We then round out the script part of the code by setting outline as a reactive statement. We will use this when we create the variant for our Chip component later in this book.

Okay – now for the more complex part! The markup looks a little complex for a simple component: in reality, we have a set of spans nested inside two div elements. We will always display at least one span, but depending on whether close is set to true or false will determine if we render the second span in the browser. Outside of this, we pass in several props to the inside div element, such as class:selected or the on:click event handler, then wrap all of the content inside the usual garnet div element.

To wrap things up, we finish by adding a bunch of styling – most of it applies to the core Chip component, but we also add some for the close button, so it reacts appropriately when we hover over it or have it in focus in the browser.

Accessibility

So far, we've developed a good set of components, but there is one thing we've not covered: accessibility.

Accessibility is an essential part of any component – with one in five people living with a disability, illness, or long-term impairment, we risk excluding up to 20% of the population if they can't use a site due to inaccessible components! It raises questions about how far we can go – we can't cater for everything from day one, so we need to add this in as resources allow. I've not included it for now, so you will see some esLint exclusions appear in the code. We'll go through this, and more, when we cover accessibility in more detail in Chapter 9.

Hooking the Component into Storybook

We've built the Chip component, so it's time for us to get it into Storybook. We will use the same process as previous components, which will help speed up the process. Let's look at the steps involved in more detail to see if the Chip component works as expected in Storybook.

HOOKING INTO STORYBOOK

To get our Chip component working in Storybook, follow these steps:

1. First, go ahead and create a new file, then add this import – this brings the Chip component into the Storybook file:

```
import Chip from "./Chip.svelte";
```

2. Next up, we need to add a template – in a similar manner
   to other components, this will display default values in the
   absence of anything specific set in each story:

```
export default {
    title: "Garnet UI Library/Navigation
    Components/Chip",
    component: Chip,
    props: {
        close: false,
        outline: false,
        chipContent: "Test chip",
    },};
```

3. Perfect – with our default template now in place, we can add
   the main story. Go ahead and miss a line, then add this block:

```
export let Default = (args) => ({
    Component: Chip,
    props: {
        ...args,
        close: false,
        chipContent: "Test chip",
    },
});
```

4. Save the file as `Chip.stories.js`, then close the file.

5. As a last step, we need to source our Chip documentation file –
   for this, extract a copy of `Docs.mdx` from the code download,
   and add it to the Chip folder.

6. We have everything in place, so let's test it! Switch to a Node.
   js terminal session, then set the working folder to our garnet
   project area.

7. At the prompt, enter npm run storybook and hit Enter – if all is well, we should see Storybook launch and display in our browser at http://localhost:6006/. Click the Default link under the Chip entry on the left to display the component we just created, as shown in Figure 4-3.

Figure 4-3. *The Chip component running in Storybook*

8. Leave Storybook running in the background for now – we will return to it shortly.

Excellent – we can now see our Chip component working! Granted, it's only a small component, but a useful one – we could use it to tag related content on blog sites or even provide a link to similar products for sale, such as screwdrivers (assuming you're running a hardware ecommerce offer!).

Okay – let's crack on: even though this was a relatively simple component, it still has an important role to play. We've used some critical functions in our component code, so let's take a moment to explore the code in more detail.

Understanding the Changes Made

To get our chip component hooked into Storybook, we started by importing the Chip component, before creating a default template. This template contains properties you will be familiar with by now, such as the title (used for building the index in Storybook) and the name of the component. We also have our argTypes entry; this time, we're using it to create an oninput handler for the component.

It's worth noting that if you look through the code for each component, you will notice that it seems like there's a certain degree of repetition for those that use event handlers! Truth be told, it does feel like it, but we have to add these event handlers in several places – the component itself, the default template, and the Default (or other) templates that use the component. Think of the one in the default template as a pass-through from the Storybook entry to the component itself – without it, you will find a component doesn't do anything!

As a reminder – we use both default and Default when naming templates. It's easy to confuse the two: the first takes care of what happens if an overriding value is not provided. The Default is more for what happens out of the box when we don't change the default configuration. Ideally, I would choose different names for at least the latter. I'll return to this in Chapter 11 when we tidy up the components, ready for release.

Returning to the Storybook file, we have our Default template present – here, we set similar properties to those shown in default, but this time, we add the event handler we want to use. The default template references the type of event handler to expect; we then set the actual handler in the on: property within each story.

As we're using Storybook, all of the windows.alert entries will appear in the Actions tab, not as a separate alert window.

To finish things off, we extracted a copy of the Docs.mdx file as our documentation, saved everything, and previewed the results of our work in a browser.

Building Two Variants

Variants – for a small component, is it possible to have any, let alone more than one?

The answer is yes: while building a disabled version might not suit this component (unlike others), we can still change the styling and appearance. An obvious one we could do is add a close button – this would be perfect for those occasions when we want to filter out irrelevant products or reset the filters to show everything. We could change the styling, too – let's look at two variants I've created as a starting point.

ADDING TWO VARIANTS

To build our two variants, follow these steps:

1. First, go ahead and crack open the Chip.stories.js file – scroll to the bottom, then add this block to display a close button in our chip:

```
export let CloseButton = (args) => ({
  Component: Chip,
  props: {
    ...args,
    close: true,
    chipContent: "Test chip",
  },
});
```

2. This second variant changes the standard design of the chip from a solid-filled one to one with an outline only:

```
export let Outline = (args) => ({
  Component: Chip,
```

```
      props: {
        ...args,
        outline: true,
        chipContent: "Test chip",
      },
    });
```

3. Save, then close the file. Switch to your instance of Storybook, and then refresh the page. If all is well, we should see two new variants appear, as shown in Figures 4-4 and 4-5.

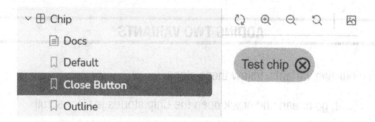

Figure 4-4. *Displaying the Close button variant*

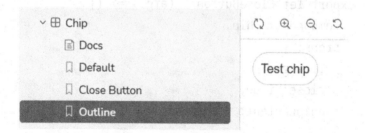

Figure 4-5. *Displaying the Outline variant*

Perfect – this is just the start, though, as there are a few more ideas for variants that come to mind:

- Adding an avatar or picture of someone, maybe as the author of a series of posts or articles on a site.

- We could even turn the Chip into a Status chip: What about adding someone's name but showing a Teams, Slack, or social messaging status? You might not want to alert all visitors to the status of your availability online, so it's something we should use with care! At the moment, I'm only thinking about the technical how-to for this; deciding if it is something you want to do will be up to you...

- I've used an SVG icon of a delete symbol in one variant, but what about experimenting with the Iconify code we created for the Breadcrumbs component? I'll bet there are a few versions we could make using it!

- Here's another idea: How often have you seen pills created that contained color names or showed off themes, such as red for warning or green for success? It's a slightly different concept, but the code will likely be similar and only need minor changes.

Hopefully, these will get you started with something – the great thing about Svelte is its light touch on code, allowing us to create all manner of different variants with only superficial changes to code.

Okay – let's move on to the third and final component for this chapter: Tabs. Yes, you know the kind: they are everywhere! It's a great way to display (and navigate to) content quickly and easily, so let's dive in and take a look at the steps needed to build a Tabs component.

Constructing the Tabs Component

If you buy anything online, such as books or products from the likes of Amazon, I can guarantee you will see instances of our next component: Tabs. Tabs components may only serve one purpose, but they serve it well – they are a perfect way to display lots of information in a small area while allowing you to view specific tabs as your needs dictate.

For the last component in this chapter, we will build a simple Tabs component. The basic structure centers around an unordered list, but we need some Svelte magic to make it hang together – let's look at how we create such a component in our next exercise.

BUILDING THE TABS COMPONENT

To construct our Tabs component, follow these steps:

1. To start, go ahead and create a new folder called Tabs inside the \src\lib\components folder within our project area.

2. Next, crack open a new file and add this code – we set several variables for export, such as the active tab (activeTabValue), our data source (items), and vertical, used later in Storybook:

```
<svelte:options customElement = "garnet-tabs" />
<script>
  export let activeTabValue = "0";
  export let items;
  if (items == null) {
    items = tabItems;
  }
  const handleClick = tabValue => () =>
  (activeTabValue = tabValue);
</script>
```

3. Next up, miss a line, then add the markup to render our Tabs
    component:

```
<div class="garnet">
  <ul >
    {#each Object.entries(items) as [id]}
      <li class={activeTabValue === id ? 'active' : ''}
      data-testid="tabHeader">
        <!-- svelte-ignore a11y-click-events-have-key-
        events -->
        <!-- svelte-ignore a11y-no-static-element-
        interactions -->
        <span on:click={handleClick(id)}>
          {JSON.stringify(items[id].name).replace
          (/['"]+/g, "")}
        </span>
      </li>
    {/each}
  </ul>
  <div class="content" data-testid="tabContent">
    {#each Object.entries(items) as [id]}
      {#if activeTabValue === id}
        {JSON.stringify(items[id].text)
        .replace(/['"]+/g, "")}
      {/if}
    {/each}
  </div>
</div>
```

4. To finish off the component, we need to add some basic styling – we first add our library's theme colors, followed by some rudimentary styling:

```
<style>
  .garnet-tabs {
    display: flex;
    flex-direction: column;
    font-family: Arial, Helvetica, sans-serif;
  }
  ul {
    display: flex;
    flex-wrap: wrap;
    padding-left: 0;
    margin-bottom: 0;
    list-style: none;
    border-bottom: 1px solid #dee2e6;
  }
  li {
    margin-bottom: -1px;
  }
  span {
    border: 1px solid transparent;
    border-top-left-radius: 4px;
    border-top-right-radius: 4px;
    display: block;
    padding: 8px 16px;
    cursor: pointer;
  }
```

```
span:hover {
  border-color: #dee2e6;
  border-bottom-color: #ffffff;
}
li.active > span {
  color: #ffffff;
  background-color: #733635;    border-color: #dee2e6
  #dee2e6 #fff;
}
.content {
  padding: 10px;
  min-height: 300px;
}
```

5. Save the file as `Tabs.svelte` in the same Tabs folder and close it.

Great – that's the first part done! We now have a Tabs component ready to pull into Storybook and test that it works as expected. This next stage should be relatively familiar by now, so let's crack on with adding the new component to Storybook without further ado.

Exploring the Code Changes

In some ways, building a Tabs component is almost a game of two halves – although we are creating one component, we have to construct code for the tab header (or tab itself) and the tab content area. Fortunately, Svelte makes this very easy, with not too much markup required!

We started by creating the requisite folder before adding code to what would become our core component – the first block imported styles before setting up two exported values – `items[]` and `activeTabValue`. At the same time, we added the `<svelte:options>` directive to tell Svelte we are creating a web component. We also add a `handleClick` event handler to switch between each tab, based on which `tabvalue` we set.

Next, we added the markup for our component based on an unordered list. We first check that our `items` object is of type array before iterating through each item and setting an `active` class on the list item, depending on whether we've clicked the tab. At the same time, we display `item.name` as the header for each tab, then iterate through `items` and use `ActiveTabValue` to determine which content area to display as the tab in our browser.

You will notice the presence of `.replace(...)` when we display the text – this is purely to remove the quotes around each text entry from the JSON file. It's a little hacky, so we can't display quotes in the tab panel, but it works!

Hooking the Component into Storybook

With the component now constructed, adding the Tabs component to our Storybook instance should be straightforward. We will use the same process as previous components, which will help speed up the process. Let's look at the steps involved in more detail to see if the Tabs component works as expected in Storybook.

HOOKING INTO STORYBOOK

To get our Tabs component working in Storybook, follow these steps:

1. First, go ahead and create a new file, then add these imports – the first brings in our Tabs component, and the second brings in a block of test data to display on-screen:

```
import Tabs from "./Tabs.svelte";
import tabItems from "./tabsdata.json";
```

2. This next bit should be very familiar by now – leave a line blank, then add this export block. As before, it adds a title, sets the component we want to use, and defines the types of arguments we will use by default in each story unless specified otherwise:

```
export default {
  title: "Garnet UI Library/Navigation
  Components/Tabs",
  component: Tabs,
  argTypes: {
    vertical: false,
    items: tabItems,
  },
};
```

3. We can now render our component. For this, we will create a default function similar to what we did earlier in the book. Go ahead and add this block:

```
export const Default = {
  args: {
    vertical: false,
    items: tabItems,
  },
};
```

4. Save the file as `Tabs.stories.js`, then close the file.

5. As a last step, we need to source our Tabs documentation file – go ahead and extract a copy of `Docs.mdx` from the code download and add it to the Tabs folder.

6. We have everything in place, so let's test it! Switch to a Node.
js terminal session, then set the working folder to our garnet
project area.

7. At the prompt, enter `npm run storybook` and hit Enter – if
all is well, we should see Storybook launch and display in our
browser at `http://localhost:6006/`. Click the `Default`
link under the Tabs entry on the left to display the component
we just created, as shown in Figure 4-6.

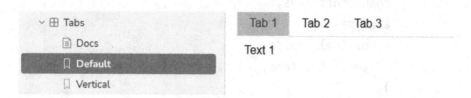

Figure 4-6. *The new Tabs component on display in Storybook*

There – that doesn't look too shabby, does it? Granted, it doesn't have
all the features other Tabs components may have, but that will come in
time; we've created a solid base for further development.

That isn't the end of it, though – there is scope to add a variation of
our component, which we will do momentarily (you can see a hint of it in
that last screenshot). Before we do so, let's pause for a moment to review
the code changes we just made to see how the Tabs component renders in
Storybook in more detail.

Understanding the Changes Made

By now, I'm sure you will be familiar with how we can add our component
to Storybook – so much so that with a little trial and error, we might be at
a point where you can almost do it without needing help! Don't worry,
though – I'm not going to leave you just yet: let's break that code apart to
see how it all hangs together.

We started by adding the now-familiar import call, this time for our Tabs component. We then also imported tabItems, which is some dummy data I've created as a JSON file. The rest of the Storybook code is very similar to other components – we include the default function block for our template and a Default function to render an instance of the Tabs component out of the box. To round things off, we also obtained a copy of the placeholder Docs.mdx documentation file before running up the Storybook development server and previewing the results in our browser.

Creating a Variant

For the last demo in this chapter, we're going to modify how our Tabs component looks – in many cases, we would display the component horizontally, but there may be occasions where displaying the tab "heads" on the side would be a preferred option.

Fortunately, the changes needed to implement our new variant are pretty straightforward; let's crack on and implement them to see how our new variant appears in Storybook.

CREATING A VERTICAL VARIANT

To add our variant, follow these steps:

1. First, crack open the Tabs.svelte file, then add this line immediately below the last export:

   ```
   export let vertical = false;
   ```

2. We also need to add a Svelte reactive statement for this property, which tells Svelte to update it every time the value changes. Add this below the handleClick event handler and just before the closing </script> tag:

   ```
   $: vertical = vertical
   ```

3. Next, scroll down to the opening `<div>` tag for the markup and amend the code as highlighted:

```
<div class="garnet-tabs" class:vertical>
```

4. We also need to do something similar for these three lines (at various places in the code) – add `class:vertical` as indicated:

```
<ul class:vertical>
...
<span class:vertical on:click={handleClick(id)}>
...
<div class="content" class:vertical data-testid=…
```

5. Scroll down toward the bottom of the page, then add these three rules before the closing `</style>` tag:

```
/* variant */
.garnet-tabs.vertical { display: flex; flex-
direction: row; }
ul.vertical{
    display: flex;
    flex-direction: column;
    border-right: 1px solid #dee2e6;
    border-bottom: none;
    margin-top: 0;
}
ul.vertical span { border-radius: 0; border-right: 0;
border-color: #dee2e6;
    }
```

6. Save the file and close it. Switch to the `Tabs.stories.js` file, then scroll to the default template block:

7. Amend the `argTypes` function to this:

```
argTypes: {
    vertical: false,
  items: tabItems,
},
```

8. In the Default block just below it, amend the `args` block to this:

```
args: {
    vertical: false,
    items: tabItems,,
  },
/>
```

9. Leave a line blank after that story, then add this new block for our variant:

```
export const Vertical = {
  args: {
    vertical: true,
    items: tabItems,
  },
};
```

10. Save the file and close it. We have everything in place, so let's test it! Switch to a Node.js terminal session, and make sure the working folder is set to our garnet project area.

11. At the prompt, enter npm run storybook and hit Enter – if all is well, we should see Storybook launch and display in our browser at `http://localhost:6006/`. Click the `Vertical` link under the Tabs entry on the left to display the component we just created, as shown in Figure 4-7.

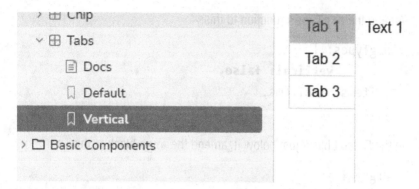

Figure 4-7. *The new variant for the Tabs component*

Perfect – with only a few minor changes (most of which were CSS based), we have a new variant for our Tabs component! Sure, this is only one variant, and with some work, we could add more variants (such as different tabs, language support, support for disabling tabs, and so on). It does show that with minimal changes, we can turn an existing component into something different and usable by developers consuming our library.

So, how did we get here? We started by adding an exported variable vertical – this would trigger the component to display our tab set horizontally or vertically (and which is controlled by the Svelte reactive statement in the block). We then updated the opening <div> tag, the <ul> element, and the internal <span> tags using the class: directive; this tells the component to include the vertical class if our variable vertical is true.

Next up, we added a new markup block for our variant – into this, we passed the vertical variable, which we set to true (and amended the Default story to include this new parameter.) We then added a handful of styles to re-render the Tabs in a vertical format. That's one of the great things about Svelte – we do most of the work using CSS, with only minimal markup required to refactor our component!

Summary

And that's the end of this journey, ladies and gentlemen. I hope you've enjoyed what you've seen...

Creating excellent navigation for a site is essential – it's the bread and butter we need to help customers find what they want and keep them within the confines of our site. To help with that, we've created three navigation components for our library; each has its respective page in our Storybook instance. We're now over halfway, with only one more component category to add to our library! Before we get on building the next category of components, let's take a moment to review what we have learned in this chapter.

As we saw in the previous chapter, we focused on adding each component to our library and setting it up in Storybook. We started with creating the Breadcrumbs trail component before swiftly moving on to building a Chip component – one that looks simple but belies the complex code behind it!

We explored setting up a Tabs component for the third and final tool in our toolbox. It was a little more involved as we examined adding a new variant – we learned that even though we use the same markup, changes in styling effectively meant we had the equivalent of a new component.

Okay, let's crack with creating the penultimate batch of components: the notification group. We'll look at creating components such as an overlay, modal dialog boxes, and more – intrigued? Stay with me, and I'll reveal it all in the next chapter...

CHAPTER 5

Creating Notification Components

I spend many an hour reading and researching material for the books I've written – I've come across all manner of different articles, views, and ideas; too many to count! There was, however, one thing that I found that I think is very apt for this chapter:

You can be happy with less and miserable with more.

This little gem from the author and entrepreneur Robert Gill is perfect for the following few pages – particularly when I say we will look at creating notification components! One hopes that we never get any indicating an error of some kind; indeed, the less we get, the more we're happy!

Keeping that thought, we will create three more components – an Alert, Dialog, and Tooltip. Much of what you are about to see will reuse many of the principles we've already covered, so without further ado, let's crack on with creating the first, which is the Alert component.

Creating the Alert Component

An essential part of the user experience for anyone browsing a website is making sure we keep them informed. While we expect things to run smoothly, there will be occasions when we must notify our customers

© Alex Libby 2025
A. Libby, *Developing Web Components with Svelte*,
https://doi.org/10.1007/979-8-8688-1180-7_5

if there is a problem! We need an alert component – we will develop a suitable tool for our component toolbox using the standard HTML5 dialog element.

We could build something from the ground up, but there's no need to do so when most recent browsers natively support the `<dialog>` element. In our next exercise, we can use that to construct our alert component. Before assembling the code, we should cover one small point relating to the icons we use in the exercise.

Sourcing the Icons

Our alert component will use the SVG markup from icons chosen from the Ionicons library at `https://ionic.io/ionicons`. I've picked two and edited versions of them for the exercise; the (renamed) originals will be available in the code download.

If you want to use different ones, head to the website and enter "alert" or "warn" in the search box. It will come back with at least two options – to download the SVGs, click one of the icons, then hit the SVG icon to the right of the brown box at the foot of the screen in Figure 5-1.

Figure 5-1. *The download icon on the Ionic website*

You will need to update the SVG markup used in one of the files in the next exercise – I will point out which one, at the appropriate point. Okay – with that in mind, let's begin with the next exercise to construct our alert component.

Building the Component

Although we're building for what should be a simple alert component, the code we need to use is a little more complex than some of our other components! We will have to create a few files and add the SVGs we talked about just now, so let's start with creating the core component first.

BUILDING THE ALERT COMPONENT

To construct our alert component, follow these steps:

1. First, create a new folder called `Alert` at the root of the components folder.

2. Next, crack open a new file and add this code — we'll start with setting our usual `customElement` tag, then importing an Icon component, and setting a few variables for export:

    ```svelte
    <svelte:options tag="garnet-alert" />

    <script>
        import Icon from './Icon.svelte';
        export let show;
        export let showIcon = true;
        export let type = "";
        export let title = "";
        export let description = "";
        export let showAnimation = true;
        let typeClass;
    ```

3. Next, leave a line blank, then add the second part of our script block, which will determine which style to use for our alert component:

    ```
    switch (type) {
      case "warn":
    ```

```
          typeClass = "alert-warn";
          break;
       case "dark":
          typeClass = "alert-dark";
          break;
       case "error":
          typeClass = "alert-error";
          break;
       case "info":
          typeClass = "alert-info";
          break;
       case "success":
          typeClass = "alert-success";
          break;
     default:
          typeClass = "";
     }
     const classes = ["alert", typeClass, showAnimation ?
     "fade-in" : ""]
       .join(" ");
```

4. The last part of our script will take care of closing the alert
    when triggered by clicking the X in the modal:

```
    const closeAlert = () => {
      show = false;
    };
</script>
```

5. We can now add the markup for our component – much of this
    standard HTML markup, but with a few Svelte tags. Miss a line,
    then add this block:

```
<div class="garnet">
  {#if show}
    <!-- svelte-ignore a11y-click-events-have-key-
    events -->
```

136

```svelte
<!-- svelte-ignore a11y-no-noninteractive-element-
interactions -->
<dialog class={classes} role="alert">
  <div class="icon">
    {#if showIcon}<Icon iconType={type} />{/if}
  </div>
  <div class="message">
    <strong>
      {title}
    </strong>
    {description}
  </div>
  <div>
    <button on:click={closeAlert}>&#x2716;</button>
  </div>
</dialog>
  {/if}
</div>
```

6. We have one more section to add, which is the styling. For
    this, leave a blank line after the code from step 4, then add
    this block:

```svelte
<style>
  dialog {
    min-width: 300px;
    display: flex;
    justify-content: space-between;
    font-family: Arial, Helvetica, sans-serif;
    border: none;
  }

  button {
    background: none;
    border: none;
```

```
      font-size: 21px;
    }

    .icon {
      margin-right: 10px;
    }

    .message {
      display: flex;
      flex-direction: column;
      line-height: 24px;
      min-width: 300px;
    }

    .fade-in {
      animation: fade-in 2000ms both;
    }

    @keyframes fade-in {
      from {
        opacity: 0%;
      }
    }

    .alert-warn {
      background: #ffeb3b;
      color: #000000;
    }
  </style>
```

7. Save the file as `Alert.svelte`, then close it. Next, crack open a new file and add this code – this time, we first need to set three exported variables before adding what will be the markup for the first of three icons we add to our component:

```
<svelte:options customElement="garnet-icon" />

<script>
```

```
export let width = "24px";
export let height = "24px";
export let iconType = "";

let icons = [
  {
    box: 512,
    name: "warn",
    svg: `<path d="M85.57 446.25h340.86a32 32
0 0028.17-47.17L284.18 82.58c-12.09-22.44-44.
27-22.44-56.36 0L57.4 399.08a32 32 0 0028.17
47.17z" fill="none" stroke="currentColor"
stroke-linecap="round" stroke-linejoin="round"
stroke-width="32"/><path d="M250.26 195.39l5.74
122 5.73-121.95a5.74 5.74 0 00-5.79-6h0a5.74 5.74
0 00-5.68 5.95z" fill="none" stroke="currentColor"
stroke-linecap="round" stroke-linejoin="round"
stroke-width="32"/>
<path d="M256 397.25a20 20 0 1120-20 20 20 0 01-20 20z"/>`,
  },
```

8. Next up, add these lines – this will form the second icon for our demo:

```
let displayIcon = icons.find((e) => e.name ===
iconType);
</script>
```

The markup is available in the code download, so you don't have to edit manually! Although I've only included markup for one icon, we will add more later in this chapter when we look at variants for this component.

---

9. With the SVG markup in place, we now need to call it – for this, miss a line, then add this markup, which will take care of choosing the right icons based on the name passed in when calling the component:

```
<svg
  class={$$props.class}
  {width}
  {height}
  viewBox="0 0 {displayIcon.box} {displayIcon.box}">
    {@html displayIcon.svg}
</svg>
```

10. Save the file as `Icon.svelte` in the Alert folder, and close it and any other open files.

Great – our component is in place and ready to test! Although much of the code consists of standard HTML markup and CSS styling, there are a few interesting points where we use Svelte syntax. Before we add our component to Storybook, let's take some time to review the code and understand how it all works – I know the SVG part will appear a little confusing at first!

Understanding What Happened

In an ideal world, we would never need to display alerts to people using a site or online application – everything would run smoothly, customers get what they want and where they need to be, and leave happy and content...

However, the reality is that it is all a pipe dream and that we still need to display the occasional alert! With that in mind, and to construct our component, we started by creating the usual component folder before setting some variables for export. At the same time, we imported an Icon component and set a handful of variables for use internally, such as show, type, and title.

Next, we set up a somewhat lengthy `switch` statement for type – this determines what class to set based on the value assigned to `type`. For example, if we had passed in "warn," we would apply the class `alert-warn` to the component, and so on. We then concatenate all classes together, ready for use in our component.

You will notice that, unlike other components, we've not used `createEventDispatcher` in this component. In this case, I don't believe it's necessary – the event handler serves a single purpose: to close the alert. No matter how we write the code, it still serves the same purpose! In this case, it *should* be sufficient to run this internally; if circumstances change, we can always come back and expose this event handler.

We then moved on to adding the markup for our component – this is where things get a little more complex. We wrap everything in a Svelte `if` block inside our parent `garnet` div element; we show or hide the component based on the value of `show`. We built the core part of the component around an HTML5 `dialog` element, passing the classes we set earlier and setting an on-`click` event handler to close the alert. The rest of the markup is standard HTML, except for the second Svelte `if` block and the event handler assigned to the close button. To round off that part, we add some basic styling, including a simple animation to render the alert.

Right – let's crack on: we still have plenty to do! It's time we tested our component to ensure it works, so as with others, let's dive in and hook our component into Storybook.

Adding the Component to Storybook

So far, we've created the core Alert component, added some styling, and sourced three SVGs to act as icons when displaying the Alert. We're now at a stage where we can test the component, so as before, let's crack on with adding an instance to Storybook so we can prove it works as we expect.

ADDING TO STORYBOOK

To get our alert component working in Storybook, follow these steps:

1. First, go ahead and create a new file, then add this import:

```
import Alert from './ Alert.svelte';
```

2. This next part of the process should be very familiar by now – we need to create a default template that contains values to display, should we not override them in specific stories:

```
export default {
  title: "Garnet UI Library/Notification
  Components/Alert",
  component: Alert,
  argTypes: {
    type: { control: "string" },
    title: { control: "string" },
    description: { control: "string" },
    showIcon: { action: "boolean" },
  },
  parameters: {
    docs: {
      story: {
        height: "100px",
```

```
      },
     },
    },
};
```

3. Next, leave a line blank, then this code – it's the `Default` story, to render our Alert component as is (largely) with default values:

```
export const Default = () => ({
  Component: Alert,
  props: {
    show: true,
    type: "info",
    title: "Simple Info",
    description: "An info description",
    showIcon: "true",
  },
});
```

4. Save the file as `Alert.stories.js`, then close the file.

5. You will see from the code that we've specified a file as our documentation but haven't yet added it. We need to extract a copy of `Docs.mdx` from the code download and then drop it into the Alert folder.

6. We have everything in place, so let's test it! Switch to a Node. js terminal session, then set the working folder to our garnet project area.

7. At the prompt, enter `npm run storybook` and hit Enter – if all is well, we should see Storybook launch and display in our browser at http://localhost:6006/. Click the Default link under Alert on the left to display the variant we just created, as shown in Figure 5-2, as a blue dialog box.

Figure 5-2. *Displaying the new Alert warning in Storybook*

Excellent – we now have a working component ready for others to use. It's a simple affair (even if the code might say otherwise) but an essential addition to our library!

However, if we had to display any alerts, they wouldn't just be information ones – what about warnings or success messages, for example? Fortunately, these are easy to add as variants – we will add a couple shortly. Let's first examine the code we created to get the component working in Storybook in more detail.

Exploring the Code Changes

Much of this component follows a similar pattern to the others we've already created – we started with the now-familiar import for the component, followed by creating a default template to render each story in the absence of any overriding values.

In the default template, we have the `argTypes` block, which we've used before – here, we're setting the types of values to expect for `type`, `title`, `description` (all strings), and `showIcon` (boolean). There is an additional feature, though, and one we've used before: `parameters`. Here, we need to use it to enlarge the canvas for each story in Storybook – without it, they are too small! This setting only applies to Storybook and will not feature as part of the component itself.

Okay – let's move on: cast your mind back to the end of the last section but one. Remember how I said adding different variants for the Alert component is easy, such as displaying a warning message instead?

Creating a Variant

When adding variants, the structure of our Alert component might not change much (if at all), but the appearance will be different. To achieve this, we need to add new markup into the `Alert.stories.js` file and some extra styling rules.

This change will just be a small start, though; with a bit of imagination, we could add more variants – what about adding a (configurable) border or maybe reworking the Icon functionality to use the Iconify library we've used elsewhere in this book? As they say, "...we gotta start somewhere, so let's dive in an' start with our two variants... "

CONSTRUCTING THE VARIANTS

To add our variant, follow these steps:

1. First, crack open `Alerts.stories.js`, then scroll to the bottom of the page.

2. Add a blank line, then this code – this will display a warning style message in our component:

```
export const Warn = () => ({
  Component: Alert,
  props: {
    show: true,
    type: "warn",
    title: "Simple warning",
```

```
        description: "A warning message",
        showIcon: "true",
    },
});
```

3. Next, miss a line under the last block and add this variant – it
   will show an error dialog:

```
export const Error = () => ({
    Component: Alert,
    props: {
        show: true,
        type: "error",
        title: "Error message",
        description: "An error message",
        showIcon: "true",
    },
});
```

4. We need to add some extra icon markup for the new variants,
   so crack open Icon.svelte and add this code immediately
   before the closing square bracket:

```
    {
        box: 512,
        name: "info",
        svg: `<path d="M248 64C146.39 64 64 146.39 64
        248s82.39 184 184 184 184-82.39 184-184S349.61
        64 248 64z" fill="none" stroke="currentColor"
        stroke-miterlimit="10" stroke-width="32"/><path
        fill="none" stroke="#ffffff" stroke-linecap="round"
        stroke-linejoin="round" stroke-width="32" d="M220
        220h32v116"/>
        <path fill="none" stroke="currentColor" stroke-
        linecap="round" stroke-miterlimit="10" stroke-
        width="32" d="M208 340h88" /><path d="M248 130a26
        26 0 1026 26 26 26 0 00-26-26z" fill="#ffffff" />`,
```

```
  },
  {
    box: 512,
    name: "error",
    svg: `<path d="M448 256c0-106-86-192-192-192S64
    150 64 256s86 192 192 192 192-86 192-192z"
    stroke="currentColor" fill="none" stroke-
    miterlimit="10" stroke-width="32"/>
    <path d="M250.26 166.05L256 288l5.73-121.95a5.74
    5.74 0 00-5.79-6h0a5.74 5.74 0 00-5.68 6z"
    fill="#ffffff" stroke="currentColor" stroke-
    linecap="round" stroke-linejoin="round" stroke-
    width="32"/><path d="M256 367.91a20 20 0 1120-20 20
    20 0 01-20 20z" fill="#ffffff" />`,
  },
```

Don't worry – this markup is in the code download, so you don't have
to add it manually!

---

5. We also need to add two new style rules to complement this
    markup. Open Alert.svelte, then scroll to the bottom and
    add these rules before the closing </style> tag:

    ```
    .alert-info {
      background: #2196f3;
      color: #ffffff;
    }

    .alert-error {
      background: #ff0000;
      color: #ffffff;
    }
    ```

6. We have everything in place, so let's test it! Save and close the open files, then switch to a Node.js terminal session, and make sure the working folder is set to our garnet project area.

7. At the prompt, enter npm run storybook and hit Enter – if all is well, we should see Storybook launch and display in our browser at http://localhost:6006/. Click the Warning link under the Alert entry on the left to display a yellow dialog box with appropriate text and icon, as shown in Figure 5-3.

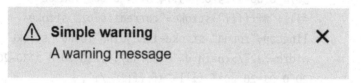

Figure 5-3. *Displaying the Warning variant of our Alert component*

8. Click the No Border entry below the Warning entry – this will display a red error dialog variant (Figure 5-4).

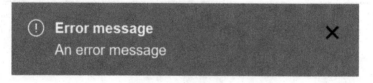

Figure 5-4. *Displaying the error dialog variant*

Perfect – with only a few styling changes (and the message we display), we can express something that looks a little different and customize it to our needs.

A question, though: Notice anything about the styling, say…how we achieved it? Some of you will undoubtedly see that we added some switching rules to choose which style to use and the appropriate classes.

While this works, it isn't the best method we could use. Could we have done better? It is a great question – let's take a moment to explore that and the rest of the variant code in more detail.

Breaking Apart the Code

As demos go, this is probably one of the simplest we've created so far – we've not even had to add any styles, as we made these available when we created the original component!

Most of the work hangs off steps two and three, where we added Story blocks to display two new variants – one a warn variant and the other to display an error variant. In both cases, we changed only the type parameter; the rest stayed the same as the original default Alert (okay, yes, we also changed text, but that's not the critical part of this – the type prop controls what icon to display!).

Thinking back to that question we asked just now – could we have improved our code? I think so: Instead of using a switch statement, what about refactoring our code to include alert as a single class (already in the join statement) but concatenating it with names such as warn, info, and error? We could remove the switch block as we already include alert as a class separately – the join statement would remain as is. We would then end up with something like Figure 5-5.

```
▼ <div class="garnet s-4Y75ZjC11XWf">
   ▼<dialog class="alert info fade-in s-4Y75ZjC11XWf" role="al
     t">  flex   == $0
```

Figure 5-5. *An example of reworked classes for Alert*

The downside is that there is no checking available as such, if we remove the switch block. That said, if a class doesn't exist in the style sheet, it won't be applied anyway!

Let's move on: we still have two more components to add to our library. The next one we'll look at is (ironically) also a dialog-based component intended for more complex occasions when you need to present more information to your user. Every library should have some form of dialog component, so let's look at how we can add one to our project in more detail.

Creating the Dialog Component

Although we've already added a dialog-based alert component to our library, it's meant more for displaying notices, where clicking the X will acknowledge and close the alert.

For more complex uses, we need something more substantial, where we can add more text and (hopefully) some markup. Depending on our needs, we might want to display a dialog with multiple buttons, such as OK or Cancel, or perhaps something more specific.

Creating a basic dialog isn't complicated; the key will be adding our content and responding to any events we generate, such as clicking OK. We need to start somewhere, so let's create a simple dialog that closes when we click an X symbol. We can always come back and add more functionality at a later date.

BUILDING THE DIALOG COMPONENT

To build our Toast component, follow these steps:

1. First, create a new folder under `\src\lib\components`, called `Dialog`.

2. Extract a copy of the `Close.svelte` file from the code download that accompanies this book, and drop it into the Dialog folder. This component will act as our close icon in the component.

3. Next, crack open a new file and add this code – we have a
    good chunk to cover, so we will add it in sections, starting with
    setting three exported variables and importing an icon file:

```
<svelte:options customElement="garnet-dialog" />

<script>
  import CloseIcon from "./Close.svelte";
  export let showDialog = true;
  export let showBackground = false;
  export let modalTitle = "Modal title";
  export let modalText = "Click on the X to close me";
</script>
```

4. Next, leave a line blank, then add this markup:

```
<button on:click={() => (showDialog = !showDialog)}>Show
dialog</button>

{#if showDialog}
  <div class="garnet">
    {#if showBackground}<div id="background" />{/if}
    <div id="modal">
      <div class="header">
        <h3>{modalTitle}</h3>
        <button
          type="button"
          class="close"
          on:click={() => (showDialog = false)}
        >
          <CloseIcon />
        </button>
      </div>
      <p>{modalText}</p>
    </div>
  </div>
{/if}
```

5. We also need to add some basic styles, so miss a line and add
    this code:

```
<style>
  .garnet-dialog {
    font-family: Arial, Helvetica, sans-serif;
  }

  @keyframes fadein {
    from {
      opacity: 0;
    }
    to {
      opacity: 1;
    }
  }

  #background {
    position: fixed;
    z-index: 1;
    top: 0;
    left: 0;
    width: 100vw;
    height: 100vh;
    background-color: rgba(0, 0, 0, 0.7);
    backdrop-filter: blur(5px);
    animation: fadein 1s;
  }

  #modal {
    position: fixed;
    z-index: 2;
    top: 50%;
    left: 50%;
    transform: translate(-50%, -50%);
    background: #fff;
```

```
    padding: 10px;
    width: 400px;
    height: 250px;
    border: 1px solid #c4c4c4;
    box-shadow: 2.5px 5.0px 5.0px hsl(0deg 0% 0% / 0.42);
  }

  .header {
    display: flex;
    justify-content: space-between;
    border-bottom: 1px solid #c4c4c4;
  }

  button {
    background-color: #733635;
    border: none;
    color: white;
    padding: 15px 32px;
    text-align: center;
    text-decoration: none;
    display: inline-block;
    font-size: 16px;
  }

  button.close {
    background-color: #ffffff;
    padding: 10px 0 10px 0;
  }

  button.close:hover {
    color: #d19c9b;
  }
</style>
```

6. Save the file as `Dialog.svelte`, and close it (and any other files) – construction is complete.

Great – we have a component in place, but I can imagine what your first question will be: What does it all do? We've covered quite a bit of code over the last few pages, so let's kick back for a moment and take a closer look at the changes we made to understand how it all hangs together.

Understanding What Happened

So, what did we achieve in that last demo? We kicked off by first creating the now-familiar component folder and file before extracting a copy of the CloseIcon file from the code download – this we will use in our component. We then set up a script block in the component file, to import CloseIcon and set exported boolean variables showDialog, modalTitle, and modalText – we'll use the latter two to display a title and text in the dialog component.

Next, we set our markup. We started by defining a button element with an event handler to show or hide the Dialog component each time we click the button. In the main markup, we wrap our code in a Svelte {#if}... {/if} block – this controls when the code is rendered based on the value of showDialog.

Inside the dialog markup, we set a title, a button to close the dialog, and some content within, using the modalTitle and modalText variables we created at the start of the demo. We then round out the demo with some basic styling to set elements such as animation and the background for the modal dialog.

Okay – let's move on: at this point, we now have a working component, so we need to test it. Let's hook it into Storybook to see how it works before adding a couple of variants later in this chapter.

Adding to Storybook

Adding a component should by now become a familiar process – granted, each component may require some tweaks to allow it to run, but the basic process is the same.

In this instance, we'll add two variants: one will display the modal closed when first rendered, and the other will display the modal without any background. Let's dive in and look at the steps involved in more detail.

ADDING TO STORYBOOK

To get our Dialog component working in Storybook, follow these steps:

1. First, go ahead and create a new file, then add this line to import our Dialog component into Storybook:

    ```
    import Dialog from "./Dialog.svelte";
    ```

2. This next bit should be very familiar by now – leave a line blank, then add this block. As before, it sets up a default template, adds a title, sets the component we want to use, and defines the types of properties to expect:

    ```
    export default {
      title: "Garnet UI Library/Notification Components/
            Dialog", component: Dialog,
      argTypes: {
        showDialog: { action: "boolean" },
        modalTitle: { action: "string" },
        modalText: { action: "string" },
      },
    };
    ```

3. With the initial configuration in place, we can now focus on
    rendering our component. Skip a line, then add this block
    in – it's similar to previous examples, with only minor changes
    to the title and properties being passed into the component:

```
export const Default = {
  component: Dialog,
  args: {
    showDialog: true,
    modalTitle: "Modal title",
    modalText: "Click on the X to close me",
  },
  parameters: {
    docs: {
      story: {
        height: "300px",
        width: "300px",
      },
    },
  },
};
```

4. Save the file as `Dialog.stories.js`, then close the file.

5. We need to add a documentation file for our users, so for this,
    extract a copy of `Docs.mdx` from the code download, then drop
    it into the Dialog folder.

6. We have everything in place, so let's test it! Switch to a Node.
    js terminal session, then set the working folder to our garnet
    project area.

7. At the prompt, enter `npm run storybook` and hit Enter – if
    all is well, we should see Storybook launch and display in our
    browser at http://localhost:6006/. Click the Closed On Open link
    under Dialog on the left to display the variant we just created,
    as shown in Figure 5-6.

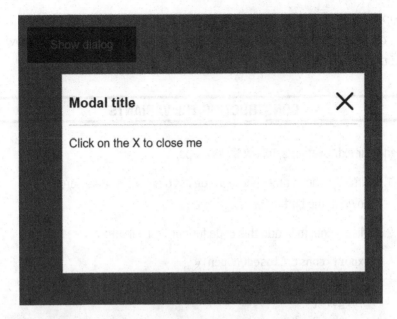

Figure 5-6. *Displaying our Dialog alert component*

Why do I love what I see but still feel hungry at this point? In the words of the great 1968 movie, *Oliver!*, "...please, can I have some more...?" Okay, enough with the puns, methinks – let's keep things going and add a couple of variants into the mix.

Creating Variants

Adding the variants for this component will seem like a walk in the park now that we have the basics in place – it's just a matter of changing a couple of properties!

It makes it super easy to create new variants, although it does make it incumbent on us to ensure we build in the options beforehand. I know this won't necessarily happen from the get-go in reality, but hey – code

development is about iterating, so we can always add them in later...
Okay – on that note, let's go ahead and add those extra variants in now, as
part of the next exercise.

CONSTRUCTING THE VARIANTS

To add our extra variants, follow these steps:

1. First, go ahead and open `Dialog.stories.js`, then scroll
    down to the bottom of the page.

2. Miss a line, then add this code for our first variant:

```
export const ClosedOnOpen = {
  component: Dialog,
  args: {
    showDialog: false,
    modalTitle: "Modal title",
    modalText: "This modal is closed on launch",
  },
  parameters: {
    docs: {
      story: {
        height: "300px",
        width: "300px",
      },
    },
  },
};
```

3. We also need to add the code for the second variant – miss a
    line, then add this block. It will look very similar to the previous
    one, as we only need to change a couple of properties to create
    this variant:

```
export const NoBackground = {
  component: Dialog,
  args: {
    showDialog: false,
    showBackground: false,
    modalTitle: "Modal title",
    modalText: "This modal doesn't show a background",
  },
  parameters: {
    docs: {
      story: {
        height: "300px",
        width: "300px",
      },
    },
  },
};
```

4. Next, we need to update the documentation file. Crack open Docs.mdx from the Dialog folder, then scroll to the end and add these lines:

```
## ClosedOnOpen

This state shows the Dialog closed, when launched:

<Canvas of={DialogStories.ClosedOnOpen} />

## NoBackground

This state shows the Dialog displayed without a
background:

<Canvas of={DialogStories.NoBackground} />
```

MDX is space-sensitive, so please add the code as shown above; otherwise, it might not appear correctly in the browser!

5.   Save and close any open files. We have everything in place, so let's test it! Switch to a Node.js terminal session, then set the working folder to our garnet project area.

6.   At the prompt, enter npm run storybook and hit Enter – if all is well, we should see Storybook launch and display in our browser at http://localhost:6006/. Click the Closed On Open link under Dialog on the left to display the first variant we created, ● as shown in Figure 5-7.

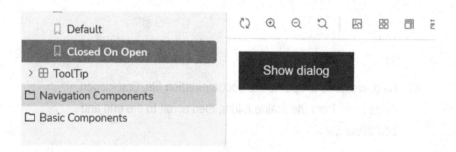

Figure 5-7. *The first variant for the Dialog component*

7.   Go ahead and click the No Background link under Dialog on the left. We should see our second variant if all is well, as shown in Figure 5-8.

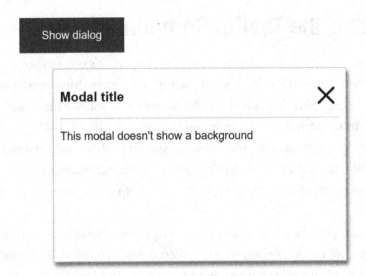

Figure 5-8. *The second variant for the Dialog component*

Perfect – that's the first iteration of our Dialog component, which is done and ready for use. Adding the two variants was easy enough; we inserted two stories and changed the parameters passed to each story. You will notice that we've also used the parameters block again to resize the canvas in Storybook – this was necessary as our dialog is a little too large to display without this change! As before, this only affects Storybook and will not be an issue when rendering in normal code.

Okay – we're almost done with creating components for the Notifications part of our library; before we move on to the next category, there is one more we'll develop. This next component might seem an intriguing choice for some, but it does notify people – and you have to have one in your toolkit at some point! I'm talking about the Tooltip component – over the next few pages, we will develop our own version for the library.

Creating the Tooltip Component

The ubiquitous tooltip has been around for years – it's one of those components that just works. It's not meant to offer anything outrageously different or complex, but it is still valuable as a tool for our toolbox.

This time, though, we're not going to use a standard HTML5 element like <dialog> (primarily as one doesn't exist for tooltip), but, instead, build our component from scratch. We're also not going to create a standard Tooltip component, but one we might use to help guide visitors through our site.

For example, if we had to ask age (for age-restricted sites, such as breweries), we could explain why we need the information. It is a little more complex, but most of the code required is standard HTML – let's dive in and take a look.

BUILDING THE TOOLTIP COMPONENT

To set up our Tooltip component, follow these steps:

1. First, create a new folder called Tooltip at the root of the \ components\src\lib folder.

2. Next, crack open a new file and add this code – we'll start with importing the fade function from Svelte, creating a few variables for export, and setting three internal variables for use within the component:

```
<svelte:options customElement="garnet-tooltip" />

<script>
  import { fade } from "svelte/transition";
  export let id = "tooltip";
  export let label;
  export let tip;
```

```
export let timeout = "400";
export let showHTML = false;

let active = false;
let enterTrigger;
let leaveTrigger;
```

3. We still need to add the second half of our script. For this, leave a line blank and then add this code. We have four functions that take care of when the mouse or keyboard is used – the first two are the equivalent of onMouseEnter and onKeyboardDown:

```
function handleKeydown(e) {
  if (e.key === "Escape") {
    active = false;
    e.target.blur();
  }
}

function handleMouseEnter() {
  enterTrigger = setTimeout(() => {
    active = true;
  }, parseInt(timeout, 0));
}
```

4. Leave a line blank, then add the remaining two functions – they deal with onMouseLeave and handling interaction:

```
function handleMouseLeave() {
  if (enterTrigger) {
    clearTimeout(enterTrigger);
    enterTrigger = null;
  }
  leaveTrigger = setTimeout(() => {
    active = false;
  }, parseInt(timeout, 0));
}
```

163

```
function handleInteraction() {
  if (leaveTrigger) {
    clearTimeout(leaveTrigger);
    leaveTrigger = null;
  }
}
</script>
```

5. We can now add the markup for our component – much of this
    standard HTML markup, but it does include some Svelte tags.
    We'll do it in two sections – first, leave a new line blank, then
    add this code:

```
<div class="garnet-tooltip">
  <div>
    <button
      aria-describedby={id}
      type="button"
      class="trigger"
      on:click={() => (active = true)}
      on:keydown={handleKeydown}
      on:mouseenter={handleMouseEnter}
      on:mouseleave={handleMouseLeave}
    >
      ?
    </button>
```

6. Immediately after the previous block, add the remaining code
    for our markup:

```
<div aria-hidden={!active} {id} role="tooltip" aria-
label={label}>
    {#if active}
      <!-- svelte-ignore a11y-no-static-element-
      interactions -->
      <div
```

```
        transition:fade
        class="content"
        on:mouseenter={handleInteraction}
        on:mouseleave={handleMouseLeave}
      >
        {#if showHTML}
          {@html tip}
        {:else}
          {tip}
        {/if}
      </div>
    {/if}
  </div>
</div>
```

7. For the last part of this component, we need to style it – we only need a handful of styles, so leave a line blank and add these rules:

```
<style>
  .garnet-tooltip {
    position: relative;
    z-index: 2;
  }

  .trigger {
    padding: 0;
    margin: 0;
    width: 19px;
    height: 19px;
    line-height: 15px;
    font-size: 17px;
    text-align: center;
    background-color: transparent;
```

```
        border-radius: 50%;
        border: 3px solid #733635;
        color: #999999;
        cursor: pointer;
        font-weight: bold;
    }

    .content {
      all: initial;
      position: absolute;
      left: 0;
      top: 100%;
      width: 300px;
      margin-top: 10px;
      padding: 10px;
      border-radius: 8px;
      box-shadow: rgba(0, 0, 0, 0.24) 0 3px 8px;
      font-size: 14px;
      font-family: Arial, Helvetica, sans-serif;
    }

    .trigger:focus {
      outline: 2px solid #000000;
    }

    [role="tooltip"]:empty {
      display: none;
    }
</style>
```

8. Save the file as Tooltip.svelte, then close the file.

Excellent – we have our component in place: the next task is to try it to make sure it works! As before, we'll work through adding it to our Storybook instance. Before we get to that, let's take a moment to review the code changes made – most of it should be self-explanatory, but some interesting Svelte techniques within the code are worth exploring in more detail.

Understanding What Happened

As components go, this is probably one of the more complex components to put together for our library – it's a real mix of HTML markup and Svelte script! Most of it hangs around exported variables and some reasonably standard markup.

We created our file before adding those exported variables, such as showHTML, label, and id. At the same time, we also set some internal variables for use within our component. Next, we added four event handlers to respond to mouse events – handleMouseEnter/Leave, handleKeyboardDown, and handleInteraction – which fire when triggering or exiting a tooltip. Notice that we define a value for setTimeout (and its partner, clearTimeout); these add a short delay before triggering the tooltip.

With the script functionality out of the way, we then turned our attention to the markup; it looks a little complex at first, but in reality, it is just a set of nested #if…/else statements. The inside one determines if we want to show rendered HTML, while the parent if block will control the tooltip display if active is set to true.

While most of the rest of the code is standard HTML, there are a couple of interesting Svelte keywords in use. The first one is transition:fade (in the nested div statement) – this shorthand defaults to a delay of 0, duration of 400ms, and an easing value of linear. We also have two event handlers using the Svelte on:… format; these hook up to the handleMouseEnter and handleMouseLeave handlers, respectively. The third keyword of note is @ html, which we use in rendering the HTML markup. This keyword escapes any markup we provide but does **not** sanitize it – that's something we have to do as developers! We finish the component with some basic styling so it will at least look presentable when displayed in a browser.

Adding the Component to Storybook

You should hopefully know the drill by now – it's time to test our component!

As with other components, we'll add the now-familiar `default` template to render a preset version of the Tooltip out of the box. For the variant (which will come shortly), we will add a story to Storybook that displays rendered HTML in the tooltip. Let's start by setting up the default instance of our Tooltip component in Storybook.

ADDING TO STORYBOOK

To get our Tooltip component working in Storybook, follow these steps:

1. First, go ahead and create a new file, then add this code – as before, we have a reasonable chunk to add. Let's start with the initial `<script>` block to import the component and documentation, along with some functions from Storybook and a test function for the button we will use in our example:

    ```
    import Tooltip from ". /Tooltip.svelte";
    ```

2. With the initial configuration in place, we can now focus on our component – as before, we first need to add a template. Skip a line, then add this block in – it's similar in structure to previous examples but adapted to suit our component:

    ```
    export default {
      title: "Garnet UI Library/Notification Components/
      ToolTip", component: Tooltip,
      argTypes: {
        tip: '<p>This is an informational tooltip - to learn
        more <a href="/tutorial">click here</a></p>',
        showHTML: false,
    ```

```
      timeout: "400",
      label: "more info",
    },
    parameters: {
      docs: {
        story: {
          height: "120px",
        },
      },
    },
  };
```

3. We can now render our component. For this, we will create a
   default object for our story. Go ahead and add this block:

```
export const Default = {
  args: {
    tip: '<p>This is an informational tooltip - to learn
    more <a href="/tutorial">click here</a></p>',
    showHTML: false,
    timeout: "400",
    label: "more info",
  },
};
```

4. Save the file as `Tooltip.stories.svelte`, then close
   the file.

5. You will see from the code that we've specified a file as our
   documentation but haven't yet added it. We need to extract a
   copy of `Docs.mdx` from the code download and then drop it
   into the Tooltip folder.

6. We have everything in place, so let's test it! Switch to a Node.
   js terminal session, then set the working folder to our garnet
   project area.

7. At the prompt, enter npm run storybook and hit Enter – if all is well, we should see Storybook launch and display in our browser at http://localhost:6006/. Click the Default link under Tooltip on the left to display the variant we just created, as shown in Figure 5-9.

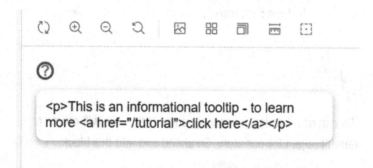

Figure 5-9. Displaying the Tooltip component in Storybook

Great – we should now have our Tooltip component displayed in Storybook! It is a valuable addition to our library and one we should be able to expand in the future; we might want to control where the tip displays, for example. However, that's for another time –let's take a moment to review the code changes before cracking on with the next component.

Exploring the Code Changes

Adding our Tooltip component will be a walk in the park – we've added a few components already, which all use the same process, so adding Tooltip would not have been any different!

To get us started, we created our story file before adding the now-usual import for our component. We then set up a default function, which acts as our template without overriding specific variables such as title or text. In this block, we provided the title for our story (which acts as the navigation in Storybook) and an `argTypes` block with entries for `showHTML`, `timeout`, and `label`.

You will see that I've also added the same `parameters` block as in previous examples (albeit with a different height value) – we have the same issue as before, where our demo is just a little too large for Storybook's default canvas size!

Next, we then dropped in an exported object for `Default` – this is to show users what is available out of the box, changing too many settings. Remember that although we use `default` and `Default`, they are technically two separate items! The former is the default setup that fills in gaps and sets what types of values to expect, while the latter is the starting view in Storybook before we add any variants. You will see that, here, we've provided values for both – the former really should be updated to show the value type (i.e., Boolean) and not the value itself.

With all that done, all that remained was to save and close the file, then run up Storybook in a browser so we could preview the results and make sure everything rendered as expected. We can now move on and add variants – I have two in mind, so let's dive in and see what we need to do as part of the next demo.

Creating a Variant

Throughout the last few chapters, we've created a host of different variants for our components – in most (if not all) cases, we've added various properties that we can change, such as `iconName` (Breadcrumbs) or `step` (for the Slider component).

However, there is something we need to be mindful of when creating our Tooltip variant – did you spot what this might be? There's a big clue in Figure 5-8: Notice how we were rendering raw HTML? There is a reason why we will need to be careful here; I'll come back to this shortly, but for now, let's look at setting up that variant in Storybook.

CONSTRUCTING THE VARIANT

To add a variant for the Tooltip component, follow these steps:

1. First, go ahead and crack open `Tooltip.stories.js` – scroll down to the bottom of the file, then add this block:

    ```
    export const CustomHTML = {
      args: {
        tip: '<p>This is an informational tooltip with custom
        markup - to learn more <a href="/tutorial">click
        here</a></p>',
        showHTML: true,
        timeout: "300",
        label: "more info",
      },
    };
    ```

2. Save and close any files open.

3. We have everything in place, so let's test it! Switch to a Node. js terminal session, then set the working folder to our garnet project area.

4. At the prompt, enter npm `run` `storybook` and hit Enter – if all is well, we should see Storybook launch and display in our browser at http://localhost:6006/. Click the Custom HTML link under Tooltip on the left to display the variant we created, as shown in Figure 5-10.

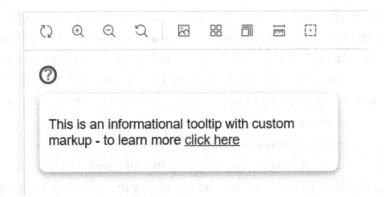

Figure 5-10. *Displaying the custom version of our Tooltip component*

Excellent – we've completed our Tooltip component and tested it: it's now ready for use. If you were expecting more code, I'm sorry to disappoint – earlier versions of Storybook might have meant adding a few more lines, but not in Storybook 8!

On that note, it brings us to the close of this chapter, where we move on to the next batch of components to add...but before we do so, let's quickly cover the changes made in this last demo.

The only change we had to effect was to change showHTML from false to true; this triggers the showHTML check in our code, allowing us to use HTML. The rest of the code is the same, albeit with a slightly different result; you will notice, though, that it renders the markup correctly this time, not as plain text in our demo.

Summary

No one likes getting more notifications than necessary – getting the balance right is essential. Otherwise, we are likely to end up irritating our customers! We still need to have something available, and while getting the balance right is something that only comes with testing, we can at least ensure we have suitable components available for use.

173

To help with that, we've created three components for our library; each has its respective page in our Storybook instance. It brings us up to the penultimate component group in our library, with only one more component category to add to our library! Before we build the final category of components, let's take a moment to review what we have learned in this chapter.

As we saw in the previous chapter, we focused on adding each component to our library and setting it up in Storybook. We started with creating the Alert trail component before swiftly moving on to building the more complex Dialog component. Both follow the same principle of displaying a notification, but Alert works one way, whereas we can use Dialog to develop something that allows for more interaction.

We then explored setting up a Tooltip component as this category's third and final tool. For this one, we were a little more limited in what we could offer – tooltips can only display information and allow us to click on links. This constraint means we only have one variant, which is to render custom HTML properly; that said, we can always look at styling options for different tooltip designs in future iterations!

Okay, let's crack with creating the final batch of components: the Grids group. It will depart a little from the usual practice as we're only going to make a single component this time! But this component will be flexible and allow us to create different layouts. Intrigued? Stay with me, and I will explain all in the next chapter.

CHAPTER 6

Creating Grid Components

So far, we've created a reasonably sized collection of components, all of which we've added to Storybook and checked that they run as expected in a browser. We have two more sets of components to create before we update the documentation in Chapter 8 – over the next few pages, we'll look at the penultimate batch of components, which are...an Image Grid.

Hold on a moment. That's just one component, right? Well, yes – and no: it *is* one component as such, but due (in part) to how Web Components work in Svelte, we need to make it from no less than three components!

I'm sure you're probably a little confused by now – don't worry; we will still use the same approach as before, but this time, I'll show you how, with a bit of planning, we can bring all three components together to create a starting point for our Image Grid component. Let's begin with setting the scene for the construction of this component.

Determining the Approach

When I started researching for this chapter, I had initially planned to create a layout grid component (or set of components). However, this soon proved too large for this book's scope – it would have meant subsuming

© Alex Libby 2025
A. Libby, *Developing Web Components with Svelte*,
https://doi.org/10.1007/979-8-8688-1180-7_6

a large part of the CSS Grid or CSS Flexbox layout concepts, which could almost form a book itself! So, how can I scale this back to something more manageable?

I was still keen to use native CSS standards where possible and not use third-party libraries to help keep the component light and dependency-free (so to speak). One component came to mind that fitted the bill – what about an Image Grid? We can use these in ecommerce sites to display products; this is a perfect fit for using CSS Grid to build a working component. So, where to start?

To keep things light, I decided to split our component into three smaller ones – in the middle will be a Cell component, to house our content. We'll wrap this in a Grid component, which will build out a grid of cells, and then wrap everything in a container, which will be our Table component. As it so happens, this will help us when it comes to displaying it in Storybook. Ideally, we would use a template in Storybook, but its current documentation isn't solid in this area. To get around it, we can render the Table as a single component in Storybook, which will then call the other two when needed.

With this in mind, let's begin with building the first of our three components – the Table component – which will act as our container for the ImageGrid.

Building the Table Component

As always, we must start somewhere – we know Storybook doesn't make it easy to display composite components in the same format as individual ones, so it makes sense to create our container component for the Image Grid.

This first component will be a relatively lightweight one, to begin with, but one I am sure we can develop in the future – along with the two child components we will create later in this chapter. Let's dive in and look at what is involved in more detail.

176

BUILDING THE TABLE COMPONENT

To construct our table component, follow these steps:

1. First, create a new folder called Table at the root of the `\src\lib\components` folder.

2. Next, open a new file and add this code – save it as `Table.svelte`. We'll start with setting the `svelte:options` tag, followed by importing two components and a bunch of variables for export:

```
<svelte:options customElement="garnet-table" />
<script>
  import Grid from "./Grid.svelte";
  import Cell from "./Cell.svelte";
  export let columnCount = 4;
  export let rowCount = 4;
  export let itemCount = 0;
  export let border = "";
  export let displayImages = false;
  export let label = "Test Label";
  export let imageLabel = "untitled";
  export let displayImageLabels = false;
</script>
```

3. Next, we have the markup – first, miss a line, then add this block of code:

```
<h1>{label}</h1>
<Grid columns={columnCount} rows={rowCount} {border}>
  {#each { length: itemCount } as _, i}
    <Cell
      {displayImages}
```

```
        imageLabel={imageLabel}
        displayImageLabels={displayImageLabels}
    />
    {/each}
</Grid>
```

4. We have one more block to add – miss a line, then add this style rule:

```
<style>
  h1 {
     font-family: Arial, Helvetica, sans-serif;
     border-bottom: 0.8px solid rgba(38, 85, 115, 0.15);
  }
</style>
```

5. Save the file and close it.

That was a short exercise – it doesn't look like it does much at face value! It still performs an important role, though – to understand how it fits into the larger picture, let's take a moment to review the code changes in more detail.

Understanding What Happened

Although this last exercise was brief, it serves an important role. You may remember my earlier comments about Storybook not making it easy to host a component made up of subcomponents, such as ours. In this case, we managed to get around it by using the Table component as a container for everything else. We may use the Cell and Grid components too, but as far as Storybook is concerned, we host everything inside Table.

In terms of code, there is very little going on in this component – we set the now-familiar `svelte:options` tag before importing both the Grid and Cell components into our component. We then set eight variables for export, including `columnCount`, `rowCount`, and `border`.

The (other) important part of this component, though, is in the call to `<Grid...>` – here, we pass into it values for `columnCount` (number of columns), `rowCount` (number of rows), and `border` (dictates if one should be displayed). We then iterate through `itemCount`; for each instance of `itemCount`, we call the Cell component and tell it whether it should display placeholder images when viewing the component in our browser.

Okay – let's move on: we've referenced the Grid and Cell components in our last demo, but the Table component won't work yet, as neither Cell nor Grid exists! That's easy to fix: let's dive in and look at setting up both; we'll start with Grid as the next component.

Creating the Grid Component

With the container component now complete, we can focus on the second component for this chapter – the Grid component. It will act as a container, too, but this one reformats each cell into the correct order based on what we set using Flexbox. Setting up this component is a little more complex than the previous one, so let's dive in and take a look.

CONSTRUCTING THE GRID COMPONENT

To set up our Grid component, work through these steps:

1. First, create a new file called `Grid.svelte` inside the `\src\lib\components\Table` folder.

179

2. Next, crack open a new file and add this code – we'll start with
    setting the `svelte:options` tag, followed by setting four
    variables for export and two for internal use in the component:

```
<svelte:options customElement="garnet-grid" />
<script>
    export let columns = 2;
    export let rows = 4;
    export let border = "1px solid #000000";
</script>
```

3. Next, we need to add the markup for our component – skip a
    line, then add this code:

```
<div
    style="
      grid-template-rows: repeat({rows}, 1fr);
      grid-template-columns: repeat({columns}, auto);
      border: {border};
    "
>
    <slot />
</div>
```

4. To finish off the component, let's add some styling – we're
    hard-coding most of the properties for now, but with the
    intention that if we develop the component further, we can
    make them dynamic:

```
<style>
  div {
      font-family: Arial, Helvetica, sans-serif;
      display: grid;
      grid-column-gap: 10px;
      grid-row-gap: 5px;
```

```
    grid-auto-flow: column;
    border: 1px solid #000000;
  }
</style>
```

5. Go ahead and save and close the file – the changes for this
    component are complete.

Excellent – that's two components down, one left to complete our
Image Grid! We base most of this component around standard HTML
markup and CSS styling, but we've used a couple of exciting code features
from Svelte. Let's review our code changes to understand how they work in
more detail.

Breaking Apart the Code

There is one thing I love about Svelte – we could have spent time creating
an elaborate Grid component, but, instead, Svelte allows us to use existing
techniques, such as CSS Grid, with very little need for extra coding to make
it all work!

To build our Grid component, we began first by adding the now-
familiar svelte:options tag before creating three variables for export:
columns, rows, and border. These will take care of the number of columns
we should display, the number of rows that should be present, and
whether our table should have a border.

The key part of this component comes next – most of the hard work
is done using CSS styling, which makes it superefficient. We set a <div>
element to which we apply the CSS Grid grid-template-rows and grid-
template-columns attributes. We use these to define the number of rows
and columns to display on the page, using 1fr to set cells of equal spacing
in each case. At the same time, we also set some typical CSS styling that

181

you might see when using CSS Grid elements – such as `display: grid` or `grid-row-gap`. These are hard-coded for now, but there is no reason why we might not want to make them more dynamic sometime in the future.

You will also notice the presence of `<slot />` – this we use to display whatever HTML or text is rendered inside the call to Grid when using the component.

Right, let's crack on – we have one more component to create, which is Cell.

Creating the Cell Component

At this stage, we now have two of the three components in place – there is one more component left to add: the Cell component.

This one isn't as complex as Grid – here, we need to create a container representing the cell of our grid and determine if we want to show a placeholder image or leave it blank.

Admittedly, the former is something we might want more control over, but that's the beauty of creating a component – it's something we can develop further at a later date. For now, though, let's focus on building the base cell component, which we will do as part of the next exercise.

CONSTRUCTING THE CELL COMPONENT

We've reached the third and final component for this chapter – to set it up, follow these steps:

1. First, crack open a new file, saving it as `Cell.svelte` in the `\src\lib\components\Table` folder.

2. Next, go ahead and add this code to the top of that file:

```
<svelte:options customElement="garnet-cell" />
<script>
  export let displayImages = false;
  export let imageLabel = "untitled";
  export let displayImageLabels = false;
</script>
```

3. We need to add markup for our component – miss a line after
    the code from step 2, then add this:

```
<div class="cell">
  {#if displayImages}
    <div class="container">
      <img src="https://loremflickr.com/320/240/
      camera" alt="placeholder" data-
      testid="placeholderImage" />
      {#if displayImageLabels}
      <div class="description">
        <span class="labelText">{imageLabel}</span>
      </div>
      {/if}
    </div>
  {:else}
    <slot />
  {/if}
</div>
```

4. As the last part, let's finish our component off with some
    styling:

```
<style>
  .cell { border: 1px solid #000000; min-height:
  100px; }
```

```
.container { position: relative; }
.description {
  padding: 10px 0;
  position: absolute;
  bottom: 0%;
  left: 50%;
  transform: translate(-50%, 0%);
  background-color: rgba(0,0,0, 0.7);
  color: #ffffff;
  font-size: 16px;
  width: 100%;
}
span { padding-left: 10px; }
img { display: block; width: 100%; height: auto; }
</style>
```

5. Save the file and close it – we have completed all necessary changes for now.

Perfect – we have everything in place, ready to link into Storybook! Although this last component wasn't substantial, we can still gain some valuable tips from this code, so let's review it in more detail before moving on to the next stage.

Understanding What Happened

In that last demo, we created the Cell component, which means we now have all the constituent elements we need for our ImageGrid component. This final component was a little more involved than the others – to construct it, we first added the usual svelte:options tag before setting three variables for export, namely, displayImages, imageLabel, and displayImageLabels.

We then set a div element as a container before using `displayImages` to determine if the component should display markup for a placeholder image. If so, we include an image that uses the LoremFlickr website to pick a random image as our placeholder; I've set it to use the camera as a search term, but we could change it to something else if required. The critical thing to note is that if a placeholder image is not needed, we use `<slot />` to render whatever markup is between the component tags. At the same time, I use a similar process to determine if we should also display a label – this we control with the `displayImageLabels` property, which determines whether to render the markup on-screen.

Our next task is to add our new ImageGrid component to Storybook so we can see how it looks in practice – before we do that, there is one small point I want to cover: `displayImages`.

You will see from the cell component markup that we've added an option to display placeholder images or our own but have not yet used it. The reason for this is that we will use it in Storybook when we come to add a variant later in this chapter. It's all about preparation and thinking ahead – as you will see, it makes adding our `displayImages` variant much easier!

Adding to Storybook

By now, I suspect this next part should be somewhat familiar to you – we've added all of our components (except one) to Storybook, so there isn't likely to be anything too new for our next task. We're now at a stage where we can test the Image Grid component. As before, let's crack on adding an instance to Storybook so we can prove it works as we expected.

```
┌─────────────────────────────────────────────────────────┐
│                  HOOKING INTO STORYBOOK                   │
└─────────────────────────────────────────────────────────┘
```

Although we've created a component, we won't see how it works until we get it into our demo. To do so, follow these steps:

1. First, create a new file, then add this code – as before, we have a reasonable chunk to add. Let's start with the initial block to import the component and documentation, along with some functions from Storybook:

    ```
    import Table from "./Table.svelte";
    ```

2. As in previous demos, we also need to add a template – go ahead and miss a line, then add this default declaration:

```
export default {
    title: "Garnet UI Library/Grid Components/Grid",
    component: Table,
    label: "Example ImageGrid",
    argTypes: {
        val: 1,
        min: 0,
        max: 100,
        step: 10,
        ticks: false,
    },
    parameters: {
        docs: {
            story: {
                height: "100px",
            },
        },
    },
};
```

3. We can now add the Story to our file, which will render the
    component on the page (largely) out of the box:

```
export const Default = {
  args: {
    columnCount: 1,
    rowCount: 4,
    border: "none",
    displayImages: false,
    itemCount: 12,
    label: "Example Grid",
  },
};
```

4. Save the file as `Table.stories.js` in the `Table` folder, then
    close the file.

5. You will see from the code that we've specified a file as our
    documentation but haven't yet added it. We need to extract a
    copy of `Docs.mdx` from the code download and then drop it
    into the Table folder.

6. We have everything in place, so let's test it! Switch to a Node.
    js terminal session, then set the working folder to our garnet
    project area.

7. At the prompt, enter `npm run storybook` and hit Enter – if
    all is well, we should see Storybook launch and display in our
    browser at http://localhost:6006/. Click the Default link under
    Table on the left to display the variant we created, as shown in
    Figure 6-1.

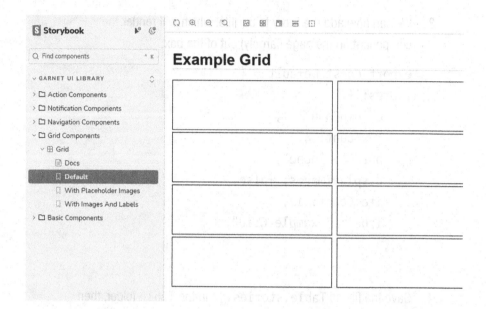

Figure 6-1. *Our newly created Image Grid component in Storybook*

Great – we now have a working Image Grid component available in our
component library! We've covered a good chunk of code in this last demo,
so while most of it will be similar to what we've already used earlier in the
book, let's take a quick look through it as a bit of a refresher.

Exploring in Detail

By now, you will hopefully be familiar with most of the steps we've used
to add our component to Storybook – using the same format may seem a
little repetitive, but the flip side is that it does make it quicker to replicate
for other components. In our case, we set up an instance of the Storybook
page for the ImageGrid component, even though we're using Table as
the main container for our component (and specify it as such in the
configuration).

We added a single import, namely, the Table component, and then created a default template to render the component (largely) out of the box, so you can see what it will look like without too many changes! You will notice that I've had to set the `height:` parameter again, as we have done before: Storybook's canvas is too short to display all of the component in our desired format. All of the values we pass are arbitrary – getting a feel for what it will look like when rendered on-screen is more important.

Adding a Variant

We now have our ImageGrid displayed in Storybook – it looks good and resizes well (or at least within the confines of Storybook). The trouble is it seems a little...well, plain. Can we do anything about this?

As it happens, yes, we can – you've probably guessed it: we could add a variant at this point! I think two would work well here – what about adding a placeholder image and maybe a label?

ADDING A VARIANT

To add in both an image and a label will require some changes to the story we set up in Storybook – to see what needs changing, follow these steps:

1. First, crack open `Table.stories.js` from within the Table folder – take a copy of the entire "Default" story block and paste it below, leaving a line blank between each story. Amend the properties passed to the story, as shown below:

```
export const WithPlaceholderImages = {
  args: {
    columnCount: 1,
    rowCount: 4,
```

```
      border: "none",
      displayImages: true,
      itemCount: 12,
      displayImageLabels: false,
      label: "Example Grid with Placeholder Images",
    },
  };
```

2. Next, leave a line blank and do the same with this block:

```
export const WithImagesAndLabels = {
  args: {
    columnCount: 1,
    rowCount: 4,
    border: "none",
    displayImages: true,
    itemCount: 12,
    displayImageLabels: true,
    imageLabel: "This is a test image",
    label: "Example Grid with Placeholder Images and
    Labels",
  },
};
```

3. Save the file, then close it.

4. We need to test the change – to do so, revert to a Node.js command prompt, then make sure the working folder is set to our project area if it is not already there.

5. At the prompt, type npm run storybook, then press Enter.

6. Storybook's development server should fire up – if all is well, we can preview the results of our change at http://localhost:6006/. Find the Grid entry on the left, then click Image Grid ➤ With Placeholder Images or With Images and Labels to view the new variants (Figures 6-2 and 6-3).

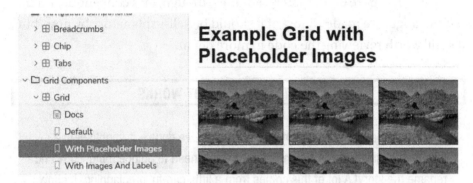

Figure 6-2. *The new Placeholder Images variant showcased in Storybook*

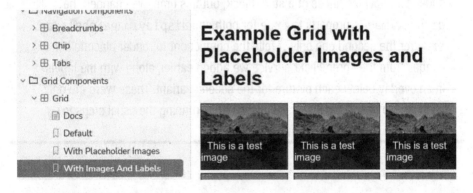

Figure 6-3. *The new Placeholder Images and Labels variant showcased in Storybook*

This change looks a little more enticing, wouldn't you agree? There will be cases where we aren't ready to display our images, so having something in place gives a little more visual interest.

As you will have seen, we've used an image placeholder service, so images are not instant – this would be a perfect candidate for updating to a fetch feature (more on this later). For now, though, let's concentrate on the code changes we made – most of it should be self-explanatory by now, but it's still worth reviewing the code in more detail.

UNDERSTANDING HOW IT WORKS

This last demo has to be one of the simplest we've done – it might seem a little long at seven steps, but in reality, we only need to do one thing: copy and rename the story! A lot of this comes from a little careful preplanning; it shows that thinking ahead makes a repetitive task more straightforward to complete.

Even though we only made one change, it's still an important one – we added two new instances of a story block, but this time, we changed the `displayImages` property to `true` for both and `displayImageLabels` to `true` for the second one only. It tells the component to render placeholder images from the LoremFlickr service we added earlier, along with the labels in an overlay below each picture for the second variant. These were the only changes we needed to make – we finished by running the usual steps to preview the results in our browser.

Summary

Adding the ImageGrid/Table components marks a significant milestone – we only have one set of components left to set up in our library and make available in Storybook! It might have taken a while, but we are indeed there. Or are we? I'll return to that question in a moment, but we've covered some important material in this chapter, so let's pause to review what we have learned.

We briefly looked at how we would approach this particular group. We noted that Storybook's documentation doesn't make things easy for us, so we created an ImageGrid component as a basis for the subcomponents in this chapter.

In total, we created three components based on the CSS Grid framework supported natively in most browsers, which makes them more lightweight and easier to develop. We started first with Table, which acts as our entry point for Storybook, and followed this with Grid, then Cell – all three used minimal markup, with styling that you might typically use when styling with CSS Grid.

We then rounded off the chapter by looking at how to hook the components into Storybook as the ImageGrid before adding a simple variant to display placeholder images in our component.

Phew – almost all components are now up and running; what's next? We have one group left to add: animation components! If all goes well (and I have no doubt it will!), we will add a Collapsible DropDown component, an Animated ProgressBar, and a Switch component. Once all three of these are in, we will finally have all our components in place: stay with me, and I will take you through creating all three in the next chapter.

CHAPTER 7

Creating Animation Components

To animate or not to animate, that is the question, your honor...

Some of you may recognize the (somewhat) modified quote, based on the original in *Hamlet*, written by the famous bard himself, William Shakespeare – it's from Act 3, Scene 1, in case you're wondering! English literature aside, you might be wondering why I started with that modified quote: there is a good reason for doing so. Let me explain.

When using animation in code – and Svelte is no different – we face that perennial question: Should we animate or not animate? How much should we animate? I'll add to that by saying that if we want to use animation, should we use JavaScript (in this case, Svelte), pure CSS, or a mix of both?

As I am sure you will know, there is no right or wrong answer: the most straightforward answer is that "it depends." It sounds like a cop-out, but there is no right or wrong answer: the best rule of thumb is usually CSS for simple animations and JavaScript for when you need more control or create more complex effects. It gets more interesting if you use a cubic-bezier-based animation (see `https://www.cubic-bezier.com`) or the new `linear()` in CSS – the latter particularly looks like it should only be used in JavaScript!

© Alex Libby 2025
A. Libby, *Developing Web Components with Svelte*,
https://doi.org/10.1007/979-8-8688-1180-7_7

To learn more about the linear() function, head over to `https://developer.mozilla.org/en-US/blog/custom-easing-in-css-with-linear/` for more details.

Fortunately, Svelte can use either – over the following few pages, we'll work through adding three more components to our library; one will use Svelte-only animation, the second CSS, and the third will use both forms. Let's start by animating a progress bar as our next component.

Animating a Progress Bar Component

Although our next component contains a fair chunk of code, there are only two elements we can animate when working with progress bars – the progress itself and any labels we use to indicate progress.

For this next demo, we're going to steer away from using a native `<progress>` element so we can insert text inside the bar – at the same time, we'll animate both the progress element (a `div` in our case) and that label, using pure Svelte animation.

CREATING THE PROGRESS BAR COMPONENT

To see how we can animate our component, follow these steps:

1. First, go ahead and create a new folder called `ProgressBar` at the root of the `\src\lib\components` folder.

2. We can now create our component – for this, crack open a new file in your editor, then add the following code, which sets up a bunch of declarations and imports two animation functions from Svelte:

    ```
    <svelte:options customElement="garnet-progressbar" />
    ```

```
<script>
  import { cubicOut } from 'svelte/easing';
  import { tweened } from 'svelte/motion';

  export let progressAmt = 52;
  // export let precision = 0;
  export let tweenDuration = 400;
  export let animate = true;
  export let labelInside = true;
  export let labelTextOutside = "This is a test";
  export let easing = cubicOut;
  export let color = '#733635';

  const progress = tweened(0, {
    duration: animate ? tweenDuration : 0,
    easing
  });

  $: progress.set(Number(progressAmt));
</script>
```

3. Next, leave a line blank, then add this markup – this takes care
    of creating the progress bar, with the label inside or outside,
    depending on the properties we set:

```
<div class="garnet-progressbar">

  <!-- Adds label inside progressbar -->
  {#if labelInside}
    <div class="labelInsideClass">
      <div class="progressbar" style="width:
      {$progress}%; background-color: {color}">
        <span class="progress">
          {$progress.toFixed(precision)}%
        </span>
      </div>
```

```
    </div>
  {:else}
  <div class="labelOutsideClass">
    <span class="labelTextOutside">{labelTextOutside}
    </span>
    <span class="progress">
      {$progress.toFixed(precision)}%
    </span>
  </div>
  <div class="progressbar" style="width: {$progress}%;
  background-color: {color}; height: 10px;"></div>
{/if}
  </div>
```

4. We have one more block of code to add, which is the styling – after all, we need to make sure our progress bar looks somewhere near presentable! It won't win any style awards – add these styles to get us started:

```
<style>
  .garnet-porgressbar {
    display: flex;
    flex-direction: column;
    font-family: Arial, Helvetica, sans-serif;
  }

  .progress {
    font-size: 14px;
    line-height: 20px;
    font-weight: 500;
  }

  .progressbar { border-radius: 9999px; }
```

```
.labelInsideClass {
  display: flex;
  flex-direction: column;
  font-size: 12px;
  line-height: 16px;
  font-weight: 500;
  text-align: center;
  padding: 0.5rem;
  border-radius: 9999px;
  color: #000000;
}

.labelOutsideClass {
  display: flex;
  justify-content: space-between;
  margin-bottom: 1px;
  color: #000000;
}
</style>
```

5. Save the file as `ProgressBar.svelte` in the ProgressBar folder – the component is now built and ready for testing, which we will do in the next demo.

Excellent – we have our core component ready for testing: we can now progress to adding it to Storybook! Puns aside, this can now test our component in Storybook! It is one of three components we will create for this chapter, using a mix of animation principles; let's take a moment to explore how we set it up in more detail so we can get a feel for how the animation works from Svelte.

Exploring the Code Changes

At the start of this book, I made a promise to use native HTML elements where possible – and in particular, HTML5 ones! You will notice that we've not kept that promise for this component, but it's with good reason: we want to be able to put a label inside the progress bar, and the best way to do it is to use the `<div>` elements we have used in our component.

So, how did we create our component? We started with setting the now-familiar Web Component tag, using `svelte:options` and specifying a name of `garnet-progressbar` as our `customElement`. Next, we imported two animation functions from Svelte – `cubicOut` from `svelte/easing` and tweened from `svelte/motion`. At the same time, we also created various variables – `progress`, `precision`, and `animate`, to name but three – which we will use within the component or when we render it in Storybook.

Moving on, we set a const called `_progress`, which gives a numerical representation of where our progress is. This part is a little more complex, as we use tweened to animate it; we only do this if `animate` is set to true; otherwise, it is not animated. We then store this value in a reactive statement (the `$:` line just below), forcing Svelte to update it every time the value of `progress` changes.

The next block is our markup for the component – it looks complex, but it will be easier to understand if you look at it as a sizeable conditional `{#if}...{:else}...{/if}` block. Most of the code is standard HTML markup, but we use the if...else... block to first check if `labelInside` is true. If so, we put our progress value inside the bar; if not, we set it outside, along with a span that contains the `labelTextOutside` text. We finish the component with a set of basic styles – `.garnet` takes care of the parent container, followed by `progress` for the text, `.progressbar` to style the progress bar, and the two `.label...` classes that look after the text displayed in the component.

Adding to Storybook

We now have our progress bar component ready for testing, so our next task is to add it to Storybook – we'll create our usual Storybook file, followed by a default fallback template and the first of several stories. It's no different from the other components we've already added to our Storybook instance, so let's crack on with our next demo.

ADDING TO STORYBOOK

To set up our progress bar component in Storybook, work through these steps:

1. First, crack open a new file in your editor, then add these imports:

```
import ProgressBar from "./ProgressBar.svelte";
import { fn } from "@storybook/test";
import { action } from "@storybook/addon-actions";
```

2. Next, miss a line, then add this default fallback template, which tells Storybook what properties to use if we don't override any:

```
export default {
  title: "Garnet UI Library/Animation Components/
  ProgressBar",
  component: ProgressBar,
  argTypes: {
    disabled: { control: "boolean" },
    label: { control: "string" },
    oninput: { action: "changed" },
  },
  on: { change: fn().mockName("on-change") },
};
```

3. Next, leave a line blank, then add this block of code – this will be our Default story, which renders our component with (largely) out-of-the-box properties:

```
export const Default = (args) => ({
  Component: ProgressBar,
  props: {
    ...args,
    labelTextOutside: "ProgressBar",
    disabled: false,
    color: "red",
    on: { change: fn().mockName("on-change") },
  },
});
```

4. Save the file as `ProgressBar.stories.js` in the Alarm folder, then close the file.

5. You will see from the code that we've specified a file as our documentation but haven't yet added it. We need to extract a copy of `Docs.mdx` from the code download and then drop it into the Alarm folder.

6. We have everything in place, so let's test it! Switch to a Node. js terminal session, then set the working folder to our garnet project area.

7. At the prompt, enter `npm run storybook` and hit Enter – if all is well, we should see Storybook launch and display in our browser at `http://localhost:6006/`. Click the Default link under ProgressBar on the left to display the variant we created, as shown in Figure 7-1.

Figure 7-1. *Our animated progress bar component*

Perfect – granted, the choice of color is perhaps not one I would use, but hey, it's more to prove that we can choose what color we want to use and not be limited to any particular choice!

It's a shame we can't see the animation run in print, so you'll have to believe me that it runs – in the meantime, let's pause for a moment to explore how the code hangs together and, in particular, the way we have used animation to create our progress bar.

Understanding the Changes Made

By now, you will hopefully be familiar with most of the steps we've used to add our component to Storybook. I appreciate that using the same format might bring a case of déjà vu, but practice makes perfect!

For this component, we first imported our component, followed by two modules from Storybook – these we use to help render our component in our Storybook instance. We then set our default fallback template to render if properties are not otherwise provided before adding the Default story to give us a feel for how the component will render (largely) out of the box. To finish, we fired up Storybook before checking to ensure our component rendered as expected in the browser.

Adding Variants

We've now added our component to Storybook and seen it render as expected – what's next?

Well, it's all good having a single instance of our component running, but as I am sure you will appreciate from earlier demos, a component only becomes useful if we can create different variants! Our progress bar component is no different – for our next demo, I'll take you through modifying Storybook to show a new variant where the label sits outside the component.

ADDING VARIANTS

To enable our variant, follow these steps:

1. First, crack open `ProgressBar.stories.js`, then scroll to the bottom – go ahead and add this code:

```
export const LabelOutside = (args) => ({
   Component: ProgressBar,
   props: {
     ...args,
     labelInside: false,
     labelTextOutside: "This is a test progress bar",
     disabled: false,
     color: "blue",
     on: { change: fn().mockName("on-change") },
   },
});
```

2. Save and close the file – revert to a Node.js terminal prompt, and make sure the working folder is set to our project area.

3. At the prompt, enter npm run storybook and hit Enter – if
    all is well, we should see Storybook launch and display in
    our browser at http://localhost:6006/. Click the Label
    Outside link under ProgressBar on the left to display the variant
    we created, as shown in Figure 7-2.

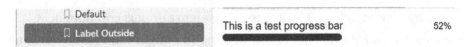

Figure 7-2. *A variant for our ProgressBar component*

Excellent – we have our variant in place and working. Granted, it is
only one, but this is intentional: I want to see what you can come up with!
What variants do you think we could use here? Let me give you a couple of
examples as a starter for ten:

- The animation: We used cubicOut as one of the
  animations, but how about choosing a different one?

- We've defined a height for our progress bar, but what if
  we wanted a thinner (or even thicker) one?

- We set a single color for the background, but could we
  adopt a striped background? It would require using
  something like a repeating-linear-gradient()
  function in CSS – could we create something abstract?

- It's a little more complex, but what about setting a color
  for the label text? If we have it inside the progress bar,
  it should be light-colored, while outside, it could be
  darker (or even black).

These are just some ideas I came up with – I'm sure you can think
of more! In the meantime, let's take a moment to break apart the code
changes from that last demo to see how it all hangs together.

We added a new story, which we called `LabelOutside`. You may or may not have noticed that we already included this entry in our `Docs.mdx` file, similar to the one for Default. Inside this variant, we set `labelInside` to `false` and `labelTextOutside` to a test label – this tells Storybook to switch from showing the progress amount inside the bar to showing it outside the component.

Okay – let's crack on: it's time to move on to our next component, which will be an alarm. No – not something you might want to hurl halfway across the room at some ungodly hour in the morning, but something more delicate: a way to tell you if you've got a new message. Let's dive in and take a look in more detail.

Creating the Alarm Component

We live in an age where so much is happening – dozens of jobs to do, people to see, and places to go. It's impossible to manage without some form of notification; we've already covered some notification components that would be a perfect tool.

However, there is one more we can add – what about an alarm? No – I'm not thinking of something to wake you up in the morning (and yes, we all need that), but something to tell you of a new message or alert. We're not going to create a static alarm but an animated one; it's a perfect opportunity to mix in a little animation from Svelte. Let's take a look at how, in the next demo.

BUILDING THE COMPONENT

To create our alarm component, follow these steps:

1. First, go ahead and create a new folder called `Alarm` at the root of the `\src\lib\components` folder.

2. We can now create our component – for this, crack open a
    new file in your editor, then add the following code, which
    sets up some declarations and imports an animation function
    from Svelte:

```
<svelte:options customElement="garnet-alarm" />

<script>
    import { scale } from 'svelte/transition'

    export let notifications = 26;
    export let label = "This is a test label";
    export let countColor = "#733635";
    export let countBackgroundColor = "#f4f4f4";
    export let filled = false;
    export let small = false;
</script>
```

3. Miss a line, then add this markup – this forms the basis of our
    component:

```
<div class="garnet-alarm">
  <h3>{label}</h3>
  <div class="notifications">
    <div class="count {small ? 'small': ''}" style="--
    countColor: {countColor}; --countBackgroundColor:
    {countBackgroundColor}">
      {#key notifications}
        <span in:scale>{notifications}</span>
      {/key}
  </div>
```

4. The second part of the markup is a little more complex – this
    looks after the markup for the bell SVG, and whether certain
    properties will be set, based on what we provide to the
    component:

```
<svg
  class="bell {small ? 'small': ''} {filled ?
  'filled' : 'outline'} {notifications > 0 ?
  'ring': ''}"
  xmlns="http://www.w3.org/2000/svg"
  viewBox="0 0 24 24"
  stroke-width="1.5"
  stroke="currentColor"
>
  <path
    d="M14.857 17.082a23.848 23.848 0
    005.454-1.31A8.967 8.967 0 0118 9.75v-.7V9A6 6 0
    006 9v.75a8.967 8.967 0 01-2.312 6.022c1.733.64
    3.56 1.085 5.455 1.31m5.714 0a24.255 24.255 0
    01-5.714 0m5.714 0a3 3 0 11-5.714 0"
    stroke-linecap="round"
    stroke-linejoin="round"
  />
</svg>
</div>
</div>
```

5. With the basic markup in place, we can now focus on the all-
    important styling. Leave a blank below the markup and then
    add this style block – there is a fair bit to add, so we'll do it
    in sections, starting with one for the title and the notifications
    container:

```
<style>
  h3 {
    font-family: Arial, Helvetica, sans-serif;
  }

  .notifications {
    position: rclativc;
    font-family: Arial, Helvetica, sans-serif;
  }
```

6. Next, add these rules – the first takes care of styling the
    number of notifications on display:

```
.notifications .count {
    position: absolute;
    left: 120px;
    top: 5px;
    display: grid;
    place-content: center;
    padding: 16px;
    font-size: 20px;
    font-weight: 700;
    color: var(--countColor);
    background-color: var(--countBackgroundColor);
    border-radius: 50%;
    width: 22px;
}
```

7. For this component, we're using a mix of CSS and Svelte
    animation – this next block is a keyframe animation called ring,
    which we will use to animate the bell:

```
@keyframes ring {
0% { transform: rotate(0); }
1% { transform: rotate(30deg); }
3% { transform: rotate(-28deg); }
5% { transform: rotate(34deg); }
7% { transform: rotate(-32deg); }
9% { transform: rotate(30deg); }
11% { transform: rotate(-28deg); }
13% { transform: rotate(26deg); }
15% { transform: rotate(-24deg); }
17% { transform: rotate(22deg); }
19% { transform: rotate(-20deg); }
21% { transform: rotate(18deg); }
23% { transform: rotate(-16deg); }
25% { transform: rotate(14deg); }
27% { transform: rotate(-12deg); }
29% { transform: rotate(10deg); }
31% { transform: rotate(-8deg); }
33% { transform: rotate(6deg); }
35% { transform: rotate(-4deg); }
37% { transform: rotate(2deg); }
39% { transform: rotate(-1deg); }
41% { transform: rotate(1deg); }

43% { transform: rotate(0); }
100% { transform: rotate(0); }
}

.ring {
  animation: ring 4s .7s ease-in-out infinite;
}
```

8. These last few styles are primarily for variants – they control
    both size and whether the icon is filled in, depending on the
    variant selected:

```css
.notifications .bell {
  width: 140px;
  height: 140px;
}

.filled{
  fill: #000000;
}

.outline {
  fill: none;
}

svg.bell.small {
  width: 70px;
  height: 70px;
}

.count.small {
  font-size: 12px;
  position: absolute;
  top: -20px;
  left: 65px;
  padding: 10px;
}
```
</style>

9. Save the file as `Alarm.svelte` in the Alarm folder – the
    component is now built and ready for testing, which we will do
    in the next demo.

Excellent – we can now test our component in Storybook! Even though this was a small component, we've created a fair chunk of code – before we test it all, let's pause for a moment to review what we created in more detail, ready to see it in action.

Breaking Apart the Code

To create our component, we first set our `customElement` tag before importing the `scale` animation function from `svelte/transition`. We then set a bunch of variables such as `notifications`, `label`, and `filled` – some of these will be for the core component, while others will be more for use in displaying our component in Storybook.

Next up, we then created the markup for our component – most of this is standard HTML, but we include checks such as whether `small` is set to `true` (so rendering the smaller version of our component) or determining which background color to use from `--countBackgroundColor`. You will notice that I've prefixed some variables with a double hyphen; this allows us to set the value at the top and will filter down wherever we use it in the component. The addition of export means we can also set the property from outside the component!

At the same time, we set an `in:scale` property for the span that contains notifications – this should slide numbers down each time we update them, but it's not working as well as expected, so something we should target in a future version!

Moving on, we then set up the markup for our SVG – here, we set three properties in addition to the markup for the SVG: `small`, `filled`, and `notifications`. The first controls the size (which we will use as a variant), and `filled` determines whether the icon should be opaque. We use the notifications properties to add a `.ring` class if the count is greater than zero.

The last part of this component is the somewhat lengthy style sheet we set to style our component. The rules we set cover areas such as the text of the notification, the label's position, and the keyframe animation for our bell. You will see that I've used CSS variables in a couple of places to expose that value outside of the component so we can specify what that value should be. For example, I set `--countColor` in the `.notifications` `.count` rule – we use this to determine what the text color for the number of alerts should be. The remaining rules are primarily for the variants – we use them to determine if the icon should be an outline, filled in, or whether we want to display a smaller size than the current default of 140px.

Adding to Storybook

By now, you're probably familiar with the process we've been following – we create our component (or components, in the case of Grid we created earlier) before adding them individually to Storybook.

The process won't be any different for Alarm – we'll create our usual Storybook file, followed by adding a default fallback template and the first of several stories. So, without further ado, let's crack on and set up our component in Storybook.

ADDING TO STORYBOOK

We have a component ready for use, but we can't use it until we set it up in Storybook! To do so, follow these steps:

1. First, crack open a new file in your editor, then add these imports:

```
import Alarm from "./Alarm.svelte";
import { fn } from "@storybook/test";
import { action } from "@storybook/addon-actions";
```

2. Next, leave a line blank, then add this export – this creates a
    template to determine what Storybook should render by default
    as a fallback:

```
export default {
  title: "Garnet UI Library/Animation
  Components/Alarm",
  component: Alarm,
  argTypes: {
    disabled: { control: "boolean" },
    label: { control: "string" },
    small: { control: "boolean" },
    oninput: { action: "changed" },
    notifications: { control: "integer" },
  },
  on: { change: fn().mockName("on-change") },
};
```

3. With our default template in place, we can now turn our
    attention to *the* Default template we've seen before – this
    shows off the Alarm component using (mostly) out-of-the-box
    settings:

```
export const Default = (args) => ({
  Component: Alarm,
  props: {
    ...args,
    id: "1",
    label: "Alarm with label",
    notifications: 12,
    disabled: false,
    filled: false,
```

```
    on: { change: fn().mockName("on-change") },
  },
});
```

4. Save the file as `Alarm.stories.js` in the Alarm folder, then
    close the file.

5. You will see from the code that we've specified a file as our
    documentation but haven't yet added it. We need to extract a
    copy of `Docs.mdx` from the code download and then drop it
    into the Table folder.

6. We have everything in place, so let's test it! Switch to a Node.
    js terminal session, then set the working folder to our garnet
    project area.

7. At the prompt, enter `npm run storybook` and hit Enter – if
    all is well, we should see Storybook launch and display in our
    browser at `http://localhost:6006/`. Click the Default link
    under Alarm on the left to display the variant we created, as
    shown in Figure 7-3.

Alarm with label

Figure 7-3. *The default variant of our Alarm component*

Perfect – if all is well, we should see an alarm ringing after a few moments; it's a shame I can't show you in print! That all aside, we've covered some valuable tips in the last demo, some of which I know you will have seen in earlier demos.

It's still a great opportunity, though, to explore the changes we made just now, so grab a drink, and let's go break apart the code to see how it all hangs together in more detail.

Exploring the Changes

To get our alarm ringing (so to speak), we had to work through a series of steps that will no doubt be reasonably familiar by now – we first imported our component, followed by two modules from Storybook, to help render the component in our Storybook instance.

We then set our default fallback template to render if properties are not otherwise provided before adding the Default story to give us a feel for how the component will render (largely) out of the box. In this instance, we provided the name of our component, plus set a handful of properties with the appropriate values – such as marking disabled to false – so that Storybook knows how to render our component. To finish off, we fired up Storybook before checking to ensure our component rendered as expected in the browser.

Adding Variants

At this point, we should now have a working alarm bell that rings just like the real thing (but without the noise!). It looks a little dull, though – what can we do to add a little variety?

Well, as a starting point, we could change whether we use an outline or a filled icon; what about the size of the icon, too? To see how we could do this, let's dive into our next demo.

216

ADDING VARIANTS

To add our new variants, follow these steps:

1. First, crack open `Alarm.stories.js`, and scroll to the bottom of the file.

2. Next, add this block of code – this will change the icon we use from an outline version to a filled one:

```
export const Filled = (args) => ({
  Component: Alarm,
  props: {
    ...args,
    id: "1",
    label: "Alarm with label",
    notifications: 12,
    disabled: false,
    filled: true,
    on: { change: fn().mockName("on-change") },
  },
});
```

3. Leave a line blank, then add this second block of code – the name of the story will give it away: this will resize the icon to something smaller.

```
export const Small = (args) => ({
  Component: Alarm,
  props: {
    ...args,
    id: "1",
    label: "Alarm with label",
    notifications: 12,
```

```
            disabled: false,
            filled: true,
            small: true,
            on: { change: fn().mockName("on-change") },
        },
    });
```

4. Save and close the file. Switch to a Node.js terminal prompt, and make sure the working folder is set to our project area.

5. At the prompt, enter npm run storybook and press Enter. Go ahead and browse to http://localhost:6006/ – if all is well, we should see two new variants listed on the left under Alarm ➤ Default – Filled and Small. The first of these is shown in Figure 7-4.

Alarm with label

Figure 7-4. *The Filled variant of our Alarm component*

6. We can see the second one for Small, shown in Figure 7-5.

Alarm with label

Figure 7-5. *The Small variant for our Alarm component*

Superb – our progress bar component is now starting to come to life! Even though we only added two more blocks, this is enough to show off what is possible with this component – we've used the same format as other components but set slightly different properties to give us our new variants.

For the first variant, we set the filled property to true – this tells Storybook to apply a `fill:` to the SVG we use as the bell icon. We've not set a fill color property as such; instead, we use the outcome of `filled: true` to set a `filled` CSS property, in which we tell it to use #000000, or black.

In the second variant, we use the same principles to set the size – here, we set the small property to apply a small class to the SVG to reduce its size by 50%. As part of this, we also reduced the count circle size and repositioned it to allow for the new size.

While these (and other) components may be limited in scope and variants, they do show one important point – they are not the finished article by any stretch of the imagination. Indeed, I'm a big fan of the MVP approach, where we can create a basic version to start with and iterate so it becomes a more refined article. If it works, that's OK – people can still use it!

To add to that point, here's an example of what we can and should do: What about adding a property for fill color so it is controllable?

Okay – let's crack on: we have another component to create in this chapter. We've so far used Svelte-only animation and a mix of both: for this last component, it's time to switch to using CSS only....

Creating a Switch Component

Ouch – that was a terrible pun: given the nature of what we're about to do, I'm sure you can appreciate why I included it!

Yes, we will create a classic switch for the last component in this chapter; these are essential for instances such as turning on or off properties in an online account. Our component will be a little more complex than others, so let's crack on exploring the code in the next demo.

BUILDING THE SWITCH COMPONENT

To get started with creating our Switch component, follow these steps:

1. First, create a folder called Switch under `\src\lib\components`.

2. Next, go ahead and add the following code into a new file – we have a fair amount to get through, so we will start with the now usual `customElement` tag and variable definitions:

   ```
   <svelte:options customElement="garnet-switch" />

   <script>
     export let id = "";
     export let label = "";
     export let css = "";
     export let size = "";
     export let isChecked = false;
     export let disabled = false;
   ```

3. We also need to add a reactive statement and a function:

   ```
   $: switchContainer = [
       "switch-container",
       css ? css : "",
   ```

```
    disabled ? "disabled" : "",
  ].filter(c => c).join(" ");

  let classes = ["switch", size ? `switch-${size}` :
  ""].join(" ");
</script>
```

4. With our script in place, we can turn our attention to the
    markup – go ahead and add this block:

```
<label class={switchContainer} for={id}>
  <input
    type="checkbox"
    class="switch-input"
    id={id}
    bind:checked={isChecked}
    disabled={disabled}
    on:change
    on:input
    role="switch"
  />
  <span class={switchSpan()}></span>
  <span class="switch-label">{label}</span>
</label>
```

5. Excellent – we have one more stage to complete: styling! We
    do have a lot of styles to add, but that's only to be expected as
    we're building from the ground up:

I've compressed the code for space reasons: I'd recommend copying
and pasting this from the code download accompanying this book!

```
<style>
  .switch-container { display: flex; min-height: 36px;
  width: 100%; padding: 8px; position: relative;
  align-items: center; }

  .switch-container:hover { cursor: pointer; }

  .switch::before,
  .switch::after { border: 1px solid #ccc; content:
  ""; position: absolute; top: 50%; transform:
  translateY(-50%); }

  .switch::after { background: #fff; border-radius:
  100%; width: 22.4px; height: 22.4px; right: 22.4px;
  transition: right 200ms ease-in-out; }
  .switch::before { background: #eee; border-radius:
  28px; width: 44px; height: 28px; right: 4px;
  transition: background 300ms ease-in-out; }

  .switch-input:checked + .switch::after { right:
  6.4px; }

  .switch-input { margin: 0; opacity: 0.01%; position:
  absolute; left: 0; top: 0; width: 100%; height: 100%;
  pointer-events: none; }

  .switch-input:focus + .switch::before {
  box-shadow: 0 0 0 3px rgb(55 149 225 / 50%); }
  .switch-input:checked + .switch:not(.switch-
  border)::before { background: #733635; }

  .switch-input[disabled] + .switch,
  .switch-input[disabled] + .switch-label,
```

```
.switch-container.disabled { color:#717171;
appearance: none; box-shadow: none; cursor:
not-allowed; opacity: 80%; }
</style>
```

6. Save the file as `Switch.svelte`, in the Switch folder – the component is now built and ready for testing, which we will do shortly in the next demo.

Perfect – our switch is ready: we just need to "switch it on" in Storybook (groan!). Okay, leaving aside my terrible jokes, we now need to set up an instance of it in Storybook to see if it works as expected. Our demo contains some valuable tricks worth exploring in more detail, so before we crack open Storybook, let's dive into the codebase again to see how our component hangs together in more detail.

Breaking Apart the Code

For a component that only took five steps to create, we sure covered a lot of code! A lot of it will follow the same format as for other components, namely, setting variables first, followed by markup and finishing with styles.

To get us there, we first set seven different variables, such as `label`, `css`, and `size`; all of these we marked for export, so they are available externally. We then created a reactive statement (the block starting `$: switchContainer = [...]`), which we use to pull together some of the style properties for our component and, more importantly, make sure they are updated if values change. Note how, in this instance, we are only focusing on what we might call *outside (or container)* properties – in this case, a generic `switch-container`, plus `disabled` and any external properties we want to set. These properties will likely need to change more often than those set internally, hence setting them in a reactive statement.

Moving on, we perform a similar operation, but for classes `inside` the Switch – these are pulled together and assigned to classes. Here, we concatenate a generic `switch` class with `size` – we're not using that latter style for the moment, but we could easily use it to create a new variant later.

Next up comes the markup – here, we used a standard `<label>` element with an `<input>`. We format the latter as a checkbox to form the basis for our switch. You will notice that we provide a set of standard properties, such as `class`, `type`, and `id` – three of these properties are Svelte-specific. We used `on:change`, which is the same as `onChange={handleChange}`; `bind:checked`, which ties the value of `checked` to `isChecked` so we can pipe out the result if needed, and `on:input`, which equates to `onInput={handleInput}`. We then finished up by supplying a host of styling rules for our Switch component, before previewing the results of our work to make sure it functions as expected in a browser.

Okay – let's crack on: we've created our component, so it's time now to add it to our Storybook instance. It should be a relatively straightforward process by now, so let's dive in and take a look at how we do it in more detail.

Adding to Storybook

By now, you're probably familiar with the process we've been following – we first create the component (or components, in the case of Grid) before adding them one by one to Storybook.

As before, we'll continue with that process for Switch – it will contain our usual Storybook file, with a fallback template and the first of our two-Story setups. So, without further ado, let's crack on and set up our component in Storybook.

ADDING THE SWITCH COMPONENT TO STORYBOOK

Setting up our Switch component to run in Storybook requires a little more work than previous demos – to see how, follow these steps:

1. First, open a new file, then add this markup:

```
<div>
  <slot />
</div>

<style>
  div { width: 300px; font-family: Arial,
  Helvetica, sans-serif; border: 1px solid #d4d4d4;
  display: flex; }
</style>
```

2. Save the file as `SwitchDecorator.svelte`, then close it. We will only use this in Storybook, but it doesn't become part of the component.

3. Next, we need to create our Storybook file. For this, crack open a new file, then add the following code, starting with some imports:

```
import Switch from "./Switch.svelte";
import { fn } from "@storybook/test";
import { action } from "@storybook/addon-actions";
import SwitchDecorator from "./SwitchDecorator.svelte";
```

4. Next, leave a line blank, then add this story – as we have done in previous demos, this will provide default values if we don't specify any in a story:

```
export default {
  title: "Garnet UI Library/Animation Components/
  Switch",
  component: Switch,
  decorators: [() => SwitchDecorator],
  argTypes: {
    disabled: { control: "boolean" },
    label: { control: "string" },
    oninput: { action: "changed" },
  },
  on: { change: fn().mockName("on-change") },
};
```

5. Last but by no means least, we need to add the Default story,
    which will render our Switch component with a (largely) out-of-
    the-box configuration:

```
export const Default = (args) => ({
  Component: Switch,
  props: {
  ...args,
    id: "1",
    label: "Switch with label",
    disabled: false,
    on: { change: fn().mockName("on-change") },
  },
});
```

6. Save the file as Switch.stories.js in the Switch folder,
    then close the file.

7. You will see from the code that we've specified a file as our documentation but haven't yet added it. We need to extract a copy of `Docs.mdx` from the code download and then drop it into the Switch folder.

8. We have everything in place, so let's test it! Switch to a Node.js terminal session, then set the working folder to our garnet project area.

9. At the prompt, enter `npm run storybook` and hit Enter – if all is well, we should see Storybook launch and display in our browser at `http://localhost:6006`. Click the Default link under Switch on the left to display the variant we created, as shown in Figure 7-6.

Switch with label

Figure 7-6. *Our new Switch component*

Nice – we now have our Switch component in place and tested; hopefully, it worked just as well for you as it did for me!

It does, however, mean that we have reached a milestone in this project since we have now created all of the initial components for our library. We still have one more task to complete before moving on to the next stage of this project – we have one more variant to add to our Switch. It's a simple change to make, so let's crack on with adding it so that we can wrap up the component creation process.

Creating a Variant

For this last variant, we will keep it simple and add a Disabled story – this will show what the component looks like if we disable it from running in code. This is a simple change: we need to add a new story and set the `disabled` property to `true` – let's take a quick look at how as part of our next demo.

ADDING A SWITCH VARIANT

To add what will be the last variant for our project, follow these steps:

1. First, crack open `Switch.stories.js`, then scroll to the bottom.

2. Leave a line blank, then add this block – it does as it says on the tin; it will render a disabled version of our Switch component:

```
export const Disabled = (args) => ({
  Component: Switch,
  props: {
    ...args,
    id: "1",
    label: "Disabled switch with label",
    disabled: true,
    on: { change: fn().mockName("on-change") },
  },
});
```

3. Save and close the file. Revert to a Node.js terminal session, then make sure the working folder is set to our project area.

4. At the prompt, enter `npm run storybook` and hit Enter – if all is well, we should see Storybook launch and display in our browser at `http://localhost:6006/`. Click the Disabled link under Switch on the left to display the variant we created, as shown in Figure 7-7.

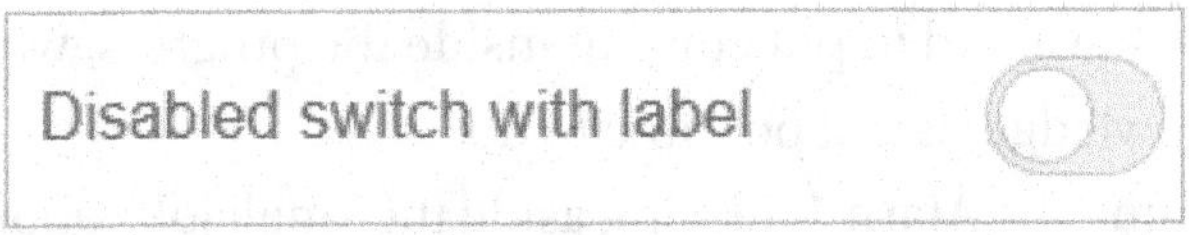

Figure 7-7. The variant for our Switch component

And there we are – our final variant in place, at least for now! To get us here was a quick process, similar to one we've already used on other components elsewhere in this book.

We added a new story to the `Switch.stories.js` file, which uses the same config object as the Default, but this time with disabled changed from false to true. Sorry to disappoint if you were hoping for more, but that's the beauty of Storybook – in most cases, we only need to alter the properties set each time! Granted, if you use a composite component like the Grid components we developed in Chapter 6, things become slightly more complex. In the main, though, it's still passing values, provided you set up the architecture of your components to support a parent/child structure.

Summary

Phew – we covered a lot over the last few pages!

Animation is a crucial topic in today's modern world – long gone are the days of torrid gray pages with HTML marquee tags dotted everywhere (yes – anyone remember those?); we have to strike a delicate balance between animating enough content to provide interest and not too much to put people off.

It is why I deliberately kept animations simple in this chapter – we worked our way through three examples of components for our library, but with emphasis on using pure CSS in one, Svelte-only animations in another, and a mix of both in the third component.

We started by looking at how we might animate a progress bar – it's a common element, but one where we had to take a different route to building it as we wanted to put content inside the progress, which (to the best of my knowledge) is not possible to do.

Next up came the Alarm – leaving aside the small joke about wanting to throw it somewhere early in the morning(!), we explored how to use a keyframe animation to make a bell ring realistically while at the same time providing a visual indication that we had a notice that should be read. We used pure CSS and a Svelte transition; Svelte is happy to work with both, and given that it has some built-in animations, it is effortless to use!

The third and final component for this chapter was a Switch – for this one, we used pure CSS to animate the sliding effect; this ties in with providing enough animation to give a component extra polish but not to get in the way of the user experience and ultimately put people off!

Okay – we've come to the end of the construction process: it's time to move on to the next area! We have all of our components in place, but one thing that we've not really spent any time on is that all-important documentation! Let's put that to rights by exploring how some of the documentation files hang together and using the opportunity to make sure it's all shipshape in the next chapter.

CHAPTER 8

Writing Documentation

Throughout this book, we've created a host of new components to form our component library – they may only be simple ones, but as they say, we must start somewhere!

There is one important task we need to perform, and that is to document how these components work. Given that we're using Storybook, we can add documentation files to each component, accessible from the Docs tab at the top of Storybook, as shown in Figure 8-1.

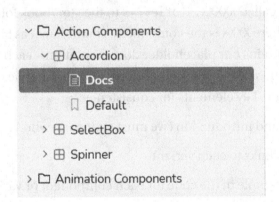

Figure 8-1. *An example of the Docs tab in Storybook*

© Alex Libby 2025
A. Libby, *Developing Web Components with Svelte*,
https://doi.org/10.1007/979-8-8688-1180-7_8

You will undoubtedly notice that we've already done this for most (if not all) components. The trouble is that many of them are a little rough around the edges and could use a little tidying! This updating is easy enough to do – the placeholder pages we've added so far use Markdown, which is similar to what you might use if you're creating pages in GitHub, for example.

Don't worry if you're unfamiliar with Markdown – most of it is text based, with a relatively simple syntax for creating items such as titles. I'll take you through everything as we go through this chapter. Rather than being too prescriptive about the final article, we'll keep each relatively fluid so you can use them to expand and develop your versions in the future.

With all that in mind, let's explore the process we will use to check each documentation page to see what we can improve in our existing offer.

Setting the Scene

Cast your mind back to the last component we created – in each instance, we added a file called XXXXX.stories.js to the storybook folder for each component (where XXXX is the component's name, such as Slider).

This file contains our placeholder documentation – each will, of course, vary depending on the components and variants we create, but all should have some key elements for consistency:

- Title and introduction (we must start somewhere!)

- Jump links to each variant

- An example of the code for each component or variant

- Add-on badges to confirm status, for example, Stable, Experimental, etc.

- A list of argument types where appropriate

Okay – let's crack on: we know what we need to do, so let's make a start! We'll come to making sure the content is up to date shortly, but first, let's begin with adding some status badges for each component so we know if they are alpha, beta, or ready, and so on.

Copies of the source files will be in the code download if you get stuck.

Adding Status Badges

Our first task is to set up badges – this is one of the features we listed back in the previous section as something we want to have on all component pages. The process comes in two parts. In the first part, we'll set up the feature for use in Storybook, and then I'll show you how to add labels to the documentation page for each component.

In the first edition of this book, I used a package called `storybook-addon-badges`, by @geometricpanda – this was not working in Storybook 8, at the time of writing. It hadn't had an update for some time, so I used a forked version which works fine; the original may now have SB8 support by the time this book goes to print.

ADDING STATUS BADGES

To add status badges, follow these steps – we'll use the Checkbox component as our example:

1. First, we need to install the storybook-addon-badges package. To do this, crack open a Node.js terminal session, then change the working folder to our project area.

2. At the prompt, run this command:

    ```
    npm install storybook-addon-badges
    ```

3. Node will go away and install it – minimize the session, as we will need it later in this exercise.

4. Once we've installed the package, switch to your editor and open the `main.js` file in the `\.storybook` folder.

5. We need to tell Storybook about our new package, so add the highlighted line as indicated:

    ```
    "addons": [
      "@storybook/addon-links",
      "@storybook/addon-essentials",
      "@storybook/addon-interactions",
      "storybook-addon-badges",
    ],
    ```

6. Next, open `Breadcrumbs.stories.js` in your editor, then add this line immediately after the last import statement at the top of the file:

    ```
    import { BADGE } from "storybook-addon-badges";
    ```

7. Scroll down to the end of the Default story, then add the line
   as shown:

```
    ],
  },
});
Default.parameters = { badges: ["beta"] };
```

8. Save and close all open files. Revert to the Node.js terminal
   session from earlier, then at the prompt, enter npm run
   storybook and browse to http://localhost:6006/. If all is well,
   we should see the Experimental badge shown in Figure 8-2,
   with a BETA tag to the top right of the image.

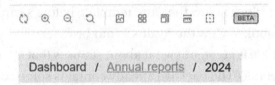

Figure 8-2. *An example of a Storybook add-on badge*

Great – we can now add badges to our site! Adding a BETA tag like this
one might scare a few people, but we must remember that our components
are not yet production-ready, and there will be things we need to do or test
before we hit that stage.

It's a realistic indication of where we are, so people know what to
expect. Either way, it's a valuable feature to have in Storybook, so let's
spend a few moments reviewing the changes in more detail.

Understanding What Happened

Since I started working with Storybook several years ago, adding badges has always been one of my top tasks for customizing Storybook. It gives a clear, unambiguous way to show what state a plugin is in, such as stable, experimental, or even (dare I say it) deprecated!

It is an easy plugin to install – we first ran a typical `npm install` command to download and set up the plugin as a development dependency. The install is only part of the story, though, as next we had to tell Storybook about the plugin; we added it to the list of add-ons in the `.\storybook\main.js` configuration file. To finish the demo, we added an import statement to `Breadcrumbs.stories.js` (our demo file for this exercise). We followed this by setting the badge configuration in the `parameters:` block below the story template before saving the file and restarting Storybook to view the results in our browser.

Adding a badge is great, but what about statuses that are not included as options by default? The package already contains some common options, but we might want to add something like Alpha as a possible option. Fortunately, it's straightforward to customize the plugin – let's take a look at how, as part of the next demo.

Customizing the Badges Plugin Configuration

Okay, we can now add a status label to each component as needed; we've done one for the Default version of the Breadcrumbs component, which works well.

There is one question I'm sure will be on your minds, though: What if we want a label that isn't one of the predefined batches available with this add-on? It's pretty easy to add one for whatever we need – we need to define how it will look and add the configuration for it into the `preview.js` file. Let's take a look at how, in the following demo, where I will add one for an ALPHA status.

When adding a custom badge, you need to decide your color scheme – you need to have suitable colors for a border, background color, and text color. We'll use three shades of yellow for this demo as our scheme. If you need inspiration or color values, then `https://www.colorhexa.com` is a good place to start!

ADDING A CUSTOM LABEL

To add a custom label, follow these steps:

1. First, go ahead and crack open `preview.js` in the `\.storybook` folder – immediately below the controls: {} line and before the matching closing bracket, add this code as highlighted:

```
/** @type { import('@storybook/svelte').Preview } */
const preview = {
  parameters: {
    controls: {},
    badgesConfig: {
      Alpha: {
        title: "Alpha",
        styles: {
          backgroundColor: "yellow",
          borderColor: "#ffbf00",
          color: "#000000",
        },
      },
    },
  },
};
export default preview;
```

237

2. Save and close the file. Next, open the `Breadcrumbs.`
    `stories.js` file and add these lines immediately after the
    import for `Breadcrumbs.svelte`:

```
import { BADGE } from "storybook-addon-badges";

const BADGES = {
  ...BADGE,
  ALPHA: "Alpha",
};
```

3. Scroll down to the `CustomImage` variant. Miss a line, then add
    this line:

```
CustomImage.parameters = { badges: [BADGES.ALPHA] };
```

4. Save and close all open files. Revert to a Node.js terminal
    session, enter npm `run` `storybook`, and press Enter. Browse
    to http://localhost:6006/ – if all is well, we should see the
    ALPHA badge appear, as shown in Figure 8-3 with an ALPHA
    tag to the top right of the image.

Figure 8-3. *A newly defined custom label in use*

Perfect – to quote a phrase, the world is our oyster! Okay, so I'm probably thinking a little too loftily about what we're doing, but we now have a mechanism to add any label we need. We've covered some essential tips in this demo, so let's pause for a moment to review the changes we made in more detail.

If you need practice, why not try to add the same badge to each of the other variants? Hint: If you add to the default entry (and **not** the Default entry), it will automatically add all variants in that file.

Breaking Apart the Changes

At first glance, it might take a moment to work out how it all hangs together, but it's simpler than it might appear. All of the action happens in preview.js; inside this file, we have the badgesConfig object, where we can add as many badge types as we require.

Our example has one at present, which is Alpha – we might want to add labels such as Discontinued, Windows Only, Mac Only, and so on. Whatever labels we add will entirely be based on our requirements, although I recommend not adding more labels than necessary!

The key to making it all work is two properties – styles and title. Both should be self-explanatory, but to confirm, styles contain the CSS styles for the badge and title the name for each label.

As a test, try changing the Alpha set against title: to something else (say, Node 18+) in preview.js – the code changes would look something like this:

```
...
badgesConfig: {
  "Node 18+":{
    title: "Node 18+",
```

```
    styles: {
      backgroundColor: "#b1b1ff",
      borderColor: "#3b3bff",
      color: "#000000",
    },
   },
  },
},
...
```

and like this for `Breadcrumbs.stories.js`:

```
const BADGES = {
  ...BADGE,
  NODE18PLUS: "Node 18+",
};
...more code...

CustomImage.parameters = { badges: [BADGES.NODE18PLUS] };
```

If all is well, we should see the ALPHA label replaced with a NODE 18+ one, as shown in Figure 8-4.

Figure 8-4. *Displaying a Node 18+ version label*

The remaining styles for each label are just standard CSS color properties – this will vary according to the color palette you're using for your site. I would recommend using HEX or name values, though – a quick test suggests that Storybook doesn't support RGB (or, by extension, RGBA) values!

You will see from the code that I've used NODE18PLUS as a property name – it is probably easier to spell out the title in full if you use special characters such as plus or minus symbols. If you use a name with a space, enclose the full name in quotes when adding it to `preview.js`!

Okay – let's crack on with updating the documentation! There is plenty to do, but as a fair bit is very similar, we won't work through all the steps for adding documentation. Instead, we'll go through an example to show you the kind of changes we can make so that you can apply these to the remaining files. Let's take a closer look at what is involved.

Updating the Documentation

Documentation. Everyone's least favorite topic, but it's one of those things that needs to be done!

While writing documentation isn't everyone's favorite task, Storybook makes it easier to create. There are several ways to do it, from Storybook's autodocs facility to writing in CSF format or Markdown. I prefer to use the latter – it is easier to edit, and with a good text editor, you can see it formatted properly in color, too!

Breaking Apart an Example

So, what's involved in writing documentation?

For us, it revolves around creating an MDX file for each of the 15 core components we have in our library and hooking them as metadata into the stories file for that component. Some of them have child components, but we'll return to this later in the chapter.

Most of the files follow the same format – we import a few functions, set a Meta tag, add an introduction, and then add sections for each of the variants of the component. Rather than go through all 15 (which will take a while and become tedious!), let's crack open one and walk through it step by step so you see how it hangs together in more detail as part of the next demo.

WALK-THROUGH – BREADCRUMBS

To see the format used to create our documentation files, follow these steps:

1. First, crack open the `Docs.mdx` file in the Breadcrumbs folder – once open, you should see the code begin with two imports:

   ```
   import { Canvas, Meta } from "@storybook/addon-docs";
   import * as BreadcrumbsStories from "./Breadcrumbs.
   stories";
   ```

   These imports are required for setting up the story file, which ties into the Storybook stories file and uses each story as a basis for a documentation page.

2. Next, we miss a line (line spacing is critical in Markdown) and add a `Meta of=...` statement – this links in the documentation file to the Breadcrumbs stories file in Storybook:

   ```
   <Meta of={BreadcrumbsStories} />
   ```

3. We miss another line, then start by adding an introduction for
    our component. This one says we have three variants (including
    default). Notice the block below the introduction – this is the
    Markdown syntax for named anchors, where the text in square
    brackets is displayed to the developer, and the hashtag in
    normal brackets is the link:

```
Breadcrumbs is the primary component. It has three
possible states.
- [Default](#default)
- [CustomImage](#customimage)
- [TextDivider](#textdivider)
```

4. We miss a line, then start each story with an href link – this
    is the named anchor for the story, and the ID given must match
    the text shown against the hashtag above:

```
<a id="default" />
```

Default

```
This is the default version of the Breadcrumbs
component.
<Canvas of={BreadcrumbsStories.Default} />
```

5. We miss another line and then display the next block – this time,
    it's for the custom image variant. We have the named anchor set to
    customimage, then the title and text for the story, followed by the
    Canvas object, which renders an example of the variant on-screen:

```
<a id="customimage" />
```

CustomImage

```
This version of the Breadcrumbs component displays an
icon from the Iconify library.
```

```
<Canvas of={BreadcrumbsStories.CustomImage} />
```

6. We miss another line and then display the next block – this time, it's for the text divider variant. We have the named anchor set to `textdivider`, then the title and text for the story, followed by the Canvas object, which renders an example of the variant on-screen:

```
## TextDivider

This version of the Breadcrumbs component displays
a text-based divider.

<Canvas of={BreadcrumbsStories.TextDivider} />
```

We must remember two things of note when using this approach – the first is using hash symbols, and the second is spacing.

We need to use the hash notation to determine how to format the text, so one hash is equivalent to an H1 tag, two hashes equate to H2, and so on. Using hashes is standard practice when using Markdown, but it is relatively easy to get used to once you've written a few files! The other is that Markdown is super fussy about spacing, particularly when leaving blank lines – it is tempting to compress the text, but doing so will alter how it's laid out on-screen and make it harder to view when editing the text.

Okay – enough of that, let's crack on: next up, we need to run through some checks for our documentation. While we may already have files in place, there will likely be things we can do to tidy up or improve our documentation, such as spelling, removing redundant imports, and making sure named anchors work. Let's take a closer look at what we can do – I know some of the tasks will be a formality, but hey: it's always worth checking!

Making Improvements

So far, we've been through a breakdown of one of our documentation files to see how it all hangs together – while it works well, there is always room for improvement!

Don't worry – this is not something that needs lots of resources, but we should perform some basic checks to ensure everything is as expected. At the same time, we can also add some improvements – before we get to some examples, let's quickly run through some example areas we should check in the documentation:

- The most obvious is spelling: not everyone is blessed with great spelling skills! If you've copied the files from the code download, any spelling errors should be minimal; if you've added anything, it's worth checking to ensure it is spelled correctly.

- Do all of the named anchor links in the introduction point to the correct part of the documentation file? For example, does Custom Image in the Breadcrumbs file go to the section with the same name if you click it?

- Is there any glaringly obvious issue, such as the documentation saying the Breadcrumbs component has five variants when it only has three, including the Default?

- We use the hash symbol to signify the font size, so three hashes equate to an H3, for example – have we used the correct number of hash symbols for each title?

- We will be adding a panel with all of the argument types for each component – once we do so (in the next demo), are there any issues that pop out, such as using the wrong type for a variable (string when integer might work better, for example)? Or have we used a series of props that are inconsistent across each variant, which we need to move into the default fallback so we can set reasonable defaults throughout?

Okay – let's move on: assuming our documentation content is up to scratch, let's take a moment or two to see how we can step up our documentation to the next level.

Before you start on this demo, I recommend starting up Storybook if it isn't already running, then browse through each component and its variants. Have a look at how they appear – if we get it right, we should be able to make our code more concise without affecting how they look!

IMPROVING THE DOCUMENTATION

For this next demo, we'll use the Breadcrumbs component as our example, but the changes apply to all of our components across the board. To see what we can do, follow these steps:

1. The first task is to add an `argsType` entry to each document file – this will create a table of all of the properties for a component. For this, we'll use the Breadcrumbs component as our example – go ahead and crack open the `Docs.mdx` file, then scroll to the bottom of the page.

2. In the imports, add this line:

```
import { ArgTypes } from "@storybook/blocks";
```

3. At the bottom, miss a line after the last entry, then add this code:

```
## Properties of component
```

```
Below is a list of arguments available for this
component:
```

```
<ArgTypes of={BreadcrumbsStories} />
```

4. Save and close all open files. Revert to the Node.js terminal session from earlier, then at the prompt, enter npm run storybook and browse to http://localhost:6006/. If all is well, we should see the Experimental badge shown in Figure 8-5.

Name	Description	Default
BreadcrumbItems	-	-
image	-	-
∨ PROPERTIES		
divider	string	/
iconFamily	string	" "
iconName	string	" "
breadcrumbItems	array	

Figure 8-5. *An example ArgTables table in Storybook*

5. The next change we can make is simple, but it could have implications – the name we use for each Docs page. There are a couple of ways to do this, but the easiest way is to rename the Docs.mdx file for a component or something else, such as Docs - Breadcrumbs.mdx. While this will make it easier to

determine which `Docs.mdx` file belongs to which component, it's important to bear in mind that the length will make the menu wider, and you might even end up with truncated names!

I won't make this change, as the naming convention is personal – I suggest trying a few combinations to see what works best for you.

---

6. If you click Show code to the right of each demo in Storybook, you will see it show something like this:

    ```
    <Breadcrumbs />
    ```

7. It isn't the best we can do here – granted, it shows the component's name, but what about props? To show a more accurate view of what code was used, add this to the `Default.parameters` block we created earlier in `Breadcrumbs.stories.js`, like so:

    ```
    Default.parameters = {
      badges: ["beta"],
      docs: { source: { type: "code" } },
    };
    ```

Beware – it will show what you used in the story file, so you may find it's not as good as expected! I've included it here for demonstration purposes but not in the code files – feel free to add it if you wish.

You will have noticed by now that I've also made references to both a default template and a Default template. Yes, they aren't the same thing, although they will look similar – they both serve different roles. There are some changes we can make to simplify things and make it easier to determine which is which.

8. First, let's move this block to just below the BADGES entry we
    created earlier and before the default fallback template:

```
let levels = [
  { href: "/", text: "Dashboard" },
  { href: "/reports", text: "Annual reports" },
  { href: "/reports/2019", text: "2019" },
];
```

9. We can also move the argTypes block into the default fallback
    template, like so:

```
parameters: {
  badges: [],
},
argTypes: {
  BreadcrumbItems: levels,
  image: { control: "boolean" },
},
};
```

10. To spread our configuration properties over each story, we need
    to add the meta object – look for ...args, then immediately
    below each one, add this:

```
...meta,
```

11. We have three instances of this block across the variants –
    replace the content inside the square brackets with the word
    levels so we can use the predefined block already in our
    stories file:

```
breadcrumbItems: levels,
```

12. Save and close all open files. Revert to a Node.js terminal session, enter `npm run storybook`, and press Enter. Browse to http://localhost:6006/ – if all is well, we should see no change to any of the variants for the Breadcrumbs component, but it's now running more optimized code.

Now we've made changes to Breadcrumbs – how about trying the same changes to the other components? Remember that you won't need to make the same change, but look particularly at the default and Default templates.

Can any be rationalized so we're not duplicating too much code? Note that we have to have a title in each variant, though – if you change anything else, you can always revert back!

Do not be alarmed if you can't optimize anything or if the code is such that it's not worth refining: it's more important to keep that mentality of checking and not treat it as a one-off process.

Excellent – our code looks tidier, and everything still works as expected! I'm sure there will be more changes we can make in the future, but for now, let's take a moment to review the changes we've made so far in more detail.

Exploring the Changes in Detail

Adding documentation may not be everyone's favorite task, but one of the great things about Storybook is its flexibility, particularly when writing stories! We've only touched the surface of what is possible, but even still, the changes we made will make the documentation a little better.

So, what did we do? We started by adding an `argsType` entry to the Breadcrumbs documentation file. This block shows anyone using the component what properties are available, what type of property is available, and whether we have set a default value. It's important to note that this is not available from core Storybook – we had to add this from the @storybook/blocks module.

Moving on, we then discussed how we can rename the Docs entry to make it less generic – my initial research indicated there appeared to be a name or title property you can set in each story, but can I find details? No! Instead, the simplest way to do it – at least for now – is to rename the `Docs.mdx` file for each component, as Storybook will use that name automatically when rendering the index. There isn't any absolute right or wrong approach to take, but remember that the longer the name, the more likely Storybook will truncate it. I recommend keeping it short so you can see the full name without issue.

The next change we made was to add a property to the parameters block – when rendering the component in Storybook, we can see the source code used to display that component. It frequently just shows the name of the component, though – to see the exact code used, we added `docs: { source: { type: "code" } }`, which forces Storybook to display the code we used. We touched on a downside of doing this – it will show **exactly** what you used so that unexpected results may appear!

To finish the demo, we worked through several changes to reduce some of the duplication, such as not repeating the levels block twice or moving the `argTypes` properties into the default fallback template. Although we only made the changes to the Breadcrumbs component (to keep the demo short), we could quickly make similar changes to the remaining components. Indeed, something like this should be an ongoing task to ensure we're keeping duplicated code to a minimum. We then rounded out the demo by firing up Storybook to preview the results of our changes in the browser and make sure that even though we've optimized our code, it's not had any impact on people using our components.

Summary

Documentation of how a component works is an oft-neglected but essential part of any component library; I've lost count of the number of libraries I've seen where the developer provides the bare minimum, making it awkward to work out how to achieve a task! Even though there may be gaps, it's important to have accurate documentation in one place (such as Storybook) – over the course of this chapter, we looked at how to add documentation to Storybook using MDX files, as well as provide some added extra finish with badges. Let's take a moment to review what we have learned.

We started by exploring how to add Storybook badges. We saw how this is a helpful tool for identifying the state of any component, such as experimental, stable, or (heaven forbid) deprecated. Adding this feature was a simple change; at the same time, we learned how to customize the labels to display our text.

Next up, we began the lengthy process of updating the documentation files for each component. We focused on using the Breadcrumbs component as our example and as a basis for making similar changes throughout the documentation files for the other components. We touched on topics such as rationalizing code, setting Storybook to render the complete code used for a component, and a way to rename documentation files to something more explicit – keeping in mind that conciseness works better than something lengthy.

Phew – it may seem we haven't done much in this chapter, but don't forget the importance of accurate documentation! It plays an essential part in our toolkit, as we will see in the next chapter. Get ready, my friends, for testing times (if you pardon the pun)...

CHAPTER 9

Testing Components

So far, we've spent time creating our masterpiece, but can we be sure it all works? What guarantee do we have that it won't suddenly collapse in a heap the first time someone tries to use it?

Before we release our library to the outside world, we need to test each component to ensure it works as expected. In this chapter, we will go through setting up unit testing for our library before exploring some examples of tests we can write, so end users can see how each component performs in a real-world capacity.

Setting Expectations

When it comes to testing our code, we can do a host of things – anything from simple snapshot testing to checking accessibility and even writing tests to test every feature of each component to the bitter end!

While testing is essential to the success of any library, there is a limit to what we can do in this book. Some people might not like this, but I'm a big fan of the MVP approach (which we will use in this chapter). Instead of trying to get everything done before release, we can write the basic tests and set up a starting point for our code coverage.

This way, we can release things quicker – if we're making our code available as open source, then it's always open to others to contribute changes to help improve the quality of our code and tests. From the outset,

© Alex Libby 2025
A. Libby, *Developing Web Components with Svelte*,
https://doi.org/10.1007/979-8-8688-1180-7_9

it's essential to clarify that this is the approach we will use – who knows, your initial work can become a real collaborative effort! Keeping that in mind, let's start with our testing. So, where do we start?

Setting Up the Testing Environment

Well, the first task is to choose the right testing library for our needs. I know this might sound a little odd, given you might already have a preferred tool and assume that you can use that, right?

When I wrote the first edition of this book, I decided to use Svelte Testing Library – I had wanted to go with my preferred suite, Cypress, but it barfed over the use of the `<svelte:options>` directive, making it impossible to use!

Since then, I think things may have improved – I've decided this time to go with Vitest, an upcoming test suite compatible with Jest, which is gaining wide acceptance. Given we're already using Vite, it makes sense to keep it in the family (so to speak) – it also makes it easier to install and configure! The irony is that we still need three functions from the Svelte Testing Library, but it's much less than we needed before when using that package outright. With that in mind, let's dive in and take a look at how to set up our test suite, ready for use.

INSTALLING VITEST

To get Vitest set up within our project area, follow these steps:

1. First, fire up a Node.js command prompt, then change the working folder to our project folder.

2. We need to install Vitest, so go ahead and enter `npm install -D vitest` at the prompt, and press Enter.

3. We have two more packages to install – for this, enter npm install -D jsdom @vitest/browser and press Enter.

4. While Node installs these, crack open your package.json file, then scroll down to the closing } of the scripts: block, and add this entry (as highlighted):

   "test": "vitest",
   },

5. Next, open a new file and add this line:

   import "@testing-library/jest-dom";

6. Save it as setupTest.js in the \src folder. We need to reference this file, so open vite.config.js and edit the contents as shown:

```
plugins: [svelte()],
test: {
  globals: true,
  environment: "jsdom",
  setupFiles: ["src/setupTest.js"],
},
```

7. Save and close any open files – the setup process is complete.

We now have Vitest ready for use – we will test it to ensure it works in the next exercise when we start to write tests for our library. Before we do so, it's worth spending some time going through the setup – there are some interesting points we should cover in more detail.

Breaking Apart the Code Changes

Testing our components is an essential part of the development process. To facilitate testing, I could have picked any one of several possible tools (even if the selection is a little more limited than for, say, React or Vue!). I chose Vitest as it works well with Vite – what did we do to set it up?

We kicked off by installing two dependencies, `jsdom` and `vitest/browser`, to help with the tests and, of course, `vitest` itself. Next, we added a reference to the scripts block to make it easier to run tests before setting up `setupTest.js` in the `\src` folder. This file provides some DOM utilities that are helpful with testing; as you will see later, we use it to test the Dialog component. We finished by adding a reference to the `setupTest.js` file in Vite's config so it knows how to use it when running tests.

Okay – let's crack on: with the testing suite up and running, it's time to test it to see if it works as expected. There is no better way to do this than by writing a test, so let's dive in and look at what is involved in more detail.

Testing the Components

So, what should we test? How in depth should our tests be?

These are both great questions – we'd test everything in an ideal world to ensure we have covered all possible eventualities. However, that isn't always possible (or even practical) – you can bet that someone will find a way to use a component that wasn't in the manner we intended and so could claim it's not working as expected! This "use" opens up that proverbial back-and-forth can of worms about what should or shouldn't have been tested...you get the picture.

Leaving thoughts about the scope of our testing aside for a moment, let's start creating the tests for our library. Many of the tests I've created for this book follow the same format, so I will work through Accordion as an example, and we'll extract the rest from the code download accompanying this book. With that in mind, let's crack on with the next demo.

WRITING/PUTTING TOGETHER TESTS

To get the tests set up, follow these steps:

1. First, we need to create our folder structure – for this, go ahead and add a new folder called __tests__ under the \src\lib\ components\Accordion folder.

2. Open a new file in your editor, then add this code – there is a fair bit to cover, so we'll do it in blocks, beginning with the imports:

```
import { describe, test, expect } from "vitest";
import {
  render,
  screen,
  fireEvent
} from "@testing-library/svelte";
import Accordion from "../../Accordion/Accordion.
svelte";
```

3. Next, we need to open our test suite, so miss a line and add this opening block:

```
describe("Tests for Accordion", () => {
  const mockText = "This is a Accordion";

  const props = {
    data: [
      { title: "Heading 1", text: "aaa" },
      { title: "Heading 2", text: "bbb" },
      { title: "Heading 3", text: "ccc" },
    ],
  };
```

4. This next test checks to make sure that our Accordion displays the correct titles for each drawer:

```
test("should have the correct title", () => {
  render(Accordion, props);

  expect(screen.queryByText(props.data[0].title)).
  toBeInTheDocument();
  expect(screen.queryByText(props.data[1].title)).
  toBeInTheDocument();
  expect(screen.queryByText(props.data[2].title)).
  toBeInTheDocument();
});
```

5. This test takes care of checking that the first item in our Accordion renders the correct content:

```
test("should have the correct text for the first
AccordionItem", async () => {
  render(Accordion, props);

  const AccordionObj = await screen.
  getAllByRole("button")[0];
  await fireEvent.click(AccordionObj);

  const accordionText = await screen.
  findByText(/aaa/i);
  expect(accordionText).toBeTruthy();
});
```

6. Next, miss a line, then add this block – this test is a check for the presence of aria-expanded when we click the first Accordion item:

```
test("should show aria-expanded as true when first
item clicked", async () => {
```

```
  render(Accordion, props);
  const AccordionObj = await screen.
  getAllByRole("button")[0];
  await fireEvent.click(AccordionObj);
  expect(screen.getAllByRole("button", { expanded:
  true })[0]).not.toBeNull();
});
```

```
test("get a snapshot of component", () => {
  const { tree } = render(Accordion, props);
  expect(tree).toMatchSnapshot();
});
```

7. Save and close the file. Next, extract a copy of the src folder from the code download and drop it into the root of our project folder. This folder contains the remaining tests for our components, prepopulated in the relevant folder for each component.

8. Switch to a Node.js terminal session, then change the working folder to our project area.

9. At the prompt, enter npm run test and press Enter – if all is well, we should see it run through each test, rendering results on the screen, similar to this extract:

✓ src/lib/components/Slider/__tests__/Slider.
   spec.js (3)
✓ src/lib/components/Spinner/__tests__/Spinner.
   spec.js (2)
✓ src/lib/components/Switch/__tests__/Switch.
   spec.js (4)
✓ src/lib/components/Tabs/__tests__/Tabs.spec.js (3)
✓ src/lib/components/Tooltip/__tests__/Tooltip.
   spec.js (4)

```
Test Files  17 passed (17)
      Tests  57 passed (57)
```

There will likely be some warnings/errors around unknown prop names and a deprecation warning for punycode – these are to be expected. We will explore these later in the book when we come to do the tidy-up ready for release.

Congratulations if you manage to get a successful set of results – granted, we may have seen some warnings, but the critical point is that we now have a basic set of tests in place and can start to build confidence that everything works as expected. Let's pause and explore what we created in more detail.

Exploring the Changes in Detail

Look closely at the tests we copied from the code download. Do you notice anything in particular?

I suspect many of you will say no – after all, each component is different, so surely tests will be different, right? It's a valid point and a true statement: all of the tests will be different.

However, even with us testing different components, we can still maintain a common format throughout – we can make sure tests are consistent and reuse elements where appropriate. For the tests I've created, we start by importing up to three functions from Vitest and three from the Svelte Testing Library.

It's important to note that I've written the tests to run in Vitest, not the Svelte Testing Library. The latter three functions are because Vitest doesn't have an equivalent, and the developers recommend using those from the Svelte Testing Library instead.

We finished that part by importing the relevant component for our test – in this case, it was Accordion, but the same principle applies to all of the tests.

Moving on, we then focus on writing the tests, starting with opening a describe block. Here, we define any prop values needed for the test, such as the mockText and data block for Accordion, before starting with each test assertion. In most cases, we first start with a test to ensure the component renders as expected, followed by two to three tests for specific functions, such as checking text displays when clicking an Accordion drawer. We finished by taking a snapshot before running through the tests to ensure we got a successful result for each test.

Okay, let's crack on: We've run tests on each component in isolation, but what about in a more practical context? It is possible – we need to do some work first to build them into a package suitable for testing. Before we do this, there are a few points I want to cover relating to how we can improve our tests.

Improving on the Tests

Although we now have tests in place for all of our components, I think there is scope for us to do more – after all, there is only so much we can do in the limited space we have in this book!

So far, we've followed a relatively consistent format for each test – first defining any values before making sure it renders, then running two to three tests specific to each component before finishing with a snapshot of the component. It's not a bad format per se, but there are more things we could add:

- One that should be at the top is checking variables and properties that we define – do they all work, given that we are using Web Components and may have to use string-based properties (owing to a limitation with Web Components)?

- In Chapter 10, we will look at accessibility – as part of that, we will use the vitest-axe package to perform accessibility checks using the accessibility tool Axe (albeit in a limited capacity). For now, it will be a basic check, but I suspect there will be improvements we can make there!

- We will look at adding test coverage later in this book, but for now, it's worth thinking of how much code is covered by our tests and whether there is anything we need to do to expand coverage for each component.

- One area we may need to consider is which queryBy… or getBy… methods we use with Vitest. We should mimic how users will use our components as much as possible, so the Vitest developers recommend an order of usage – queryByRole first, right down to getByTestId.

There is more on this in the official Vitest documentation at https://testing-library.com/docs/queries/about#priority.

These are just a few things we can consider – I'm sure you will come up with more! The critical point is that we must balance the number of tests with what we test. Some people will say we need to test absolutely everything, but sometimes that isn't practical – I've seen libraries and repos with over 2000 individual tests! We must be thorough, but I think 2000 may be too excessive...

But I digress. We've spent quite a bit of time putting together tests, but there is one test we need to do: What about checking our components visually?

Testing the Components Visually

So far, we've run tests using Vitest, but there is an additional step we can take – what about running some visual tests? Sure, we could use a service such as Chromatic (https://www.chromatic.com/storybook – works very well in Storybook), but this costs money.

However, we can do a lot by doing some simple testing with our eyes. To do this, we need to set up a simple demo to run our components. With that in mind, let's use the Spinner component as an example to render it on-screen as part of our next demo.

TESTING VISUALLY

To test our components visually, follow these steps:

1. First, crack open the App.svelte from the \src folder in your editor. Edit the file so it looks like this:

```
<script>
  import Spinner from './lib/components/Spinner/
  Spinner.svelte'
</script>

<main>
  <h1>Garnet UI Web Component Test Page</h1>

  <garnet-spinner
    color="#733635"
    duration="0.75s"
    size="40"
    variant="circle">
  </garnet-spinner>
</main>
```

```
<style>
  main { padding: 20px; }
  h1 { font-family: Arial, Helvetica, sans-serif; }
</style>
```

2. Save the file and close it. Next, switch to a second Node. js terminal session, then change the working folder to our project area.

3. At the prompt, enter `npm run dev` and press Enter.

4. If all is well, we should see an instance of the Spinner component running if we browse to `http://localhost:5173`, as shown in Figure 9-1.

Garnet UI Web Component Test Page

Figure 9-1. *The newly compiled Spinner component working in our demo*

This demo looks great, but how can we prove it's our new component and that it's coming from the newly built file? For the more adventurous, feel free to look at the compiled code from within a developer console. You should see something similar to that shown in Figure 9-2, where we reference the component `<garnet-spinner>` from the newly generated distribution file.

```
▼<main class="s-XsEmFtvddWTw">
   <h1 class="s-XsEmFtvddWTw">Garnet UI Web Component Test Page</h1>
  ▶ <garnet-spinner class="s-XsEmFtvddWTw"> ⋯ </garnet-spinner> == $0
  </main>
  <!--<App>-->
```

Figure 9-2. *Proof that we're using the newly compiled component*

Perfect – hoping that all went well, we've set up a simple demo and now seen it working in our browser! It was an easy demo to set up, using standard (semantic) tags – the only point of real note is that we used the *Web Component* name for our component, even though we imported it directly from our codebase.

Strictly speaking this would normally not be the correct way to import it – we should use a compiled JavaScript bundle file to reference the component, not the Svelte import we've used. I've done this deliberately for a reason – I will explain why in the next section.

It's worth noting that we passed through all of the properties as strings – in the previous edition of this book, I mentioned that this was a requirement for web components; I have seen evidence that suggests this may no longer be the case and that we could potentially use integers and Booleans instead. We're not going to change things now, but it's worth testing this in more detail nearer that time when it comes to preparing for launch.

I touched on this earlier in the book, as part of improving our testing.

Okay – let's move on; we've run a visual test – what now? We've reached the point where we can start making our code available for people to use.

Bundling the Components

With the testing complete, we can move on to the next stage, bundling our components. Bundling, I hear you ask – what exactly is that, I wonder? It is where we prepare the components for release in a format that makes it easy to drop into projects – let me explain what I mean.

So far, we've created our Svelte components using HTML, CSS, and vanilla JavaScript, and we've seen how they all work great in Storybook. However, one of the benefits of Svelte components is the ability to release them as web components that we can use in other environments, such as React. You will have seen from the previous demo too that we used the Web Component name for our component, but imported the Svelte file – this won't work if we tried to use this method in React. It worked for our demo, as Svelte is aware of the web component name specified in the component, so is able to display it correctly.

To avoid this issue of importing Svelte component files directly, and to make components available outside of Svelte, we need to bundle the code into files that we can consume outside of our development environment – in the same way, we might import a third-party library into our code. There are several ways to do this, depending on our requirements; before we explore them, let's first set up our library, ready to bundle our components.

Configuring the Build Process

Bundling our components isn't a complex process – we need to set up the main index file for them and make sure we have a place to demo them.

The latter might sound a little odd, as it's not something anyone consuming our components would need to use, but trust me: if that file is not present, Svelte will complain! With that thought in mind, let's dive in and look at what we need to do to get our library ready for bundling.

CONFIGURING THE BUILD PROCESS

To bundle our components ready for use, follow these steps:

1. First, we need to create a barrel import file – for this, fire up your editor and add this code to a new file:

```
// Main components
export { default as Accordion } from "./Accordion/
Accordion.svelte";
export { default as Alarm } from "./Alarm/Alarm.
svelte";
export { default as Alert } from "./Alert/Alert.
svelte";
export { default as Breadcrumbs } from "./Breadcrumbs/
Breadcrumbs.svelte";
export { default as Checkbox } from "./Checkbox/
Checkbox.svelte";
export { default as Chip } from "./Chip/Chip.svelte";
export { default as Dialog } from "./Dialog/Dialog.
svelte";
export { default as Table } from "./Grid/Table.svelte";
export { default as Input } from "./Input/Input.
svelte";
export { default as ProgressBar } from "./ProgressBar/
ProgressBar.svelte";
export { default as SelectBox } from "./SelectBox/
SelectBox.svelte";
export { default as Slider } from "./Slider/Slider.
svelte";
export { default as Spinner } from "./Spinner/Spinner.
svelte";
```

```
export { default as Switch } from "./Switch/Switch.
svelte";
export { default as Tabs } from "./Tabs/Tabs.svelte";
export { default as Tooltip } from "./Tooltip/Tooltip.
svelte";

// Ancillary components
export { default as AccordionItem } from "./Accordion/
AccordionItem.svelte";
export { default as Icon } from "./Alert/Icon.svelte";
export { default as Close } from "./Dialog/Close.
svelte";
export { default as Cell } from "./Grid/Cell.svelte";
export { default as Grid } from "./Grid/Grid.svelte";
```

2. Save this as `main.js` at the root of the `\src\lib\
components` folder.

Saving it here avoids conflict with a second `main.js`, which is at the root of our project area and used elsewhere; it also makes it easier to read the imports! This `main.js` file is also on the code download if you need help editing it.

---

3. We also need to add a new configuration file and update a second one – create a new file and save it as `vite.lib.config.js` at the root of the project folder. Add this code:

```
import { defineConfig } from "vite";
import { svelte } from "@sveltejs/vite-plugin-svelte";

// https://vitejs.dev/config/
export default defineConfig({
  build: {
```

```
    lib: {
      entry: "./src/lib/components/main.js",
      name: "Garnet UI Library",
    },
    output: {
      format: "es",
    },
  },
  plugins: [
    svelte({
      compilerOptions: {
        customElement: true,
      },
    }),
  ],
});
```

4. Save and close both configuration files – the configuration part
    of the process is now complete.

Excellent – we're ready to bundle! It's at this point that we will have
some decisions to make. Do we release packages for each component
individually, in groups, or one that covers all components?

If we did the latter, does that mean people have to download the entire
library if they only want one component? That doesn't seem sensible, but
we need to balance that against maintenance and where package versions
might diverge if we update one and not the other. It's just a few questions
we must ask; before we do so, let's first explore the changes we've made in
more detail.

Understanding the Changes in Detail

Throughout this book, we've created a set of functional components for our library and tested them in Storybook. This is all good, but most of these components wouldn't operate if we used them outside a Svelte environment. Why? The reason lies in our configuration – if we didn't complete the steps we've just taken, we will likely have a space or an empty page where our component should be.

To fix this, we first created a central `main.js` file – inside this file, we added exports to all the components and some child components used by a handful of the parent components.

The key to the bundling process is the changes we made to the Vite configuration. We first added a `vite.lib.config.js` file; inside this, we imported two functions from Svelte and Vite. Then, we defined a `build:` setup for Vite to specify the library's name and the main entry point for our components.

As an aside, you will see the `customElement` property we added earlier in the book. This property tells Svelte to make the component available to other frameworks. Without it, we will end up with a warning such as this one:

```
09:22:07 [vite-plugin-svelte] C:/cobalt/src/lib/
Accordion/Accordion.svelte:1:16 The 'tag' option
is used when generating a custom element. Did you
forget the 'customElement: true' compile option?
```

Right – let's crack on with running the build process. We have our configuration in place, so it should just be a matter of running a command, right? There's more to executing a single line of code – it all hangs around how we want to make our code available to others. To see what this means, let's dive in and look at the second part of this process in more detail.

Running the Build Process

Remember how we alluded to the fact that we can run this process in one of three ways? We could

- Bundle all components together: Typically producing multiple files in the same process.

- Generate a single file: Larger but more manageable to move around for portability.

- Generate single files for each component: It creates more files but keeps them smaller, with less redundant code to download.

The first two options are straightforward – we can run the first now without any further configuration, and the second only requires changing the file we run during the process. The third option is a little more complex; let's dive in and look at all three to understand what this means for us in practice.

RUNNING THE BUILD PROCESS

With the build process set up and ready to go, we can now run it – to do so, follow these steps:

1. We'll start with the option that includes everything – fire up a Node.js terminal prompt, then enter this command and press Enter:

   ```
   npm run build
   ```

2. If all is well, we should see the files listed on the screen:

   ```
   $ npm run build

   > garnetui@0.0.0 build
   > vite build
   ```

```
vite v5.2.8 building for production...
✓ 28 modules transformed.
dist/index.html                        0.39 kB |
gzip: 0.27 kB
dist/assets/index-t0rlJ_cJ.js  13.24 kB |
gzip: 5.01 kB
✓ built in 424ms
```

This output is good, but if we look closer at the number of the files we have and work the approximate total size, something won't seem right – we have approximately 160 KB of components squeezed into 13 KB. You'd be right for thinking something doesn't add up – we'll come back to why at the end of the demo. For now, let's continue with the next part.

3.   Occasionally, we might get more than one JavaScript file appearing when running that command, which is not ideal. We can use the `lib` option in the build process to generate a single JavaScript file to get around it.

4.   At the Node.js terminal prompt, run this command:

```
$ npm run build -- -c=vite.lib.config.js
```

5.   If all is well, we should see output similar to this:

```
> garnetui@0.0.0 build
> vite build -c=vite.lib.config.js

vite v5.2.8 building for production...
✓ 56 modules transformed.
dist/garnetui.js  163.74 kB | gzip: 40.91 kB
dist/garnetui.umd.cjs  104.58 kB | gzip: 33.50 kB
✓ built in 1.18s
```

This option takes the `garnetui` name from the name field in your `package.json` file.

It is better – but what if we wanted to produce a package purely for specific components? To do this:

6. We need to make a change to `vite.lib.config.js`. Crack this file open, then replace the contents of the `build:` option with this code:

```
export default defineConfig({
  build:{
    // lib: {
    //    entry: "./src/lib/components/main.js",
    //    name: "Garnet UI Library",
    // },
    rollupOptions: {
      input: ["./src/lib/components/Spinner/Spinner.
      svelte"],
    },
    output: {
      format: "es",
    },
  },
},
```

Commenting out the original code means we can always revert it if needed!

7. Switch to the Node.js terminal session from earlier in this
    demo, then at the prompt, enter this command and press Enter:

    ```
    npm run build -- -c=vite.lib.config.js
    ```

8. If all is well, we should see output similar to this appear:

    ```
    > garnetui@0.0.0 build
    > vite build -c=vite.lib.config.js

    vite v5.2.8 building for production...
    ✓ 23 modules transformed.
    dist/assets/Spinner-7EA5ytIy.js  11.96 kB |
    gzip: 4.48 kB
    ✓ built in 327ms
    ```

9. Our build file is ready for testing, which we will do momentarily.

With the build process done, it's time to test it! We already have the
demo in place (we created it as part of running the initial npm run build
command). We need to make one change to it, though, to test the new file
we've just built. Before making that change, let's pause for a moment to
review the code changes we've made to see how it all hangs together.

Breaking Apart the Changes

This is one of those occasions where writing code is arguably less
important than the decisions behind it. We could take this in several ways:
we've proven that the demo works with individual components, but as a
starting point, it (kind of) makes sense to have a single file and split it into
smaller components once we develop them. All thoughts aside, it's still
essential to understand how this part of the process works, so let's review
the code we created in the previous demo.

We started by simply running the `npm run build` command without any further changes – this was possible as it uses the `vite.config.js` file to specify how the build should run. It gave us two files, an `index.html` and a JavaScript asset file containing…well *something*. I say something, as it looks to work fine at first glance. However, there are a couple of problems with this approach:

- If we crack open the asset file, we find that everything is not as it seems: on closer inspection, I've seen that it contains our component as well as the contents of an `index.html` file and that it's just one component.

- The naming convention it uses isn't ideal, to say the least, but we can do better!

So, what gives? The first issue is that Vite builds anything set to run in the `App.svelte` file; I set this to run Spinner in a demo I ran as part of researching for this book, hence why we only have one component present and the `index.html` file (which subsequently appears empty, with only a basic HTML structure). The markup in this file doesn't look like it will run anything – this isn't the case: it's designed to run the `App.svelte` as a regular Svelte application.

We will rectify the naming convention shortly when we adapt the build process.

It's a good starting point, but what if we didn't want to download multiple files? To get around this, we switched to the alternative configuration in `vite.lib.config.js`, which we set up in the previous demo and gives us two files. In both cases, all components are bundled into one file but formatted for use as JavaScript modules (we can set this using the formats option, depending on your preference).

Let's turn this on its head – if we wanted the best of both worlds (i.e., one component, one file), can we do anything? As it so happens, there is: we set a `rollupOptions` property in the build options. Here, we can specify which components we want to include – in our example, we listed the files for Spinner, but we could list them for any component in our library. It means that we could have multiple configuration files that group several components in the same way.

By default, the build.lib options will bundle your library in two formats: es and umd (depending on how many files are created). You can configure it by adding the formats property to the lib settings. Available options are `'es'` | `'cjs'` | `'umd'` | `'iife'` – you can see more details at `https://vitejs.dev/config/build-options#build-lib`.

To round out the demo, we ran the final build option, which gave us the compiled files for Spinner. The naming is better, although it's still not perfect – we'll have to rename it at some point! Okay, let's continue. We've tested our components and bundled them into a format suitable for release. It's time to put these bundles to a proper test: let's add them to a demo to see how they perform.

Updating Our Demo

When it comes to testing our component bundle files, there are several ways we can do this. We could do it in something like a CodeSandbox demo, but we'll do that later when we test our component with React.

For this next demo, I will use what we already have – remember how I mentioned I had already updated my copy of App.svelte? Well, let's look at the changes I made to test our newly created bundle in action.

```
                  UPDATING OUR STAND-ALONE DEMO
```

To update the `App.svelte` app so it uses our new bundle, follow these steps:

1. First, we need to make a change to the `main.js` file that sits in `\src\lib\components` – comment out all but the references to Spinner and Input; this should leave you with two lines not commented out.

2. Save and close the file, then run this command to build a package with these two components:

   ```
   vite build -c=vite.lib.config.js
   ```

3. If all is well, we should see something akin to this:

   ```
   > garnetui@0.0.0 build
   > vite build -c=vite.lib.config.js

   vite v5.2.8 building for production...
   ✓ 56 modules transformed.
   dist/garnetui.js   163.74 kB │ gzip: 40.91 kB
   dist/garnetui.umd.cjs   104.58 kB │ gzip: 33.50 kB
   ```

Make sure you uncomment those components you commented out in step 1. Otherwise, your bundle might be a little on the light side for future demos!

---

4. Next, crack open the `index.html` file at the root of the project, and make sure the first script import is set to import your new bundle – in this example, mine sits in the `./dist` folder and is called `garnetui.js`:

   ```
   <script type="module" src="./dist/garnetui.js">
   </script>
   ```

5. Save and close the file. Next, open App.svelte and change the content in <main> to match the code below – we already added the spinner from earlier, but we now also add the Input component:

```
<main>
  <h1>Garnet UI Web Component Test Page</h1>

  <garnet-spinner
    color="#733635"
    duration= "0.75s"
    size= "40"
    variant= "circle">
  </garnet-spinner>

  <garnet-input label="Text:" placeholder="Enter your
  text here"></garnet-input>
</main>
```

6. At the same time, remove the import at the top of App. svelte – we replaced it with the script import we added back in step 3:

```
<script>
  import Spinner from './lib/components/Spinner/
  Spinner.svelte'
</script>
```

7. Save and close the file. Switch to a Node.js terminal session, then at the prompt, enter npm run dev and hit Enter. After a few moments, go ahead and browse to http://localhost:5173 – if all is well, we should see something akin to that shown in Figure 9-3.

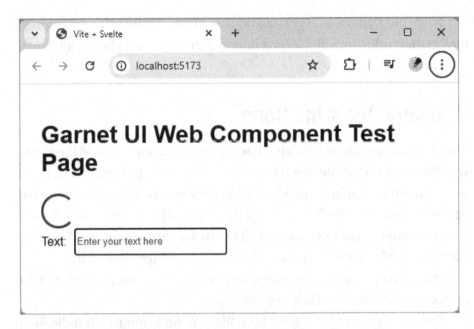

Figure 9-3. *Proof that our new component bundle works*

Okay, so it won't win any style awards any time soon, but it works! Sure, we can spend time rearranging how components appear on the page, but the important point here is that we are now displaying web components. To verify, a quick check in the browser console log shows references to our components (Figure 9-4).

```
▼<main class="s-XsEmFtvddWTw">
    <h1 class="s-XsEmFtvddWTw">Garnet UI Web Component Test Page
    </h1> == $0
  ▶ <garnet-spinner class="s-XsEmFtvddWTw"> ⋯ </garnet-spinner>
  ▶ <garnet-input class="s-XsEmFtvddWTw"> ⋯ </garnet-input>
  </main>
```

Figure 9-4. *Proof that we are using our new web components*

While our demo was very straightforward, we should still take a closer look at that code – let's pause for a moment to understand how it all hangs together in more detail.

Breaking Apart the Code

This demo is one where we didn't have to do too much – most of the hard work we've already done! For this demo, we updated the `App.svelte` page to pull in our new Spinner and Input components from the bundle created earlier in the chapter rather than as a direct import from the source files.

We started by commenting out all but two of the components from the `main.js` file in the components folder. This change allowed us to regenerate the component bundle with just these two components, not the ones we do not need in this demo.

Next up, we altered the index.html file to point to our new bundle file, which was in the `\dist` folder – for this, we used the expanded version, but you could equally have pointed to the minified version. We then updated the contents of the `<main>` object in our code to add the Input component before removing the original import statement at the top of App.svelte.

We finished by running up the page in our browser before previewing the results to confirm that we do at least have a Spinner and Input displayed, even if the page isn't styled that well!

Perfect – we've completed the initial test, but the real test is yet to come! One of Svelte's features is that any web component we create should work in a non-Svelte environment, such as a React demo. After all, it is just plain CSS, HTML, and JavaScript, so why not? Let's put this to the test and explore what might happen if we were to use one of our components in a React demo.

Testing with Other Frameworks

At this point, I must admit to a slight air of trepidation and doubt – I, like many of you, will be familiar with React components running in React demos, Angular ones in Angular, and so on, right? Svelte is an exception: it claims to run in any framework, so how can we test it?

There are a couple of ways to achieve this, but I prefer creating a CodeSandbox demo using a React template. Thanks to its predefined template options, CodeSandbox makes this a cinch to complete, so let's dive in and take a look at an example using the Spinner component.

If you get stuck, my version is available in a CodeSandbox at `https://codesandbox.io/p/sandbox/runtime-snow-9frpdj`. You will need to sign in either with a GitHub, Google, or Apple account to view the demo.

USING OUR COMPONENT IN A REACT DEMO

To set up the example, follow these steps:

1. First, browse to `https://www.codesandbox.io`, then click Create in the top-right corner once you are there.

You might be prompted to log in. A good option is to use a Google account, which will allow you to save your work.

---

2. From the list of templates that appear, click React, then wait for it to prepare a new demo.

3. We need to add a copy of our component. First, create a folder
    called `dist` at the top level, and then inside this, create one
    called `assets`.

4. Take a copy of the `Spinner-XXXX.js` file you created in the
    Running the Build demo, then drag and drop it into the assets
    folder to upload it.

You might wonder why I've replicated the same folder structure
here when it isn't entirely necessary. It's purely to replicate what we
receive when we run the bundling process – keeping it similar helps
prove that the component works as expected outside of Svelte.

---

5. With the component file imported, switch to `App.js` in the
    CodeSandbox editor. At the top of the file, add this import
    immediately above the existing one for `styles.css`:

```
import "./dist/assets/Spinner-7EA5ytIy.js";
```

Note   Replace the Spinner-7EA5ytly name with the name your
system created when you ran the build process in the earlier demo.

---

6. Next, find the line with the `<h2>` tag, and add this code
    immediately below it, as highlighted (and before the last
    `</div>` tag):

```
<h2>Start editing to see some magic happen!</h2>
<div className="layout">
  <garnet-spinner
    color="#733635"
    duration="0.75s"
```

```
      size="40"
      variant="circle"
    ></garnet-spinner>
  </div>
```

7.   Click File from the hamburger menu on the left, then Save
     to save the demo – if all is well, we should see our spinner
     running, as shown in Figure 9-5.

Hello CodeSandbox

Start editing to see some magic happen!

Figure 9-5. *The Spinner component running inside a React app*

Yay – we finally have one of our web components working in a non-
Svelte environment! It might have taken us a while to get there, but in the
tradition of "best things come to those who wait," we finally got there.

This is one of the best things about Svelte: unlike other frameworks, we
can create reusable components in any framework, including Svelte. On
a more practical matter, this demo has a few interesting points of note, so
let's review the code in more detail.

Understanding What Happened

This last demo might seem like déjà-vu, but that is to be expected – most of the hard work in bundling our components has already been done, so all that remains is to add our component to a demo.

For this demo, we created a simple React demo based on one of the templates available in CodeSandbox. We first set up an asset folder structure before uploading a copy of our `Spinner...js` bundle. We could have used a different folder structure (and in production, probably would), but replicating the existing one created in the bundling process makes it easier to build our demo.

Next, we added an import to the Spinner file in App.js before inserting the Spinner component into the React markup. Once done, we previewed the results in the mini browser window to confirm that the Spinner component worked as expected within our demo.

Adding Test Coverage

So far, we've focused on creating tests for our components – all follow a similar format, where we include tests to prove they render correctly on the screen and that we can start to perform limited checks, such as checking that the Dialog box is not present when clicking the close button of the modal.

This testing is all very good, but it leaves out an important stage – what about test coverage? Are we using all of the code in each test, or is there code that we haven't thoroughly tested yet?

This step was left out in an earlier version of this book – possibly due to issues with setting it up locally. However, using Vitest makes setting up our coverage checks a doddle – support is already partially baked in, so to see how we can get it working, let's dive into the next demo.

```
ADDING TEST COVERAGE
```

To set up coverage using Vitest, follow these steps:

1. First, crack open `vite.config.js` and add these lines as highlighted:

```
// https://vitejs.dev/config/
export default defineConfig({
  plugins: [svelte()],
  test: {
    globals: true,
    environment: "jsdom",
    setupFiles: ["src/setupTest.js"],
    coverage: {
      provider: "istanbul",
    },
  },
  compilerOptions: {
    customElement: true,
  },
});
```

2. Save and close the file. Next, switch to a Node.js terminal session and change the working folder to our project area.

3. At the prompt, enter `npm run coverage` and press Enter. You should see a message asking to install `@vitest/coverage-istanbul` — enter y when prompted:

```
$ npm run coverage
> garnetui@0.0.0 coverage
> vitest run --coverage
```

```
MISSING DEPENDENCY  Cannot find dependency '@vitest/
coverage-istanbul'
```

√ Do you want to install @vitest/coverage-istanbul? ... yes

4. After a few moments, we should see a message similar to this to confirm it's installed:

```
added 38 packages, and audited 877 packages in 10s
172 packages are looking for funding
  run `npm fund` for details
found 0 vulnerabilities
Package @vitest/coverage-istanbul installed, re-run the
command to start.
```

5. At this point, enter the same command again and press Enter – we will see a lot of entries similar to these:

```
<garnet-input> was created with unknown prop 'id'
<garnet-input> was created with unknown prop 'class'
```

These are to be expected – we will return to this later in the chapter.

---

6. We should have a set of results similar to the extract shown in Figure 9-6.

```
% Coverage report from istanbul
---------------------|---------|----------|---------|---------|--------------------
File                 | % Stmts | % Branch | % Funcs | % Lines | Uncovered Line #s
---------------------|---------|----------|---------|---------|--------------------
All files            |   81.58 |     37.9 |   78.57 |   85.36 |
 Accordion           |   90.47 |    35.29 |     100 |   93.33 |
  Accordion.svelte   |      75 |        0 |     100 |      80 | 10
  AccordionItem.svelte|     100 |       60 |     100 |     100 | 7,25-29
 Alarm               |     100 |    29.16 |     100 |     100 |
  Alarm.svelte       |     100 |    29.16 |     100 |     100 | 6-7,10,14-23
 Alert               |   81.08 |    34.61 |     100 |   81.81 |
  Alert.svelte       |      75 |    33.33 |     100 |      76 | 16-22,28-31,37
```

Figure 9-6. *Results of our coverage tests*

7. Notice that we also get an indication of how long it takes to run the process — above the results, we should see something akin to this:

```
Test Files  17 passed (17)
     Tests  57 passed (57)
  Start at  18:58:19
  Duration  16.47s (transform 9.45s, setup 21.93s,
  collect 25.04s, tests 1.92s, environment 27.94s,
  prepare 4.30s)
```

8. Leave the Node.js terminal prompt open but minimized — we will use it in the next demo.

Mmm...we now have coverage in place, even if it's not showing the best results! It's good to see that most of the results show 100% coverage, but % Branch definitely needs attention – I suspect that much of that will improve when we look at some of the uncovered lines.

In the meantime, you may have noticed that the results returned are somewhat lengthy. We can make a few tweaks to make it easier to manage getting these results, so let's take a look at how in more detail.

Refining the Results

Although it's important to show all of the results, we may not want to do so each time – it takes longer to display and contains information that isn't immediately relevant if we're working on a specific component!

To get around this, we can tweak the coverage results to only show results for one component at a time (or all of them, when needed). Vitest also includes several files that shouldn't be part of the coverage – they are the ones primarily used in Storybook, not the final component. We can set Vitest to exclude those files that are not relevant – to see how, let's crack on with our next demo.

REFINING THE RESULTS

To refine the results, follow these steps:

1. First, crack open `vite.config.js` – in the section marked coverage, add the include and exclude statements, as shown below:

```
coverage: {
  provider: "istanbul", // or 'v8'
  include: ["src/lib/components/**/*.svelte"],
  exclude: ["src/lib/components/**/*Decorator.svelte"],
},
```

2. Next, extract a copy of the file `additional test commands.txt` from the code download for this book, and copy and paste the contents into `package.json` immediately below this line:

```
"coverage": "vitest run --coverage",
```

3. Save and close the file. We need to make a series of changes to the test spec files now – this is key to making the individual tests work correctly. We'll start with Grid, so crack open `ImageGrid.spec.js` from the `__tests__` file.

4. Look for the line starting import Table from…, and change it to this:

    ```
    import Table from "../../Grid/Table.svelte";
    ```

5. Save and close the file. Switch to a Node.js terminal prompt, enter `npm run coverage`, and press Enter.

6. If all is well, the tests will all run – we should get 17 test files showing a pass, with 57 tests also showing a pass.

Do not be tempted to terminate the tests from running – we need them to execute while we complete the remaining steps in this demo.

---

7. For the remaining tests, we need to perform a similar change – crack open each in turn, then change them following this format (using Accordion as an example):

    a. Look for the line beginning import Accordion from…, where Accordion is the name of the component.

    b. Before the name of the file, change the format from `../Accordion.svelte` to `../../Accordion/Accordion.svelte`.

    c. Save and close the file.

8. Repeat step 8 for all the remaining tests, replacing Accordion with the name of the updated component.

If you encounter any difficulties, the updated files are in the code download.

9. Once the last test is updated, switch to that Node.js terminal session from the previous demo. We need to test these new commands work, so using Accordion as our example, enter npm run coverage:accordion at the prompt and press Enter.

10. If all is well, we should see some results appear similar to this:

```
% Coverage report from Istanbul
✓ src/lib/components/accordion/__tests__/Accordion.
  spec.js (5)
  ✓ Tests for Accordion (5)
    ✓ should render properly
    ✓ should show the first heading with correct text
    ✓ should have the correct title
    ✓ should show aria-expanded as true when first
    item clicked
    ✓ get a snapshot of component
 Test Files  1 passed (1)
     Tests  5 passed (5)
   Start at  19:39:05
   Duration  2.62s (transform 807ms, setup 156ms,
   collect 1.21s, tests 125ms, environment 586ms,
   prepare 195ms)
```

11. The key part is in the coverage results – notice this time how we're only showing results for Accordion (Figure 9-7).

```
% Coverage report from istanbul
------------------|----------|----------|----------|----------|-------------------
File              | % Stmts  | % Branch | % Funcs  | % Lines  | Uncovered Line #s
------------------|----------|----------|----------|----------|-------------------
All files         |   90.47  |   35.29  |    100   |   93.33  |
 Accordion.svelte |     75   |     0    |    100   |     80   | 10
 AccordionItem.svelte |  100  |    60    |    100   |    100   | 7,25-29
------------------|----------|----------|----------|----------|-------------------
```

Figure 9-7. *Coverage results for the Accordion component*

Okay – if you were expecting the results to change to 100% across the board suddenly, I'm sorry to disappoint you: we still have work to do to fix them!

However, these tweaks make it easier to view the results on a per-component basis rather than all of them in one go. We can still do the latter if we want to – this will probably be more useful once we get the results nearer 100% across the board. In the meantime, the changes we've made raise a few key points, so let's take a moment to digest the changes we've made and explore where we go from here as our next steps.

Breaking Apart the Code Changes

Adding code coverage can be a double-edged sword – while it's great for identifying dead code, it can also open up the argument of where we set the thresholds!

Some might say it should be 100% without fail, but that puts extra pressure on us to ensure it all works. Equally, is setting it at 100% a realistic prospect? Some might see setting it lower as lowering standards, but I think it's closer to reality. We can always set low and then work to increase the thresholds over time.

But I digress. To get code coverage enabled, we worked through several steps – we started by adding a block to the `vite.config.js`, to tell Vite (and Vitest) how we want to run coverage. Here, we set our provider as

Istanbul (we could choose v8 as an alternative, but `istanbul` is as good as any to start with). We then ran `npm run test` in a terminal session – this automatically recognized that coverage wasn't set up and installed the `@vitest/coverage-istanbul` package for us. We then reran the command, and this time, Vitest automatically worked out the coverage for us, displaying the results on-screen, along with a record of the time taken, the number of tests covered, and a breakdown of the times taken for each stage.

Granted, the results are not perfect, but this is to be expected – we've not spent any time refining our code yet. I'll come back to this point later in the chapter.

Moving on, we then worked on refining the setup, as coverage included files we didn't need to test, such as decorators for Storybook. To fix this, we added include and exclude statements; we set this to cover only Svelte files and exclude decorator files. We then worked through adding separate commands to test coverage for individual files – we have a fair few that take time to test; setting up individual commands makes it easier for us to test those files when needed.

We can run the entire suite anytime, but this should only be needed as a final test once we update a specific component.

At the same time, we had to adapt the imports in each component – this isn't ideal, but not doing so will result in an error if testing a parent component that subsequently calls a child component (such as Accordion). It doesn't change how the component runs but makes it easier to assess coverage at a more granular level.

Once that lengthy part was done, we finished the demo by testing the Accordion component using the new component-specific command. It showed that the tests were still successful, but the coverage was now limited to the Accordion component. Although we only tested this one, the same principle will apply to all of the others – it's meant a lot of extra commands now showing in `package.json`, but this is only because I couldn't find a better way to be more dynamic!

A Parting Thought

When I was setting up coverage on my local version of the project, it did bring up a couple of interesting points, which I think are worth sharing.

The obvious one is (at least for anyone familiar with the principles of code coverage) what level do we set it at so that it knows when to show an overall pass or failure? Something in me says that 100% would be ideal, but is this representative of what we're aiming for?

I think it's better to start relatively low and gradually build up the success rate using an MVP approach. After all, we already know from the previous demo that we have work to do, so let's get that fixed before we think about going any higher!

We set up basic coverage support in our demo, but Vitest offers more options that could help fine-tune our setup. If you would like to learn more about them, please head over to the Vitest documentation at `https://vitest.dev/config/#coverage`.

Summary

Testing is essential to creating any code, period – be it a simple one-liner right through to a whole website! We must ensure it works (to the best of our ability) and does what we expect. In this chapter, we've covered a lot of material about testing our library, so let's review what we have learned.

We started by working through the steps to set up our testing environment. We chose to use Vitest as it fits perfectly with our Vite-based project and has no problem supporting Svelte Web Components. Next, we moved on to creating tests – as many of them follow the same format, we explored one, then extracted the rest from the code download accompanying this book.

We then switched focus to exploring how to bundle our components – this is essential to preparing them for use in a production environment, although we know they are not yet ready for that stage! This process had two parts: the first was configuring the build steps before we switched to running through that process and generating the files.

In the last stage, we rounded off the chapter by looking at how to test our components in an environment outside our current project area. We updated the local demo to verify that we can see examples running before replicating something similar to a React demo. At the same time, we saw how the component worked fine in both cases, proving that Svelte works in pretty much any environment we might use!

Okay – we've come to the end of this chapter, but we have the most critical part left: release the library into production! The state of our library is such that we would have other things to do first, but it's crucial to understand how the release process might look for our library. Stay with me, and I will reveal it all in the next chapter...

CHAPTER 10

Accessibility

Crack open the `Tabs.svelte` file for a moment – notice anything interesting about two lines that look like they are commented out? The two lines I'm thinking of are these two:

```
<!-- svelte-ignore a11y-click-events-have-key-events -->
<!-- svelte-ignore a11y-no-static-element-interactions -->
```

So why have I highlighted these lines, and what makes them so unique? It all boils down to two things – linting and accessibility. Let me explain where I'm coming from.

Accessibility is one of those topics where either one of two things (or both) can happen – first, it frequently gets left until much later in the development process (as a bit of an afterthought), and second, it can often open something of a can of worms when it comes to dealing with it! What if we could do it *during the development process*?

This feature is where Svelte is different – it has accessibility linting already built into the framework, so if you were to create something that wasn't accessible, it would flag it as such. It's not perfect – and we'll return to that shortly – but it will catch quite a few things!

Accessibility testing is a whole subject in its own right, but there are a few things we can do to get started. Throughout this chapter, we'll work through some of these basic checks and tests – before we do so, let's begin with a quick experiment.

© Alex Libby 2025
A. Libby, *Developing Web Components with Svelte*,
https://doi.org/10.1007/979-8-8688-1180-7_10

A Quick Experiment

I could talk about accessibility testing in Svelte for ages, but to be honest, the best way to understand what's going on is to see it in action. With that in mind, let's run through this quick test – I will assume you're using VS Code; you should still see the same effect in other editors.

WHY IS ACCESSIBILITY LINTING GOOD IN SVELTE?

To see what makes Svelte's accessibility checking worthwhile, follow these steps:

1. Switch to that `Tabs.svelte` file you (hopefully) had open at the start of the chapter.

2. Find the two commented lines and remove them.

3. You will notice that the `<span>` block will be highlighted (with a yellow wavy line), and you will see these two issues appear in the Problems tab (Figure 10-1).

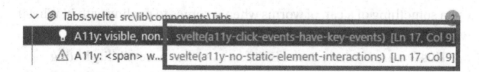

Figure 10-1. *Two accessibility linting issues in VS Code*

4. Undo the change, and you should see the issues disappear.

5. Next, try adding `role=button` above the line shown below in the Dialog component – notice how we get an immediate warning for `a11-no-redundant-roles`? We can see it appear, as shown in Figure 10-2.

```
<button

    A11y: Redundant role 'button' svelte(a11y-no-redundant-roles)

    View Problem (Alt+F8)   Quick Fix... (Ctrl+.)

    role="button"
    on:click={() => (showDialog = false)}
>
```

Figure 10-2. *Adding a redundant role flags a warning*

6. Remove the role type, and the alert will disappear.

See what I mean? The checking is already built into the development process, and it has been since we first installed Svelte. This is in stark contrast to other frameworks, where this would frequently be left as an afterthought – mainly because it can open a real can of worms that no one likes to deal with! So, now that we've seen what happens, let's dig into the details of these errors.

Understanding What Happened

Take another look at the picture in the last demo – you will notice I highlighted two entries:

```
svelte(a11y-click-events-have-key-events)
svelte(a11y-no-static-element-interactions)
```

If we hover over each of the errors in VS Code in turn (in the Problems tab), we get the following explanations:

```
A11y: visible, non-interactive elements with an on:click event
must be accompanied by a keyboard event handler. Consider whether
an interactive element such as <button type="button"> or <a> might
be more appropriate. See https://svelte.dev/docs/accessibility-
warnings#a11y-click-events-have-key-events for more details.

A11y: <span> with click handler must have an ARIA role
```

These are perfect examples of what Svelte can flag as we write code – we can deal with any that pops up in real time, not as an afterthought! I know the demo was a quick test, but it was to highlight how these checks happen in real time and not as part of any extra process we have to run to get the same results.

Setting Expectations

Okay – now we've seen something of what Svelte's accessibility checking can do, what next? It's time for us to get stuck in with testing.

As mentioned earlier, accessibility testing is a whole subject in its own right – we could easily fill a book on its own! Instead, we will focus on some of the basics to see what low-hanging fruit we can identify and fix as a starting point for our library. With that in mind, I want to outline the areas we're going to focus on for this book:

- We will use an NPM package called vitest-axe, available from `https://github.com/chaance/vitest-axe`, which uses axe under the covers. For those unfamiliar with axe, it's one of the best accessibility testing tools available. It's created by the company Deque Systems and is available from `https://www.deque.com/axe/`. There is one downside, though – we must use a pre-release version! We cannot avoid it, so I've chosen the most recent version available for use in this book.

- We'll run a simple test with the plugin to see what (if anything) it catches – based on the results, we'll go through how to fix it so the results show success. We'll use the Alert component as the basis for our tests, but at the same time, go through what we need to do to fit the same tests for the other components.

- While axe (and vitest-axe) may be one of the best tools available, it (to quote an expression) is only human and can't fix everything – it has its limits! We'll work through what these are, whether any may affect what we need to do, and whether we might have to make any changes.

Excellent – with that all in mind, let's crack on and take a look at how we can get stuck in with testing. We will look at two methods – we can use the vitest-axe package I mentioned earlier (which requires some work to set up). However, there is a quick and dirty way to run some checks – how about using a plugin directly into our browser?

Testing with the Chrome Extension

The easiest way to test our components for accessibility is to use a Chrome plugin. Deque has made one that ties in with their axe testing tool, which is available from the Chrome Store and will be the one we'll use for our next demo.

Before we get started, though, it's important to remember while we run through a project that this won't give us a 100% representative picture. We're running on a page set in time, so the results will be what axe sees at that point. If we import that component into a site, new issues, such as for contrast, may appear. That is why it's crucial to test now and again to ensure we can fix all issues where possible!

Right – let's make a start: we'll do this in two halves as there are a few steps to work through. We'll cover examining the results in the next demo, but we'll begin with setting up the browser plugin.

SETTING UP THE AXE PLUGIN IN CHROME

To set up the plugin, follow these steps:

1. First, go ahead and browse to the Google Web Store at
   `https://chromewebstore.google.com/`, then enter axe
   in the search box.

2. You should see one item listed as axe DevTools – Web
   Accessibility Testing. Click it, then click Add to Chrome on
   the right.

3. It will prompt you to confirm that you want to add the extension.
   Click Add extension. It will show a page in Chrome to confirm it
   is installed – we can close it when this appears.

4. Next, open a Node.js terminal session and change the working
   folder to our project area.

5. At the prompt, enter `npm run storybook` and press Enter –
   this will fire up Storybook, ready for testing. When Storybook
   appears, click Notification Components ➤ Alert ➤ Default.

6. When on that page, click Open canvas in new tab – it's the
   middle icon of three, at the top right of the screen. Shift+Ctrl+I
   (or Shift+Cmd+I) to open the Developer Console.

7. Click the axe DevTools tab – you will be prompted to customize
   the experience: choose Developer, then hit the checkbox by I
   accept… and the Start using… button.

8. Next, click Full Page Scan and wait a few moments for the
   results to appear.

Phew – we had to work through a few steps there, and that's only for setting up! The good thing is that the first five steps are a one-off; we only need to do steps 6–11 when testing in the future. Leaving that aside for a moment, let's take a moment to explore the results of our test and see what we need to resolve in more detail.

Understanding the Results

Once the test is completed, we end up with a set of results similar to that shown in Figure 10-3.

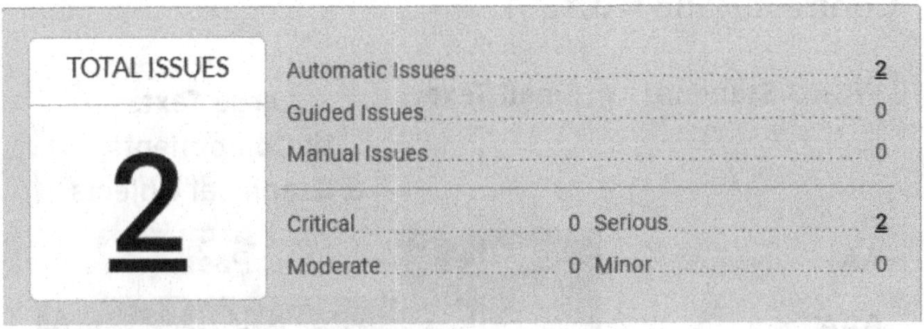

Figure 10-3. Results of running Axe Tools on the Alert component

Although we are displaying the component inside Storybook, it's only showing two issues – both relate to color contrast. If we click the arrow, we get the compiled markup and details of why it has failed:

```
<div class="message s-4Y75ZjC11XWf"><strong
class="s-4Y75ZjC11XWf">Simple Info</strong> An info
description</div>
```

Element has insufficient color contrast of 3.12 (foreground color: #ffffff, background color: #2196f3, font size: 12.0pt (16px), font weight: normal). Expected contrast ratio of 4.5:1

So far, so good? Well, maybe not. Let me explain.

301

The #2196f3 color is the blue background for our alert, which we're using against white text as our content text color. It's a reasonable combination, but here's the kicker – it's not necessarily the combination we will end up using in a project!

The problem lies not necessarily in the color we get when selecting the alert type, but in that it's hard-coded into the component, which makes it less useful. If we use the Color Contrast checker at https://dequeuniversity.com/rules/axe/4.10/color-contrast, we can see the results confirm a fail for the design we're using (Figure 10-4).

Contrast Ratio = 3.12:1

WCAG Standard	Small Text	Large Text, UI Components, & Graphical Objects
AA	FAIL	Pass
AAA	FAIL	FAIL

Figure 10-4. *Confirmation of the failing accessibility checks*

To fix this issue, the ideal solution would be to revamp the component to accept custom foreground and background colors, allowing us to use any preset color palettes we need. Alternatively, we could override the styles manually, although it's not ideal!

If we went down the route of overriding colors, we'd have to ask ourselves whether we want to go to Web Content Accessibility Guidelines (WCAG) AA level compliance or for the stricter AAA level. For the former, we'd have to change the background color to something like #0A6EBD (a darker shade of blue) – we would have to alter the latter to something like #064474, an even darker shade of blue! It's definitely something worth considering...

Tip   Sites like `https://www.colorhexa.com/` are a great help here – this site shows different shades of the target color, so with a little trial and error, you can choose a more accessible color that fits any palettes you need to use in your projects.

Okay – let's move on: we've seen some quick wins we can have with axe in the browser, but what about more complex or in-depth issues? We can still use Axe, but we must switch focus to the codebase and use a dedicated plugin. Fortunately, various people have created plugins that feed into axe, based on using Jest, Vitest, and the like. We will use one for Vitest – let's look at what's involved and how it works in more detail.

Implementing Vitest-Axe

To assess accessibility in our codebase, we will use the vitest-axe plugin, which is available from `https://github.com/chaance/vitest-axe`. The plugin is just a wrapper for axe but written to share the same API and library implementation as jest-axe, with which some of you may already be familiar.

Installing the plugin is very easy – we can do it the same way as many npm plugins, then extend our existing test setup globally or (as I prefer) on a per-test basis. Let's take a closer look at the steps required to install and configure the plugin, using the Alert component as the basis for our next demo.

In this next demo, I've set it to use the Default variant, but the principles are the same for any variant, and the code can be adapted accordingly.

SETTING UP VITEST-AXE

To set up vitest-axe in our environment, follow these steps:

1. First, crack open a Node.js terminal session, then change the working folder to our project area.

2. At the prompt, enter npm install --save-dev vitest-axe and press Enter.

3. Open Alert.spec.js, then add these two lines at the top:

   ```
   import { axe } from "vitest-axe";
   import * as AxeMatchers from "vitest-axe/matchers";
   ```

4. Next, crack open a copy of adding alert markup.txt from the code download accompanying this book. Miss a line, then add the contents.

I've added copies of the code for each component to the code download to make it easier to update your tests.

---

5. Scroll down to the bottom of the spec file, and add this before the closing brackets at the end:

   ```
   test("should demonstrate no issues with
   accessibility", async () => {
     const render = () => AlertHTML;
     const result = render();

     expect(await axe(result)).toHaveNoViolations();
   });
   });
   ```

6. Revert to the Node.js terminal session you had opened earlier, then at the prompt, run this command:

```
npm run test:alert
```

7. If all goes well, we should see a lengthy response – we'll go through what it means section by section, starting with this:

```
> garnetui@0.0.0 test:alert
> vitest --dir=src/lib/components/alert

 DEV  v2.0.5 C:/garnetui

(node:23072) [DEP0040] DeprecationWarning: The
`punycode` module is deprecated. Please use a userland
alternative instead.
(Use `node --trace-deprecation ...` to show where the
warning was created)
```

8. The next block highlights an issue we need to address with unknown props being passed or used in our component or story file:

```
stderr | src/lib/components/alert/__tests__/Alert.spec.
js > Tests for Alert > should render properly
<garnet-alert> was created with unknown prop 'icon'
<garnet-alert> was created with unknown prop 'close'

stderr | src/lib/components/alert/__tests__/Alert.spec.
js > Tests for Alert > should disappear when close
button clicked
<garnet-alert> was created with unknown prop 'icon'
<garnet-alert> was created with unknown prop 'close'

stderr | src/lib/components/alert/__tests__/Alert.spec.
js > Tests for Alert > get a snapshot of component
<garnet-alert> was created with unknown prop 'icon'
<garnet-alert> was created with unknown prop 'close'
```

9. We finally get confirmation of the results of our test – it shows
    that three tests pass, but the accessibility one fails:

    > src/lib/components/alert/__tests__/Alert.spec.js (4)
      > Tests for Alert (4)
        ✓ should render properly
        ✓ should disappear when close button clicked
        ✓ get a snapshot of component
        × should demonstrate no issues with accessibility

10. We then get details of why our test has failed – this time, it's
    because we're using a role type that is not supported:

    ──────────────── Failed Tests 1 ────────────────
     FAIL src/lib/components/alert/__tests__/Alert.spec.js
    > Tests for Alert > should demonstrate no issues with
    accessibility
    Error: expect(received).toHaveNoViolations(expected)

    Expected the HTML found at $('dialog') to have no
    violations:

    <dialog class="alert alert-info fade-in s-4Y75ZjC11XWf"
    role="alert">

    Received:

    "ARIA role should be appropriate for the element (aria-
    allowed-role)"

    Fix any of the following:

      ARIA role alert is not allowed for given element

    https://dequeuniversity.com/rules/axe/4.10/aria-
    allowed-role?application=axeAPI

11. We finish with confirmation of where the issue was triggered in
our test, and confirmation of the number of passes and failures,
as well as the time taken to run the test:

```
>
src/lib/components/alert/__tests__/Alert.spec.js:50:31
    48|      const result = render();
    49|
    50|      expect(await axe(result)).
          toHaveNoViolations();
     |                                        ^
    51|  });
    52| });
──────────────────────────────────────[1/1]-
 Test Files  1 failed (1)
      Tests  1 failed | 3 passed (4)
   Start at  18:37:48
   Duration  2.05s (transform 311ms, setup 139ms,
   collect 907ms, tests 129ms, environment 471ms,
   prepare 147ms)

 FAIL  Tests failed. Watching for file changes...
       press h to show help, press q to quit
```

Ouch – at first glance, those results look horrible! However, most of it
is clouded by the fact that we have an issue with unknown props that we
should address, in addition to the role type problem, even though it's not
strictly accessibility related! Before we look at fixing both, let's look at the
changes we made in more detail.

Exploring the Changes

So, what did we do in our somewhat lengthy demo? We kicked off by installing the vitest-axe using the typical `npm install` process – this is no different from any other package, which makes it very easy to install! Next, we added two imports for axe in `Alert.svelte` – one for axe and the other for the axe-matches package.

Moving on, we added a const value for `AlertHTML` that contained the markup for our Alert component – this we use to mount the component before running any accessibility tests. Unfortunately, there is no quick way to get this markup – the simplest is to

- Run up Storybook

- Tag on `&viewMode=story` to the URL and press Enter (this removes the Storybook markup and shows just the component)

- Open Developer Console, right-click the garnet <div> in the markup, and select Extract as HTML.

Assuming we have the markup, we then added our test at the foot of the test spec file – it contains this command:

```
expect(await axe(result)).toHaveNoViolations();
```

This statement is key to performing the check – when run, it generates a report of any accessibility issues it finds. In our case, it found two: an unsupported role type and the lack of an accessible name for our component. This, plus the issues with unknown prop names, we will look at in the next section when we come to fix the errors found in this demo.

Even though we've used the vitest-axe component, this is just a wrapper for axe – it's worth having a dig in the documentation on Deque's website to learn more about the settings. At present, we have tested the WCAG 2.1 standard, but we may want to change the specifics. How about setting it to triple AAA level to really up our game?

Fixing the Issues

Now that we've seen how vitest-axe can highlight accessibility issues, we should turn our attention to fixing them. We may not be able to resolve all problems, but we should at least consider what vitest-axe returns!

In short, we only need to make a few changes to this component – one of them isn't strictly accessibility, but hey, if we're making changes, why not fix it anyway? It's a simple fix and a good one to know about with Svelte – to see what I mean, let's dive in and look.

MAKING THE CHANGES

To fix the issues highlighted by vitest-axe, follow these steps:

1. The first issue isn't strictly one of accessibility, but given we're fixing issues, it's a good opportunity to fix this one – we have unknown prop warnings appearing when running the tests:

    ```
    <garnet-alert> was created with unknown prop 'icon'
    <garnet-alert> was created with unknown prop 'close'
    ```

2. To fix the first one, which is for `icon`, we need to change in the props const to `showIcon`, like so:

```
const props = {
    show: true,
    description: "An info description",
    title: "Simple Info",
    showIcon: "true",
    type: "info",
    close: "false",
};
```

3. The next change we need to make is to remove the entry for `close` from the same block shown in step 2 – this was likely a copy/paste issue, and as it's not needed, we should remove it. We should end up with this:

```
const props = {
    show: true,
    description: "An info description",
    title: "Simple Info",
    showIcon: "true",
    type: "info",
};
```

4. We can now fix the issues raised by vitest-axe – the first one is for an invalid role type for Alert. We used alert for this, which is not permitted – change it to `alertdialog` in `Alert.svelte`:

```
<dialog class={classes} role="alertdialog">
```

5. The next error logged by vitest-axe is due to the lack of an accessible name for the component. To fix this, add a title to the markup in `Alert.svelte`, like so:

```
dialog class={classes} role="alertdialog" title="Alert
Dialog">
```

6. Save Alert.svelte and close it. Next, look for Alert.
    spec.js.snap and delete it – it will be in the \src\lib\
    components\Alert__tests____snapshots__ folder.

7. At this point, we can rerun the tests. Switch to a Node.js
    terminal session, then make sure the working folder is set to
    our project area.

8. At the prompt, enter npm run test:alert and press Enter –
    if all is well, we should get results similar to this:

```
(node:25060) [DEP0040] DeprecationWarning: The
`punycode` module is deprecated. Please use a userland
alternative instead.
(Use `node --trace-deprecation ...` to show where the
warning was created)
 ✓ src/lib/components/alert/__tests__/Alert.
spec.js (4)
   ✓ Tests for Alert (4)
     ✓ should render properly
     ✓ should disappear when close button clicked
     ✓ get a snapshot of component
     ✓ should demonstrate no issues with accessibility

 Test Files  1 passed (1)
      Tests  4 passed (4)
   Start at  17:37:18
   Duration  3.13s (transform 531ms, setup 193ms,
   collect 1.57s, tests 164ms, environment 730ms,
   prepare 169ms)

 PASS  Waiting for file changes...
       press h to show help, press q to quit
```

If you would like to learn more about ARIA role types, then a good starting point is the documentation on the Mozilla Developer website at `https://developer.mozilla.org/en-US/docs/Web/Accessibility/ARIA/Roles`.

Excellent – I'm sure you will agree that this is already an improvement! I know the deprecation warning for punycode will still need fixing, but that will have to wait until a newer version of Storybook is available. For now, though, we've covered some important points in this demo, so let's take a moment to review the changes we made and see how we can apply them to other components in our library.

Breaking Apart the Code

Testing for accessibility is a vital part of any development process. While it can be a double-edged sword in terms of the amount of work it can create, it's still essential to make anything we produce available to all. Over the last few pages, we've worked on doing this for the Alert component, with a view to (eventually) replicating similar changes throughout the library. Let's have a look at the changes we made in more detail.

We started by fixing some unknown prop issues from the report generated in the previous demo, setting up vitest-axe. While these are not strictly accessibility related, it is still good to fix them. They cloud any issues reported by Axe, making it just a little harder to work out whether something is valid or just noise! In each case, it was a matter of either renaming an incorrect prop name or removing it completely.

Moving on, we then turned our attention to fixing the real issues flagged by vitest-axe – we had to add a missing title value and change the role name given to the component. The good thing about vitest-axe is that it usually indicates what we need to do to fix issues such as these two. For example, we could have fixed the second issue by adding one of the following:

- The `aria-label` attribute does not exist or is empty.

- The `aria-labelledby` attribute does not exist, references elements that do not exist, or references elements that are empty.

- Element has no title attribute.

In this case, I chose the `title` option, but I could equally have used either of the other two to fix the issue. We then rounded out the demo by running the `npm test:alert` command to rerun the tests – while we still got the deprecation warning (which was to be expected), it didn't complain about any accessibility issues.

Thinking further afield, we could easily apply the same fixes to other components in the library. Much of what we have to do will depend on what vitest-axe returns, but I suspect most will be invalid prop names and missing aria or title tags! I have been through all of the remaining components and added, modified, or changed code to ensure all pass basic accessibility checks.

Okay – let's move on: using Svelte to check and notify us of any accessibility issues is a great step forward, but like all processes, it's not infallible. We should be aware of some limitations when using this approach, so it will do us no harm to appreciate where we might have to make manual checks – let's look at this in a little more detail.

Limits of Testing

While one of Svelte's standout features is its checking for accessibility issues, there is a limit to how much it can catch. To put this in perspective, let me give you a figure:

> *With axe-core, you can find on average 57% of WCAG issues automatically.*

That sobering thought was taken from Deque's website while writing this book – it's quite a shock! Even though we have a great process in place for checking accessibility with Svelte, it's not as good as people expect. Don't get me wrong: it's a significant step in the right direction. But we need to be mindful that accessibility is a huge topic and that we'll never manage to get 100%, as we can't predict how our components will be used.

There is a big issue that we must be mindful of first, which did not pop up immediately when writing the tests for this book but surfaced a little later. When I ran tests, I was frequently getting this error returned for most of the components:

`"All page content should be contained by landmarks (region)"`

It turns out that Vitest treats tests as if we're working on a page, not an individual component – this behavior is undesirable if not expected. To fix it, we have to edit the test for accessibility to use this format instead – the example below is set for Alarm, but you will need to amend the `AlarmHTML` property to suit other components:

```
test("should demonstrate no issues with accessibility",
async () => {
  const render = () => AlarmHTML;
  const result = render();

  const results = await axe(result, {
    rules: {
```

```
    region: { enabled: false },
  },
});

expect(results).toHaveNoViolations();
});
```

While this is a bit of a pain, it is necessary; otherwise, the tests will still record a failure even if we've fixed any other issues that appear. Using this format also raises a few things we should fix at some point – they are as follows:

- I've included the exclusion rules here in the code for now, but, ultimately, it would be great to move these into a helper file, so we don't have to update all 17 components manually!

- In making this change, we are effectively extending axe – it would be great to do this more centrally, so we don't have to extend it in each test manually. The trouble is, I found scant documentation on how to set this up when researching for this book, so I've gone with the option of what works best for now. We can always take the MVP approach and look to improve this setup at some point in the future.

Looking further afield, Svelte can catch a fair few issues, which include

- Required attributes that are missing (e.g., no alt attribute)

- Misplaced attributes that shouldn't be there (e.g., aria-hidden on a heading)

- Invalid attributes (e.g., writing role="potato")

We can also catch a mix of issues that fall into a bag of accessibility best practices, such as not using the <marquee /> tag, autofocus, and positive tabindex values. So, what is Svelte not able to catch? One of the core developers of Svelte, Geoff Rich, has highlighted a few areas in a great article that is worth keeping in mind. They include

- Dynamic values: If we use <a href="#"> as an anchor, it will fire a warning, but if this is assigned to a constant that is later used, we won't get a warning.

- Anything that requires a larger view of the app: If you use, say, an <h2> tag in a component, Svelte won't know if you're going from <h2> to <h3> or jumping to something like <h4>; this will therefore not trigger a warning.

- Svelte won't trap styling issues related to accessibility: These need to be picked up by a dedicated Axe plugin or checked in the browser. A typical example would be color contrast, such as the one we found earlier for the Alert component.

- Svelte will only pick up those issues that are objective: for example, if you've used markup that could be improved or alt text for images isn't great, then these won't trigger an alert.

These are just a few things for us to think about! I'm sure there will be more, but let's be pragmatic – Svelte is still relatively young, and (at the time of writing) quite a few accessibility issues have not yet been resolved, so that support will improve over time.

If you want to read Geoff's original article, please visit https:// geoffrich.net/posts/svelte-a11y-limits/.

Okay, let's crack on – we've covered a lot in this chapter! There is one more topic we should cover, which is – to quote that oft-used term – "next steps." Where can we go from here? Is there anything worth exploring as a result of the issues we find in our repo?

Exploring Next Steps

So far, we've created a basic test for the Alert component and dealt with some issues – where can we go from here?

It's a great question: the answer depends (at least partly) on what results you get from the remaining components! It might not be what you expected to hear, but we can start by adding checks for specific names or properties and add these as explicit tests in our test suite. For example, we could write something similar to these:

```
expect(container.querySelector('.btn'))
.toHaveProperty(
  'role',
  'button'
);

expect(container).toHaveAccessibleName('Click me');
```

Note   These are just examples that may or may not work in Vite; please check before you add any of them!

An excellent place to start would be the options documentation on the Deque website at `https://github.com/dequelabs/axe-core/blob/master/doc/API.md#options-parameter`. Vitest-axe is just a wrapper for axe, so all options listed should be compatible if we decide to use them in our library at some point in the future.

There are a few other areas we should investigate to help improve our testing:

- Refine the exclusion setup so it is hosted centrally and doesn't require us to manually edit each test file to add or change existing rules! We may or may not need to add new ones, but doing it once, which applies automatically across all tests, is infinitely preferable to editing each file.

- I had to manually extract the (compiled) markup for the component we used in our accessibility demo. While it worked, it was not ideal. We should see if there is a way to improve this – initial checks suggested that rendering the component as <XXXX /> wasn't accepted, but I'm not sure why.

- I think the component format isn't 100% consistent – for example, do all of them have a parent `<div>` in the format of `<div class=" garnet-XXXX">`? It is critical not only for styling and separation of concerns but also because of the region landmark issue I mentioned just now – can we find a landmark tag that works better and potentially means we can do away with the exclusion rule?

These are just a couple of things to think about – I'm sure you'll come up with more! The point here is that we don't consider this done and dusted but keep iterating on what we've done until the library is no longer used and retired from active service.

Summary

Phew – we've covered a lot of valuable content over the last few pages!

I've already mentioned that testing is essential to the development process. While it is a huge topic, we've made a good start in ensuring our components work as expected in the library. We've worked through some critical steps throughout this chapter, so let's take a moment to review what we have learned.

We began with a quick experiment to see the effects of including markup in our example component that is not accessible; we noted that Svelte has accessibility checking built in, and (as we later found out) it's not perfect, but can pick up a fair few of the basic areas where accessibility can be an issue.

Next up, we moved on to testing a component with the Axe DevTools plugin for Chrome – this was designed as a quick and dirty check as it is a manual process and not one suited to lots of regular checking for more than a handful of components! That said, it picked up a valid issue with color contrast, which we delved into and figured out some of the options available for fixing the problems.

We then worked through setting up vitest-axe as an automated way of checking for accessibility – we saw how this highlighted two to three issues that were straightforward to fix and that implementing suitable changes meant we could get a 100% pass on that component when retesting it. We then rounded out the chapter with a quick look at some of the limits of testing accessibility with Svelte's built-in checker before touching on a couple of ways to take our checking further as we develop the library over time.

Okay. Big sigh – it's time, ladies and gentlemen…to release our work into the wild! Hold your horses, though, as our library isn't yet ready for that, but I will take you through the process for getting our code ready to release into the wild, as well as some options on making our components available for general use in the next chapter.

CHAPTER 11

Deploying to Production

This chapter is the most critical part: we've spent all this time creating our new library, but no one can use it unless we release it into production.

In this chapter, we will go through releasing our library into the wild and explore what documentation is required so that others can use the library for the first time. I know you'll be keen to get everything released and out for people to use, but as they say, hold your horses: the release process is critical to the success of your library, so it's essential to get it right!

It means we need to cover a little theory before getting stuck in, but it will be worth it in the long run. With that in mind, let's start with a simple task: perform some final checks to make sure all is good before release.

Performing Final Checks

Throughout this book, we've done some great work in creating our component library – it would be a shame to release it out into the wild without at least making sure we've tidied up loose ends.

We should do this task by default, but I've encountered dozens of instances where developers haven't performed this task. For example, I've

© Alex Libby 2025
A. Libby, *Developing Web Components with Svelte*,
https://doi.org/10.1007/979-8-8688-1180-7_11

seen sites containing components without documentation (or minimal at best), spelling mistakes, or poorly formatted code. I've even seen the occasional spelling mistake, too, which isn't great.

It is a symbolically important step, too – we may not need to make many (if any) final changes, but doing the last check is also a way to say, "I'm happy with what is there and ready to sign off." Let us be realistic, though: I know our library still needs work, so we won't do this until we release the site.

Leaving that aside for a moment, let's consider what we might want to do at this point. To get you started, here are a few ideas:

- Check each file in the repository: Is it still needed, or is it one that is no longer required and can, therefore, be removed?

- Do all of the component files have a consistent layout? For example, I usually start each component with the `<script>` block, followed by the markup, and finish with the `<style>` block, but you may prefer to change it.

- Are all the filenames correctly named (i.e., in title case), where appropriate? Do filenames relate to the content within? For example, we have a Grid folder, but the component inside it is called ImageGrid.

- In the test files, we import the same functions, along with the target component – are all of the imports required, or can we tidy up by removing any that are no longer needed? The same applies to components – can we remove imports if we're not using them?

- Have you pushed up any final changes in your local version?

- We have a `.gitignore` file in the book: Is this up to date, or are there any other folders or files we need to exclude?

- For each component, we used `Default` as the out-of-the-box version in Storybook – while this works technically, it's not considered standard practice to use. Ideally, we should rename any instance of Default (and note, not the `default` fallback) to something else – as long as we can come up with an appropriate option!

We might want to make more changes to tidy up, but this will depend on your circumstances. The critical point here is that we take the opportunity to make sure our library is as tidy as realistically possible before we release it into the wild. I know it's a task that ideally is done as we work, but let's be honest: Can we guarantee this happening without a cleanup/check at the end?

A minor point: This is not about tidying to the nth degree but getting things to a sensible stage, bearing in mind that we're following the MVP approach we discussed earlier in the book.

Okay – let's crack on: now that we've completed the final checks for our site, we should look at deploying our library. Getting our library out into the wild will require a few steps, such as pushing our code into a repository, releasing packages, ensuring good documentation, and more. Before we get stuck into the various tasks, let's first take a quick look at what we need to do in more detail.

Understanding the Deployment Process

Throughout this chapter, we will transition our library from being a locally hosted project into something available for others to use (and hopefully help improve and develop, too). From the outset, though, there is one thing we need to be mindful of.

Although we've done much to develop our library, I would **not** consider it production-ready. We can add plenty more, such as more extensive testing or making CSS styles more consistent – I'm sure there will be more we can do! It's important to note, therefore, that while we will cover the process, tips, and hints on deployment, we should only do these at the appropriate moment when we deem our code to be production-ready.

Okay, enough of the doom and gloom, let's move on. We've mentioned that the process of deployment will include various tasks, which will include the following:

- GitHub: If we don't upload our code somewhere, nobody will be able to use it! I've chosen to use GitHub for convenience (primarily because I already have many repos on this platform). Feel free to change it to a different platform, such as GitLab, Azure, or even Bitbucket.

- We need to release our code in a format that's easy for others to use – we have several options:

  - We can release it as one or more npm packages.

  - We also have an opportunity to bundle components as compiled JavaScript files.

- We could even push code to a Content Delivery Network (or CDN) – this would be outside the scope of this book, but it's something to consider for future projects.

- In addition to releasing code, we should also release our version of Storybook to a public hosting webspace, such as Netlify.

There's plenty to do! It might seem like a lot, but it's important to remember that much of this will be one-off. Once we complete steps such as setting up GitHub, we can switch to applying updates and new features throughout the lifetime of the component library. With that in mind, let's begin the process by getting a GitHub site set up and ready for use.

Publishing to GitHub

Although publishing content on GitHub requires quite a few steps, we can split the process into two distinct parts – the first is to create the repository and get it ready for use, while the second is uploading our code.

Let's focus first on setting up the repository: if you've already used sites such as GitHub, then much of what you will see shortly will be familiar. Before we get stuck in, though, there are a couple of points we should be aware of as part of setting up our repository:

- Although I've elected to use GitHub (and Netlify) for hosting, this part is more about the process of pushing up code into production and less about the specifics of where we host it. For this book, I will assume you are using GitHub and Netlify; please feel free to adapt where appropriate.

- The instructions over the next few pages are written for Windows, as this is the author's regular platform; please adapt if you use macOS or Linux.

For the demos, I will assume the repo's name is `garnet` and that it is available at `https://github.com/alexlibby/garnet`. Please adapt the name accordingly, depending on what you choose to use.

Okay – with that in mind, let's dive in and start setting up the library's repository.

Setting Up a GitHub Repository

At this point, things start to take shape – we are stepping ever closer to releasing our site into the wild.

The first task will be to set up a GitHub repository; I will use garnet for the account name so you can see how to configure your version, particularly if you use a different name. Setting up the repository uses the standard GitHub process – let's take a look:

SETTING UP THE REPOSITORY

To set up our GitHub Pages account, follow these steps:

1. The first step is to sign in to your GitHub account using the details you registered with before this demo; once done, browse to `https://github.com/new` to set up a new repository.

2. Once you are on the Create a new repository page, go ahead and enter your repository name (Figure 11-1).

Figure 11-1. *Creating the repository*

3. GitHub has already populated the Owner field, so leave this unchanged.

4. Next, give it a description – it's optional, so you can skip past it if you like, and it won't affect how the demo works.

5. You should see two fields present, Public and Private – GitHub has preselected the former, as private repositories are not available on a free tier.

6. Next, set all three options under the Initialize this repository with... label – you should end up with a configuration similar to that shown in Figure 11-2.

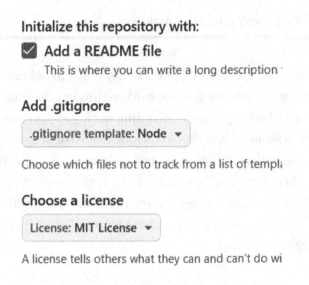

Figure 11-2. Settings to use for the new repository

7. Hit Create a repository to generate our new repository.

8. If all is well, we should end up with a new repository with a URL of `https://github.com/alexlibby/garnet` – it should look something like the screenshot shown in Figure 11-3 (allowing for your username and repository name).

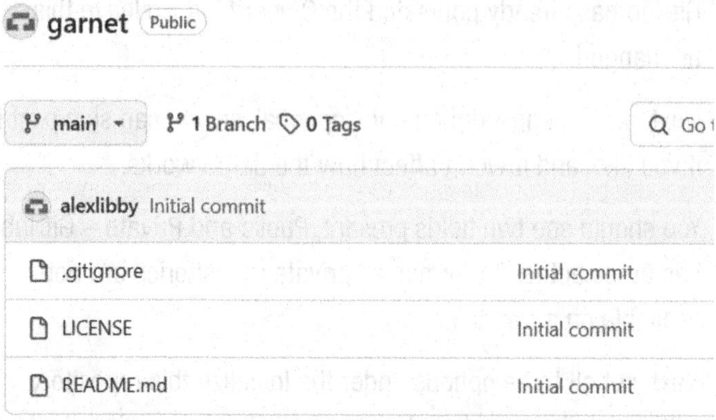

Figure 11-3. Screenshot of our GitHub repository, ready for use

9.   Our repository is ready for deployment.

Excellent – we have a working repository ready to upload content from our project area. To achieve this, we worked through the standard process for creating a GitHub repository, including setting appropriate values for entries such as name or whether to include a license or `.gitignore` file.

With our repository in place, we can now move on to the next task: upload our library code, which, fortunately, is easy enough to do using standard Git commands. I suspect some of this will be familiar to many of you already; for those new to Git, don't worry – let's dive in and take a closer look at what's involved.

Uploading Components to GitHub

With our repository set up and ready for use, it's time we turned our attention to uploading our code. We can achieve this in several ways: uploading directly from editors, Git GUI clients, or via the command line.

For this next exercise, I will keep it simple and use the Git command line; feel free to adapt if you already have a process for uploading to GitHub. Let's make a start.

UPLOADING TO GITHUB – PART 1: THE COMMIT

To upload our code to the repository, follow these steps:

1. We first need to rename the original `garnet` folder to `garnet-source` – this will allow the upload process to continue.

If you already have Git installed for your platform, please skip the next step and proceed to step 3.

---

2. Next, we need to install Git – head over to `https://git-scm.com/downloads`, then download and install the version appropriate for your platform. When asked, please accept default settings – this should be sufficient for this exercise.

3. With Git installed, fire up a Git Bash session, then change the working folder to the same level as the `garnet-source` folder we renamed in the first step.

4. Next, we need to clone the empty repository down to your PC so that we can upload content – for this, enter this command at the prompt to pull down a copy of the repository, where XXXXX is your account name:

    `git clone https://github.com/XXXXX/garnet.git`

You can also get this URL from GitHub by visiting the Code tab, then clicking Clone, and hitting the icon to the right of the URL to copy the address.

---

5. On pressing Enter, you should see something akin to this:

```
Cloning into 'garnet'...
remote: Enumerating objects: 5, done.
remote: Counting objects: 100% (5/5), done.
remote: Compressing objects: 100% (5/5), done.
remote: Total 5 (delta 0), reused 0 (delta 0),
pack-reused 0
Receiving objects: 100% (5/5), done.
```

6. Next, extract a copy of .gitignore from the code download and drop it into the root of the garnet folder.

7. Switch to your file manager, then copy all the files from garnet-source to garnet. You may be prompted to overwrite README. md and .gitignore – if so, hit Skip, as the files in the garnet repo are better versions than the local ones.

There is a reason for doing this at this stage – I will return to it at the end of the demo.

---

8. With the files copied over, revert to a Node.js terminal session, then change the working folder to the cobalt folder, and run npm install at the prompt.

9. Once this is complete, we need to add the files together, ready to push up as a commit to our repository. Run this command at the prompt:

```
git add .
```

10. With the files ready, enter git commit -m "Initial release" to bundle the code into a commit, similar to this extract:

```
[main 4d38b60] Initial release
 103 files changed, 52901 insertions(+), 106 deletions(-)
```

```
rewrite .gitignore (94%)
create mode 100644 .storybook/main.js
create mode 100644 .storybook/preview-head.html
create mode 100644 .storybook/preview.js
rewrite README.md (100%)
create mode 100644 __test__/Accordion.spec.js
create mode 100644 __test__/Alert.spec.js
create mode 100644 __test__/Breadcrumbs.spec.js
create mode 100644 __test__/Checkbox.spec.js
...
```

Excellent – that brings us to the end of Part 1, with code ready to push up. Technically, this process will be a lot slicker as we perform the first few steps as a one-off. In future iterations, we will just add the files to a commit and push it up. Take a breather for a moment, then let's continue with Part 2, which will push the code up into GitHub.

UPLOADING TO GITHUB – PART 2: PUSHING UP

To complete the process of getting the code into GitHub, follow these steps:

1. Before we can push up, we need to create a PAT (or Personal Access Token). First, browse this page: `https://github.com/settings/tokens`.

You can also access this page by clicking Profile ➤ Settings ➤ Developers setting ➤ Personal access tokens. Don't be tempted to go to the repository settings page – you must do this within your profile settings page!

2. Click Generate a new token, log in if prompted, and enter the name Garnet UI for the Note field.

3. Set the expiration as high as you feel comfortable with or is permitted in your environment, then click workflow and repo as selected scopes. Make a copy of the token – **you will need it** – then hit Generate token at the bottom of the page.

4. Switch to your desktop, then search for a Windows application named Credential Manager. Open it, then click Windows Credentials.

5. Please complete either step 6 or step 7, depending on whether you have an entry for github.com, but not both. Once done, please continue from step 8.

6. Look for an entry marked github.com – if it is there, then edit it to replace the password with the token you generated in GitHub. Hit Save and close the Manager.

7. If you do not have it, then hit Add a Windows credential and enter the details as follows:

Entry	Value
Internet or network address	github.com
Your username	The username you use to log in to your GitHub account
Your password	Your PAT token created in step 12

8. Hit Save, then close the Manager.

9. Switch back to your Node.js terminal, then at the prompt, enter `git push`.

10. You will likely be prompted to log in to GitHub. When prompted, click the Token open, paste your PAT token into your PAT token, and then hit Enter to sign in.

It may appear as a small window, which might be hidden under others – check your taskbar to see if anything appears.

---

11. Assuming your login is successful, Git will continue to push items up; if all is well, you should see something akin to this:

```
Enumerating objects: 131, done.
Counting objects: 100% (131/131), done.
Delta compression using up to 8 threads
Compressing objects: 100% (118/118), done.
Writing objects: 100% (128/128), 429.01 KiB | 5.72
MiB/s, done.
Total 128 (delta 26), reused 0 (delta 0), pack-reused 0
remote: Resolving deltas: 100% (26/26), done.
To https://github.com/alexlibby/cobalt.git
   be80a29..4d38b60  main -> main
```

12. Switch to your GitHub repository and check the Code tab to confirm that all files are present and correct, as shown in the extract in Figure 11-4.

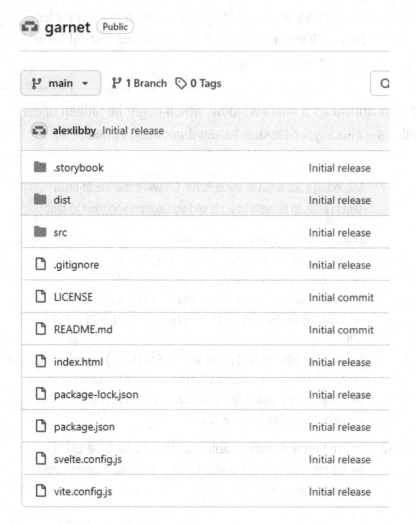

Figure 11-4. *Files uploaded to Git*

Phew – we covered a fair few steps over the last few pages! However, we have now gotten all of our content into GitHub, ready for release. It took some work, but we only need to do some of the steps as a one-off, so we won't have to do it too often.

With the content available on GitHub, we can now take a breather – the code is ready to release as component packages on npm or bundling into compiled files we can download and use in demos and projects. Before we explore that, let's take a few moments to explore what we covered in that last demo in more detail.

Exploring the Code in Detail

So, what did we achieve in that monster two-part demo?

We began this exercise with a small but essential step: rename the cobalt folder. It was necessary to allow us to clone the remote Git folder to our PC without Git complaining of a folder already present. In hindsight, though, we could have avoided the need for this, as we could have done the Git cloning step first; renaming it now means we have a backup copy just in case anything goes wrong!

Moving on, we installed Git (at least for those who didn't have it present already) before cloning the empty garnet repository down to our PC. We then copied files from our original project area to the new one before creating a commit for our new repository. At the same time, we also updated the `.gitignore` exclusion file in the new area – a few files had crept into the existing project area, which we don't need to upload; this was as good an opportunity to use the exclusion file to control what we subsequently commit to GitHub.

To push the files up, we had to set up a PAT or Personal Access Token; once done, we completed the upload before checking to see if they had successfully been committed to the repository.

Okay – let's crack on: we now have our component code in the repository, so we can release it for others to use! Other developers can access the code directly, but what about publishing a component or two to npm?

Releasing Components to npm

Yikes – releasing a component…will it work?

It's a perfectly valid question, and I'm sure you will feel a sense of trepidation as we take that leap into the unknown! But don't worry, though – while there may be a few steps involved in releasing our components, it is a straightforward process, and we will only need to do some of it for the first time. To understand what I mean, let's quickly summarize the steps involved:

- Update our component folder into a monorepo or a subrepository, ready for publishing.

- Set up a configuration file to tell Svelte how to release a compiled version of our component.

- Publish the component onto npm, ready for use.

The first two steps only need to be done once for each component – step three is the one we will repeat each time we publish a new version of our component(s) or library. Perfect – now we know what is involved, so let's get stuck! Before we get to writing code, there are a few points of housekeeping we need to be aware of:

- Please make sure you log in to `https://www.npmjs.org` with your account (including two-factor authentication, if enabled) before you start this exercise.

If you don't have an account, you will need to create one, which you can do at `https://www.npmjs.com/signup` – there is plenty of documentation online if you need assistance.

- We should complete the upload to npm after uploading to GitHub and not before – the upload process relies on GitHub.

- We will use the Checkbox component as our example – please feel free to adapt if you want to try a different component.

- Please create a new folder called dist at the root of the Checkbox component folder. We will use this to store a compiled version of the component.

We need to be mindful of another point before we get a little trigger-happy and create packages. We must remember that what we're building is still a pre-production version, and we will need to do more work before releasing a production version.

For this reason, I've marked the version in the upcoming exercise as alpha1, and it's still important to be aware of the release steps and ready for when we're ready to release it into production. With all that in mind, let's crack on creating our package to upload to npm.

RELEASING TO NPM

Before starting this exercise, there are a couple of tasks we need to perform:

- I strongly recommend logging in to npmjs.com with your chosen account – particularly if you have multiple accounts! The npm publish command will publish to whichever account is currently logged in – to log in, use npm login and follow the prompts.

- We will use some filenames that may not make sense immediately, but there is a reason for doing so. I will come back to why when we go through the changes after the demo. For now, please use the filenames given, but I recommend reading the review at the end to understand the reasons behind using the filenames and what we can do going forward.

Assuming you've completed these two steps, let's make a start – to release a component from our library to npm, follow these steps:

1. First, we need to turn our chosen component into a "monorepo"; for this, fire up a Node.js terminal session, then change the prompt to the Checkbox component folder within our project area.

2. At the prompt, enter this command and press Enter:

```
npm init --y
```

Leave the session open but minimized throughout this exercise – we will use it a few times.

---

3. It creates a `package.json` file with a few fields prepopulated – go ahead and open it, then modify it so it has these fields:

Note   Change XXXXX to your npm account name, where shown.

```
{
    "name": "@XXXXX/checkbox",
    "version": "1.0.0-alpha1",
    "description": "A simple checkbox component from the
    Garnet library, for Svelte",
```

```
    "main": "index.js",
    "scripts": {
      "test": "echo \"Error: no test specified\" && exit 1"
    },
    "repository": {
      "type": "git",
      "url": "git+https://github.com/XXXXX/garnet.git"
    },
    "keywords": [
      "svelte",
      "react",
      "custom elements",
      "web components"
    ],
    "author": "Alex Libby",
    "license": "MIT"
}
```

4. Next, switch to your editor, then create a new file and add
    this code:

```
import { defineConfig } from "vite";
import { svelte } from "@sveltejs/vite-plugin-svelte";

// https://vitejs.dev/config/
export default defineConfig({
  build: {
    rollupOptions: {
      input: ["./src/lib/components/Checkbox/Checkbox.
      svelte"],
    },
    lib: {
      entry: "/dist/assets/Checkbox-CWDZuXaz.js",
      fileName: "Checkbox-CWDZuXaz",
      formats: ["es", "cjs"],
```

```
          },
        },
        plugins: [
          svelte({
            compilerOptions: {
              customElement: true,
            },
          }),
        ],
    });
```

5. Save the file as `vite.checkbox.config.mjs`, at the root of our project area.

6. Revert to your Node.js terminal session, then from the root of the project area, run this command:

    ```
    npm run build -- -c=vite.checkbox.config.js
    ```

7. In the Checkbox folder, create a folder called `dist`. Inside the `\dist` folder at the top level, you will see two files, which start with the name Checkbox but have different file extensions. Copy both from this folder to the new folder inside the Checkbox folder.

8. Edit the entry in package.json for `main:` with this entry:

    ```
    "main": "./dist/Checkbox-CWDZuXaz.js",
    ```

9. We're almost there – just a few steps to go! The next task is to publish the component. Revert to your Node.js terminal session and set the working folder to the root of the Checkbox folder in your project area.

10. At the prompt, enter this command and press Enter:

    ```
    npm publish -access=public
    ```

Depending on how you are set up, you might get a prompt to authenticate yourself in your browser – please follow prompts as appropriate.

11. You should see something similar to this response appear, allowing, of course, for the change in account ID:

```
npm notice
npm notice 📦 @alexlibby/garnet-checkbox@1.0.0-alpha1
npm notice === Tarball Contents ===
npm notice 289B   __tests__/__snapshots__/Checkbox.
spec.js.snap
npm notice 1.9kB  __tests__/Checkbox.spec.js
npm notice 1.1kB  Checkbox.stories.js
npm notice 1.6kB  Checkbox.svelte
npm notice === Tarball Details ===
npm notice name:          @alexlibby/garnet-checkbox
npm notice version:       1.0.0-alpha1
npm notice filename:      alexlibby-garnet-
checkbox-1.0.0-alpha1.tgz
npm notice package size:  10.3 kB
npm notice unpacked size: 31.0 kB
npm notice shasum:    a259677968a6cd48d99baff4160f557
64b79fd05
npm notice integrity:  sha512-6fcQZBTFwWdMN[...
]yLJ7okL/UDDCQ==
npm notice total files:   9
npm notice
npm notice Publishing to https://registry.npmjs.org/ with
tag latest and public access
+ @alexlibby/garnet-checkbox@1.0.0-alpha1
```

12. At this point, the component is published! To check this is the
    case, navigate to `https://www.npmjs.org`, then search for
    `@XXXXX/garnet-checkbox`, where XXXXX is your account
    ID. If all is well, we should see something similar to that shown
    in Figure 11-5.

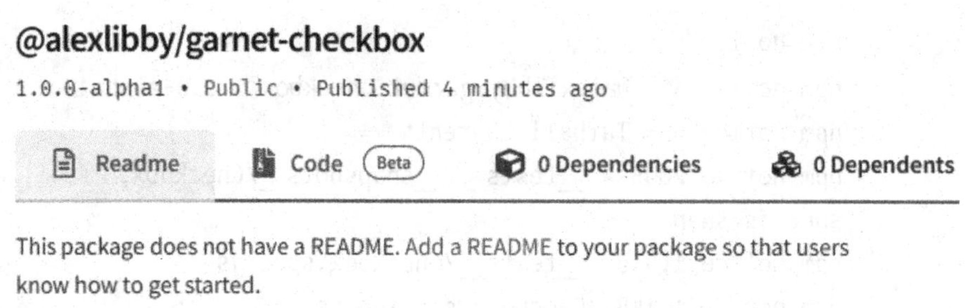

@alexlibby/garnet-checkbox

1.0.0-alpha1 • Public • Published 4 minutes ago

| 📄 Readme | 📄 Code (Beta) | 📦 0 Dependencies | 🔗 0 Dependents |

This package does not have a README. Add a README to your package so that users
know how to get started.

*Figure 11-5. Confirmation that our initial package has been
published*

Alternatively, you can find the package listed on this page: `https://
www.npmjs.com/settings/XXXXX/packages`, where XXXXX is
your account ID.

13. You will also receive a confirmation email if you have entered a
    valid email address!

Brilliant – we have published our first component! Granted, it's only an
alpha version, and we can still do more to develop and improve on it, but
it's a good step in the right direction.

Building a Demo

Of course, though, there is one thing we should do: How about testing to see if it works? We know it's now available on npm, but (as they say) the proof is in the pudding – we should test it in a demo.

This testing is easy enough, so let's dive in and look at what we need to do in more detail.

```
TESTING THE NEW COMPONENT
```

Testing our component is a quick job – to see how to follow these steps:

1. First, navigate to `https://www.codesandbox.io`, then create a new React site using their template.

2. Next, click inside the Add Dependency box on the left, and start typing the name of your component – in my case, `@alexlibby/garnet-checkbox`, but yours will be whatever name you decide to use.

3. You should see the component's name appear in a list after just a few characters – when you do, click it, then click DEV to the right, to add it as a dependency.

4. CodeSandbox will install it automatically – this will take a moment or two, so be patient!

5. Once done, click the `App.js` entry in the file list at the top of the page – add a reference to the Checkbox component as highlighted after the import for `styles.css`:

   ```
   import "@alexlibby/garnet-checkbox/dist/Checkbox-
   CWDZuXaz.js";
   ```

6. Next, add an instance of our new Checkbox component, as shown:

```
<main>
  <h1>Hello CodeSandbox</h1>
  <h2>Start editing to see some magic happen!</h2>
  <garnet-checkbox checked={true} label="This is a
  test"></garnet-checkbox>
</main>
```

7. Wait a few moments for CodeSandbox to save the change – if all is well, we should see something akin to that shown in Figure 11-6.

Figure 11-6. *The newly published component available from npm*

Yes – we have finally arrived! In the hope that this wasn't too premature, we now have a working component and have proven it works in a demo.

What is interesting to note is the use of this component's web component reference. We're not using it as <Checkbox /> (which we would in a Svelte environment), but by using <garnet-checkbox> </garnet-checkbox>. You will also notice that I've used the full name, not the shorthand; I've noticed instances where the latter doesn't work well. It is why you will see me using the longhand version when referencing components in a web component capacity.

Okay – let's move on: we covered a lot of practical steps in the previous demo, so now's a perfect opportunity to review the changes in more detail, understand how they all work, and what we need to do when releasing further changes.

Breaking Apart the Code Changes

Our last demo was a complex affair – who would have known that publishing to npm could require so many steps? In reality, many of these steps will be a one-off – if not for the repo, at least for each component package we create and publish to npm.

The key to making this process work is compiling it into a file that other developers can use. To understand what I mean, let's take a look at the changes we made.

We began by converting the Checkbox folder into a monorepo – for the uninitiated, this is effectively a repository within a larger parent. To do this, we created a `package.json`, to which we added a host of fields required for publishing the component as a package.

Next came the addition of the `vite.checkbox.config.mjs` file – this tells Svelte how to compile the component into a format we can pull into future projects. A key point here is that we created this file purely around the Checkbox component and as an ES Module. We could have included other components, too – we need to add their names and sources to a comma-delimited list in the `input:` field. The ES Module format is required to ensure that Vite bundles the files in the correct format for use in other frameworks.

We then ran the build process, which resulted in a compiled file – this we copied from the `\dist` folder into a new `\dist` folder, ready for packaging. At this point, we ran the `npm publish` command, which created a package for us on npm. To finish this part of the process, we ran a quick check to confirm that our package had been published successfully on npm and that we got a confirmation email to boot!

By comparison, the second part of this process was a far more straightforward affair – we used CodeSandbox to create a basic React site using their template. To this, we added the newly published component. Once CodeSandbox saved the update, we saw the component appear in the preview window in our browser.

Now that we've published our component on npm, there are a couple of interesting points of note that we should be aware of:

- You will notice that when we check that the component exists in npm, we only see limited information if we click through to the package's page. The package's README file provides all of this if one is available; I've gone ahead and pushed one up on my version of the Checkbox component in the library at `https://github.com/alexlibby/garnet/tree/main/src/lib/components/Checkbox`.

- We have had to use the format @XXXXX/YYYYYY to publish the package, where X is your account name and Y is the package. This naming is known as a **scoped package** – there used to be a time when we didn't have to provide the name. Since GitHub took over npm, GitHub is now enforcing the use of scoped names – in the background, we are publishing to GitHub Packages, not npm. It means that we also had to provide the `–access=public` tag. Otherwise, the component won't publish on what is a free repository.

- An essential part of the publishing process is managing the version number. I've started with 1.0.0-alpha1 to clarify that this is a pre-production version and that we should assume the usual caveats around using it. I recommend researching how to automate this manual process to apply the correct version number for each release automatically. An excellent example is the semantic-release package available on npm at `https://www.npmjs.com/package/semantic-release`.

- As a small change, you may want to add an exclusion to `.gitignore`, for the `/dist` folders – while these are needed, it's unnecessary to upload those folders as they stand, as content will be pushed up in the package anyway.

- Do you remember how I said we'd use filenames that may not initially make sense? I used the filename generated when testing the code for this book – Vite automatically adds a series of random letters to the file package during the bundling process. This name needs to be added to the local `package.json` in the component folder (Checkbox) for it to publish correctly – while this works OK for now, it would be worth trying out a few changes to see what names you can use that make more sense!

- While researching this book, I noticed a few times when newly created packages were not initially available in CodeSandbox. You may have to wait a while before they appear, so don't be alarmed if they are not present immediately. I waited overnight, which I think was more than long enough – you may not have to wait as long before the new package is listed.

Okay – what's next? Now that we have our component on GitHub, it's time to make our component documentation available for others to view online. The easiest way to do this is by publishing a static version of our Storybook instance; let's dive in and look at how we can do this as part of our next demo.

Publishing Storybook to Netlify

Wow – I'm sure you'll agree when I say that the last few pages were a little intense! Nevertheless, the steps we covered were critical to getting our first component out; we still have work to do in this respect, but that will come with time.

In the meantime, we should move on to the next important step: making our documentation available for others. We could do this in several ways, such as hosting on AWS, Vercel, Surge, or Now – I've chosen to use Netlify as I'm a big fan of this tool and have used it in the past.

Getting our content published is straightforward – Netlify links into GitHub seamlessly, so we need to complete a few steps, and our content will appear online. Let's take a look at what is involved in more detail.

PUBLISHING THE COMPONENT STORYBOOK

To publish our instance of Storybook, follow these steps:

1. We first need to export Storybook as a static application. To do this, fire up a Node.js terminal, then change the working folder to our project area.

2. At the prompt, enter npm run build-storybook and press Enter.

3. It may or may not show warnings, but we can deal with any later. The critical point is that it must not show any errors, indicating a failed build.

4. Let it churn through the process – it will finish with lines similar to this:

```
info => Manager built (1.03 min)
info => Output directory: C:\garnet\storybook-static
```

5. Node will have created a few files and folders – we need to push these up to GitHub. At the prompt, enter these commands and press Enter after each:

```
git add .
git commit -m "Add exported version of Storybook"
git push
```

Assuming no errors appeared, we have our files ready for the next part of the process: publishing the content for other developers to view and use.

At this stage, we have our Storybook exported content ready for publication – people won't see it until we hook it into our hosting. As you have already noted, I've elected to use Netlify; feel free to use a different system if you prefer. I recommend selecting one that hooks into GitHub to get the best from the next exercise.

Setting Up Netlify

Although Netlify has only been around since 2014, it has quickly become one of the most popular ways to host content. It's perfect for hosting our JAMStack-based site – all the content is already on GitHub, so we need to link it to a Netlify account and let it publish the site onto the Internet. Let's take a look at what we need to do in more detail.

If you see a reference to XXXXX in the following demo, change it to your GitHub account name.

SETTING UP NETLIFY

To set up our site, follow these steps:

1. We first need to sign up – for this, browse to `https://app.netlify.com/signup`, follow the prompts, and then, when directed, hit GitHub.

2. When prompted, click Yes to authorize Netlify to access your GitHub account.

3. Next, click Add new site, then Import an existing project.

4. At this point, select GitHub, then Authorize Netlify.

5. When prompted, enter garnet – it won't find it: don't worry, this is to be expected! It will prompt to configure Netlify so that we can give Netlify the permissions it needs to access your GitHub site.

6. Click Configure Netlify on GitHub. Scroll down on the next window to Repository Access, then choose Only select repositories ➤ Select repositories ➤ XXXXX\garnet. If all is well, you should have settings similar to those shown in Figure 11-7.

◉ **Only select repositories**
Select at least one repository.
Also includes public repositories (read-only).

[🖳 **Select repositories** ▾]

Selected 3 repositories.

🖳 alexlibby/**test-payment-api-gatsby**	✕
🖳 alexlibby/**cobalt**	✕
🖳 alexlibby/**garnet**	✕

Figure 11-7. *The settings for updating permissions for Netlify*

7. Once done, hit Save. On the previous screen, click XXXXX\
garnet, then in the Basic build settings, enter these values –
any other fields should remain unchanged (Figure 11-8).

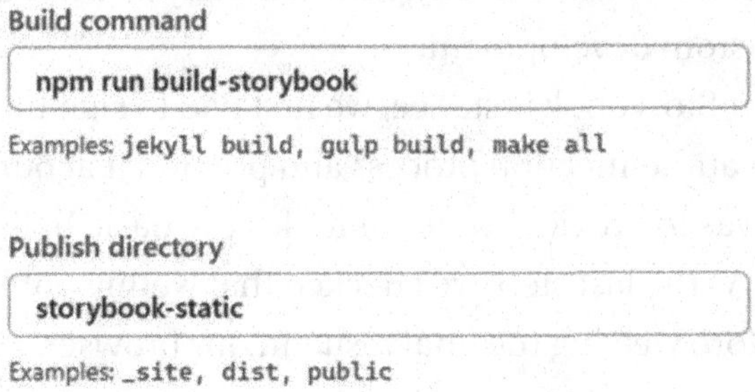

Build command

[**npm run build-storybook**]

Examples: `jekyll build, gulp build, make all`

Publish directory

[**storybook-static**]

Examples: `_site, dist, public`

Figure 11-8. *Settings to trigger the build process*

8. Once you've entered the values, click "Deploy…." If everything
goes well, you should be able to deploy and follow along with
the build log – click the Site Overview link at the top of the
page, then on the text "Site deploy in progress."

9. Assuming no errors appear, you will see a Published in green
    text in the box marked Production deploys on the Overview
    page. You will be able to see your site if you click the name of
    your site at the top of the page.

Yay – we have published our site! Publishing is only the start, as we will
need to update it as and when we make changes to our components. That
comes later, though; for now, let's review the code changes we made in
more detail to understand better how this fits into the broader picture.

Understanding the Changes Made

When releasing code onto a hosting site, dozens of different providers are
available – sometimes, it can be hard to decide which to use! Of course,
you might already use an existing system, which makes choosing one a
moot choice...

But I digress. I chose to use Netlify as it is one of the more popular
hosting systems: it also links to GitHub seamlessly and has an excellent
API for more custom development.

To set up our Storybook instance, we first had to sign up – for this, we
used its GitHub authentication process and pointed it at our repository. All
that remained was to provide some values for the basic build process and
hit Deploy site! As the last step, we checked that Netlify published the site
successfully before viewing the final result in our browser.

Adding Polish to the Repository

Now that we've set up our Storybook installation, pushed our code up into
GitHub, and released (albeit an experimental) version of our component,
it's time to start adding polish to our library so that it looks the best it can
be for people using our library.

We could do different things, such as adding more screenshots, better documentation, or creating templates for raising issues. Unfortunately, there's too much for us to do in the confines of this book, so I'm going to focus on two items:

- Adding a README for the Checkbox component file
- Installing a custom domain name for the Storybook installation

There are a few steps required for us to complete both tasks, which we will do over two separate exercises; let's dive in and look at the first, which will be adding a custom domain name.

Adding a Custom Domain Name

Before you all start worrying, I should point out from the outset that adding a custom domain name is not an essential part of running our site – the Storybook installation will run perfectly fine with the subdomain URL given to us by Netlify!

For me, though, adding a custom domain name makes it easier to access the site, as it is easier to remember; depending on what name you use, the cost isn't too expensive either! There are various ways to do this, depending on whether you want to use a custom subdomain or a top-level domain from Netlify or provide your own.

For simplicity, I will assume that if you do this step, we will register that name directly through Netlify so that it can take care of provisioning the domain for us. Before we start with the purchase and configuration process, there are a couple of assumptions we should be aware of:

- I'm assuming that the domain name you select is not already registered to anyone.
- We're purchasing directly from Netlify, so Netlify will hold the DNS and domain.

If either of the above is different for you, you will need to follow other steps, such as making sure your host points the DNS entries to Netlify.

Let's begin setting up our custom domain as part of the next exercise.

ADDING A CUSTOM DOMAIN

To add a custom domain, follow these steps:

1. From the site overview page, click Domain management.

2. Click Add a domain.

3. Go ahead and enter your chosen domain using the format shown in the text box, then hit Verify to confirm availability.

4. Click Add payment method, then enter your payment details in the modal. Note that this will auto-renew at a slightly higher price in year two; this is to be expected.

5. Enter your address, then hit Save. Back on the previous screen, hit Register domain now for…, and wait for it to complete.

    At this point, Netlify will likely state that an SSL/TLS certificate can't be provisioned to secure the site until the domain is validated. If you scroll up the page, you will see the primary DNS entry has changed and that it shows "Check DNS configuration" against it.

This process requires 24 hours for the newly created domain to propagate, so you will want to return later to complete the next part of this process.

Assuming you have waited 24 hours, follow these steps to complete the process:

6. Hit Verify DNS configuration. Assuming it returns "DNS verification was successful," click Provision certificate twice.

7. Netlify will trigger a request to Let's Encrypt to provision the certificates. You may get a "missing certificate error" – if you do, cancel and return to the previous Settings page.

8. Keep refreshing the page – if Netlify has managed to provision the certificate, you will eventually see the "Check DNS configuration" entry replaced with something similar to Figure 11-9.

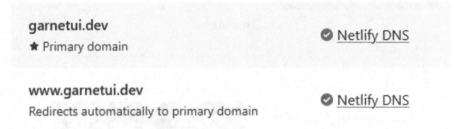

Figure 11-9. *Confirmation that DNS has been updated*

9. Take a quick look down on that page – you should also see that the SSL certificate has been successfully provisioned.

Please note this period can take up to 24 hours to complete; I was able to view these details after about 5–6 hours, but it may be longer for you.

10. The real test is to browse to the site – go ahead and browse to your new domain (in my case, `https://www.garnetui.dev`). If all is well, we should see our Storybook appear, as shown in Figure 11-10.

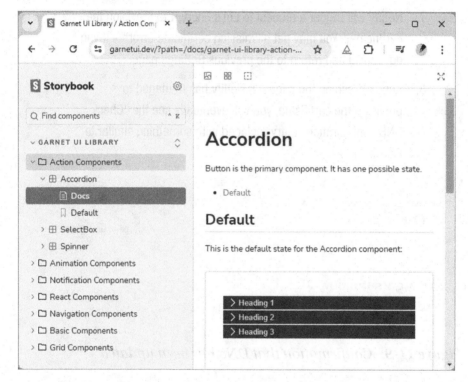

Figure 11-10. *The Storybook installation, under the new domain*

Perfect – we have a domain name that points to a working site! Although we could have stayed with the default name assigned by Netlify, I'm sure you will agree this one is a much nicer name to use.

Let's move on, and look at the second exercise we'll complete as part of this process – adding a readme file with a version badge.

ADDING A README WITH VERSION BADGE

To update the documentation readme file for our component, follow these steps:

1. We will first begin with adding a version badge for our component – head over to `https://www.shields.io/badges`, then click Version at the bottom of the list.

2. On the next page, you will see a long list of license types – scroll down until you see the entry for NPM Version and click it. It's a long list, so you might want to use the search option in your browser!

3. In the package name field on the right, enter your account ID and the name of your package in the format of @<account name>/<package> (I will assume garnet, but change it if you decide to use something different).

4. If all is well, you should see a black and orange badge with the version number of your package appear. Click the Markdown tab, then copy the contents of the field below the tab.

5. In your editor, open the `README.md` at the root of the project, then edit the file as shown:

```
# Welcome to the Garnet UI Library
```

```
This library accompanies the second edition of my
upcoming book, Creating Web Components with Svelte.
```

```
Components available:
```

```
## Checkbox - ![NPM Version](https://img.shields.io/npm/
v/%40alexlibby%2Fgarnet-checkbox)
```

Package available on NPM: https://www.npmjs.com/package/
@alexlibby/garnet-checkbox

To install, run this command: `npm install @alexlibby/
checkbox`

License: MIT

Please change the account and/or package names to match your version. Feel free to adapt the contents of the text to match your requirements – the key takeaway is the use of the Shield badge.

---

6. Save the file – we can always come back and add more later,
    but this will be enough to get us started.

7. We need to push this change up – fire up a Node.js terminal
    prompt, then change the working folder to the project area.

8. At the prompt, enter git add . && git commit -m "Add
    README", then press Enter.

9. Once done, enter git push to complete the upload.

10. To confirm all is well, browse to your GitHub site – you should
    see our updated README.md file, similar to that shown in
    Figure 11-11.

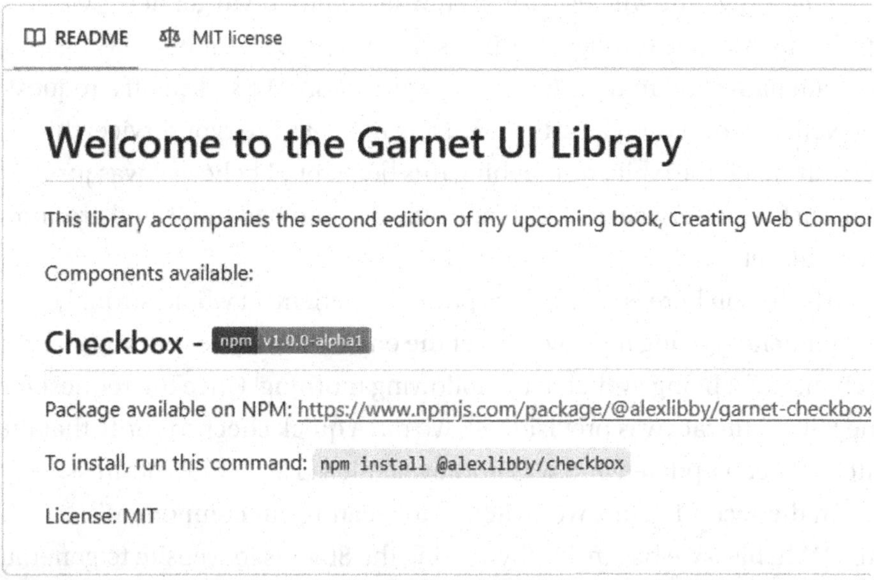

Figure 11-11. *The updated README for the Checkbox component*

Wow – we now have a working GitHub repository, a Storybook site, and we released the first version of our component to our unsuspecting audience! Congratulations if you managed to get this far; it's been a lot of work, but hopefully an enjoyable and worthwhile experience.

However, it is just the start of our journey: there is more we can do! We'll touch on some of this in the next chapter, but before we do so, let's take a moment to review the changes we made in this demo to understand how they all hang together.

Breaking Apart the Code

Adding a custom domain is one way to add that extra touch – I know many people might be happy with the default URL provided by services such as Netlify. Don't get me wrong – this is a perfectly valid option. However, going that extra distance means your library should make it more memorable and encourage people to return.

That, only time will tell – for now, what did we do to get here? We started by working through Netlify's standard process for purchasing a domain name and initiating domain registration. We kicked off a request for Netlify to provision a certificate using the Let's Encrypt service; this initially failed me while researching this book, but I believe it was just waiting for the service to kick in once the domain had replicated around the Internet.

The lesson here is that it does pay to be patient – I would strongly recommend making the payment at the end of the day so that you stand a chance of it being available the following morning! Once the request for the SSL certificate was provisioned, we ran a quick check to verify that the site had been updated and was now available via an HTTPS address.

In the second demo, we switched to creating our component's README file – we began first by visiting the Shields.io website to generate a badge with the appropriate version of the current package available on npm. We took a copy of the link for this badge as markdown text before adding it to a new README file; once saved, we committed this to the repository before checking the results in our browser.

Summary

Phew – this might have been a long chapter, but we've finally reached the point where our Storybook site and the component library will now be live! We've covered a lot of content in this chapter, so let's relax for a moment and review what we have learned.

We began way back when (yes, it does feel like a while ago!) with a quick discussion around performing the final checks. Not only did we cover some areas to consider, but we also understood that this is a symbolic way of confirming that we are ready to sign off the results and release them into production.

Next up, we moved on to pushing our code into GitHub; we first walked through setting up the repository before exploring the steps required to commit our code into our new library. We then switched to releasing a test component into the npm repository as a package – we covered that this was an alpha package and a way to explore the process; we would do this for real once we were ready to release our code.

Moving on, we worked our way through publishing the Storybook instance to a hosting site, using Netlify as our preferred platform. We first set up the authorization between GitHub and Netlify before configuring Netlify to run the build step for Storybook and create our site. As a final touch, we explored creating a new README file with a version badge and the steps we would need to take to release our site through a custom domain for our customers.

And relax! We've done most of the hard work now – the library is available on GitHub, we're hosting our instance of Storybook on Netlify, and we released our component's first instance as a package. There is still more to do, but the focus of our journey changes – it's time now to focus on how we can develop and expand our library. There's plenty we can do in this respect, so stay with me, and I'll reveal more details in the next chapter.

CHAPTER 12

Taking Things Further

Now that we've almost reached the end of the book, there is one more question we should answer: What next?

At times like this, I am reminded of the phrase, "The world is our oyster." It is up to us to decide where to go next…as well as maybe have a little fun too! To answer that question, we'll explore a range of topics, which might include

- With the library now up and running, is there anything we want to change or improve?
- What's next – how about setting a road map?
- Convert components from other frameworks.
- Revisit some of what we've already done.
- Can we optimize specific areas, such as CSS?
- Should we add themes at a component level or the target site?

These are just some of the questions we should answer – I'm sure I can think of more! To get us started, let's first review what we've done so far to see where we might have any gaps we need to fill.

© Alex Libby 2025
A. Libby, *Developing Web Components with Svelte*,
https://doi.org/10.1007/979-8-8688-1180-7_12

Reviewing the Site

Although we completed some of these tasks during the release process, I can almost guarantee that there will be things we want to add or change.

I'm not talking about adding new components, although that will come. We must also consider areas such as tidying existing code, leveling the number of variants for each component, or improving test coverage. With that in mind, let's take a quick look at a few likely candidates for improvement in the immediate future:

- Improve test coverage

- Implement a dependency update mechanism to keep the site secure and free from code vulnerabilities (where possible)

- Add more detailed documentation

- Expand the variants for each component, and level up to a minimum of three where possible

- Augment the CSS Grid properties for ImageGrid and make the filenames for this component more consistent

- Release more component packages – individually and as a whole

- Realign components into a named group for npm – not under my name, but a collective name of garnetui (or similar, depending on availability)

- Implement better chunking of Storybook to improve its speed

- Consider upgrading to Svelte 5 when available

- Use of props – should we consider using $$restprops, even though it's not really recommended, or should we be specific about what we expose?

That's just a tiny selection of what we could do to improve the codebase within the first three months of release – I'm sure there will be others! I prefer not to commit to many changes too early and to focus on our gaps before expanding with new components. (As you will see, I will break that "preference," but hey – rules are meant to be broken!) The critical point here is that we take note of what we need to do and create a plan for implementing the changes.

You can see a more extensive road map in the GitHub repository, in `roadmap.md`, at the root of the library.

The plan doesn't need to be complex – we could list everything we want to do, then put rough dates against each one (ideally quarters rather than months – it helps give yourself some flexibility). Remember that you must keep your promises in some form or another!

Setting a Road Map

Ouch – where does one start with setting a road map? The truth is that it will depend on one of two things:

- Where do you want to take the library?

- What features are others asking for?

Deciding on what to add can be a double-edged sword – there could be some no-brainer features that you have to incorporate, or you might find you want to add something that others will hate!

In some cases, others will make the decision easy – you might want to add components that your colleagues could use in a corporate environment and that releasing to the outside world will be a bonus. However, we need to balance this against those instances where you are in control of what you add – we have to prepare for those who dislike what you might have in mind. Still, as long as you are transparent about it and go with the majority decision, you will at least maintain a good audience.

Keeping all of that in mind, let's pause for a moment to consider some examples of what we might want as future components in our library:

- Avatar

- Cards – such as for product information

- HTML5 form field elements, such as email or telephone

- Popover

- ListBox

I'm sure there will be more, but as mentioned before, let's not get too ahead of ourselves! Most of our focus should be on leveling up existing components and strengthening what we've developed in our library – at least in the immediate future!

Converting Our Next Component

Okay – enough talking: we need to get stuck into some coding.

For the first demo of this chapter, we will look at our next component: Avatar. Usually, I would work through creating one, adding it to Storybook, and so on...you know the drill by now!

However, that would mean missing out on a helpful tip when creating Svelte components. If you're converting from an existing feature found on the Internet to Svelte, then forget the lift and shift approach. What do I mean by this, I hear you ask?

Well, it comes down to one simple principle: instead of focusing on the technical elements, look at the functionality offered by the component. Svelte requires a different mindset, which can be weird for developers using other frameworks. You can lift and shift values such as imports (if appropriate) or variables already declared in the React code, but that's probably as much as we can use!

To illustrate this, I've picked a React example of what our next component could be – Avatar. The original code is by the CoreUI team and is available at `https://github.com/coreui/coreui-react/blob/main/packages/coreui-react/src/components/avatar/CAvatar.tsx`; it uses standard React/TypeScript to create a simple component. Now, let's dive in and look at how this component might look if we rebuilt it in Svelte.

CREATING THE AVATAR COMPONENT

To create our new Avatar component, follow these steps:

1. First, we need to find a suitable avatar image. For this, look online to see if any image libraries have one that suits your fancy! I recommend keeping the size as close to 128px square as possible for this exercise; the file format isn't critical. Please save the file as `avatar.png`. If you change the file format or name, please adjust the code to suit.

An excellent place to try is the icon collection at `https://www.flaticon.com`, if you don't already have icons available.

2. Once you have a suitable image, drop it into the `\public` folder at the root of the garnet-source folder.

Remember, we're working on the `garnet-source` folder now that we have set up GitHub; we can always use the original garnet area as a test bed if needed!

3. We now need to create a new folder for our component – go ahead and add one called Avatar into the `\src\lib` folder.

4. Next, open your editor and create a new file, saving it as `Avatar.svelte` in the newly created Avatar folder.

5. In the file, we need to add quite a bit of code – as before, we'll do it in sections, starting with the `svelte:options` tag and a handful of export statements:

```
<svelte:options customElement="garnet-avatar" />

<script>
  export let src = "";
  export let status = "available" || "busy" || "away" ||
  "unavailable";
  export let statusSize = "small" || "medium" || "large";
```

6. Next, we need to add a reactive statement block to look after updating values if the size or status should change:

```
  $: statusClasses = () => {
    let inputClasses = [status, statusSize];
    inputClasses = inputClasses.filter((class) =>
    class.length);
    return inputClasses.join(" ");
  };
</script>
```

7. Next is the markup for our component:

```
<div class="cobalt-avatar">
  {#if src}
    <img {src} class="avatar-img" alt="avatar" />
  {/if}
  <slot />
  <span class={["base", statusClasses()].join(" ")} />
</div>
```

8. We can finish off the component with some styling – first, add
   an empty `<style></style>` block:

```
<style>
...
</style>
```

9. Next, go ahead and add the following styles inside that style
   block from the previous step – the first is the container for our
   component and a common style rule for the indicator:

```
.cobalt-avatar {
  position: relative;
  display: inline-flex;
  align-items: center;
  justify-content: center;
  vertical-align: middle;
  border-radius: 800px;
  width: 32px;
  height: 32px;
  font-size: 12.8px;
}
.base {
  border-radius: 800px;
  position: absolute;
  border: 1px solid #373737;
}
```

10. Next up, we have two styles for size – small and medium:

```
.small {
  width: 8px;
  height: 8px;
```

```
      top: 25px;
      right: 0px;
   }

   .medium {
      width: 12px;
      height: 12px;
      top: 22px;
      right: -4px;
   }

   .large {
      width: 16px;
      height: 16px;
      top: 22px;
      right: -4px;
   }
```

11. We also need some styling for availability – for this, we have
     four rules for available, busy, away, and unavailable:

```
.available { background-color: #00ff00; }
.busy { background-color: #ff0000; }
.away { background-color: #ffff00; }
.unavailable { background-color: #ffffff;
border: 1px solid #000000;}
```

12. This last style is for the avatar image:

```
.avatar-img { width: 100%; height: auto;
border-radius: 800px; }
```

13. Save and close the file – we are done with the changes for now,
     and we'll do the first test of our new component shortly when
     we link it into Storybook.

Perfect – we have a component ready to test; we'll do this shortly when we add it to Storybook. Although much of the code should be relatively familiar by now, there are some critical highlights I want to touch on – with that in mind, let's review the changes we made in the last demo in more detail.

Dissecting the Code

In our current age of social media, avatars are probably one of the most widely seen features you will see. It doesn't matter if they show letters or a fancy picture; the basic premise of identifying you as a person is still the same. We've taken the opportunity to create such a component for our library and base it on an original, built using React – let's take a moment to review the changes we made in more detail.

We began by looking for a suitable image online. We understood it needed to be around 128 pixels square where possible to ensure it works as expected in our component. Next, we created the component itself – we began setting the now-familiar `svelte:options` tag before creating three variables for export: `status`, `src`, and `statusSize`.

We then moved on to creating a reactive block, which uses the $ keyword in Svelte – as a reminder, this reacts (hence the name) to any changes in the current state or value in variables and updates them accordingly. In this instance, we're using it to update changes to the status symbol based on the availability of the person using it.

Next, we added the markup for our demo – this we kept simple for now, using a standard if block (`{#if}...{/if}`). Svelte uses this `{#if}...{/if}` to determine if we should display an image. Everything else will go in the `<slot />`, including text, markup, or other components we might use. We then finished this off with styling – we created .cobalt-avatar for the container, three styles to cover the size of the status indicator in our component, and status to cover most of the presence statuses we might want to use as developers.

371

There is one last point I want to cover from this component before we move on: the translation process from React to Svelte. While researching for this book, I found a great article on using Svelte for those who usually develop using React. It's by Sina Farhadi and available on the Plain English website at `https://javascript.plainenglish.io/svelte-for-react-developers-7edc099e03ed`. Suffice it to say, Svelte requires a different mindset to React, which can be a challenge for some; if you get it (so to speak), it often means resulting code that is cleaner and frequently faster to boot!

Adding to Storybook

So far, we've explored how to create an equivalent Avatar component in Svelte and seen that it's not just a lift and shift of existing code but that it's better to focus on functionality rather than technical code.

We now need to test our component – as we've done previously, there are two ways we can test it: writing a test case for it using Vitest and adding it to Storybook.

LINKING AVATAR INTO STORYBOOK AND ADDING A TEST

To set up our Avatar component in Storybook, follow these steps:

1. First, fire up your editor, then create a new file, saving it as `Avatar.stories.mdx` in the `\src\lib\storybook` folder.

2. We have a lot of code to add, so as usual, we'll break it into sections – we'll start with the imports and a const for Badges, similar to what we've done earlier in the book:

```
import Avatar from "../Avatar/Avatar.svelte";
import { BADGE } from "storybook-addon-badges";
```

```
const BADGES = {
  ...BADGE,
  ALPHA: "Alpha",
};
```

3. To display the component, we need a template to tell Storybook how to display it; for this, miss a line after the code from step 2 and add this block:

```
export default {
  title: "Garnet UI Library/React Components/Avatar",
  component: Avatar,
  props: {
    status: "available",
    src: "/avatar.png",
  },
};
```

4. With the template in place, we can add stories for each variant of the Avatar component we want to display. The first one is the Default, which displays a green status to show that the person is available:

```
export const Default = () => ({
  Component: Avatar,
  props: {
    statusSize: "small",
    src: "/avatar.png",
  },
});
Default.parameters = {
  badges: [BADGES.ALPHA],
};
```

5. Next, miss a line, then add this next story – this takes care of cases where the person is busy and displays a red status:

```
export const Busy = () => ({
  Component: Avatar,
  props: {
    status: "busy",
    src: "/avatar.png",
  },
});
Busy.parameters = {
  badges: [BADGES.ALPHA],
};
```

6. For this next story, we'll display the Away status, which shows a yellow circle, but this time in a larger size:

```
export const Away = () => ({
  Component: Avatar,
  props: {
    status: "away",
    statusSize: "large",
    src: "/avatar.png",
  },
});
Away.parameters = {
  badges: [BADGES.ALPHA],
};
```

7. For the last example, we'll display the Unavailable symbol in a medium size – this is a white status:

```
export const Unavailable = () => ({
  Component: Avatar,
  props: {
```

```
    status: "unavailable",
    statusSize: "medium",
    src: "/avatar.png",
  },
});
Unavailable.parameters - {
  badges: [BADGES.ALPHA],
};
```

You will notice that I've also included a parameters object to set the badge status to Alpha, similar to other components in this book.

---

8. Save and close the file.

9. We also need a copy of the Docs.mdx file as our documentation – this is available in the code download for this book, so extract a copy and put it into the root of the Avatar folder.

At this point, we should have a handful of files to push up to our repo – to get them committed, follow these steps:

10. Next, switch to a Node.js terminal session and change the working folder to our project area.

11. We need to push up all of the changes we've made so far. At the prompt, enter git add . and press Enter to pull all of our files together, and we're ready for committal.

12. Next, enter git commit -m "Add storybook support for Avatar component" to create a commit and press Enter.

13. Finally, enter `git push` to upload all of the changes to our repo – assuming you set up Netlify earlier, this will kick in and build the library.

14. If all is well, we should see updates appear on our Storybook pages, as shown in Figure 12-1.

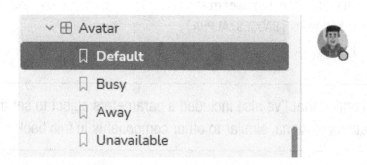

Figure 12-1. *Storybook with the updated Avatar component on display*

We have one last step to perform, which is to add some tests – as this is only a status icon, we'll keep it simple and set it to run a snapshot for now. To do this, follow these steps:

1. Crack open a new file, saving it as `Avatar.spec.js`, in the `__tests__` folder at the root of the `Avatar` folder.

2. Go ahead and add the following code into the file – we'll begin with the imports:

```
import { describe, test, expect } from "vitest";
import { axe } from "vitest-axe";
import * as AxeMatchers from "vitest-axe/matchers";
import { render, screen, fireEvent } from "@testing-
library/svelte";
import Avatar from "../../Avatar/Avatar.svelte";
```

```
const AvatarHTML = `<div class="garnet-avatar s-
q7VgqBOCP_sX"><img src="/avatar.png" class="avatar-
img s-q7VgqBOCP_sX" alt="avatar">  <span class="base
available small s-q7VgqBOCP_sX"></span></div>`;
expect.extend(AxeMatchers);
```

The code for this file is in the download, so don't worry – you don't have to enter all of it by hand manually!

3. Next up, let's add the opening part of the test – this contains a props declaration for our component:

```
describe("Tests for Avatar", () => {
  const mockText = "This is a Avatar";

  const props = {
    status: "available",
    src: "/avatar.png",
    statusSize: "small",
  };
```

4. We should test it renders correctly – for that, miss a line, then add this assertion:

```
test("should render properly", () => {
  const result = render(Avatar, { props });
  expect(() => result).not.toThrow();
});
```

5. Next, we're going to add a test to make sure that it shows the
    right CSS property when displaying a busy status:

```
test("show show a label with a red busy
status", () => {
  const result = render(Avatar, { ...props, status:
  "busy" });

  const element = document.querySelector("span");
  // element has a class
  expect(element.classList).toContain("busy");
});
```

6. This next test is a snapshot, which we can use for visual testing
    and to see where any differences may come from:

```
test("get a snapshot of component", () => {
  // Create a new container for the test and mount
    component
  const host = document.createElement("div");
  document.body.appendChild(host);
  const instance = new Avatar({ target: host, props:
  props });

  // check that all rendered OK
  expect(instance).toBeTruthy();

  // Take snapshot
  expect(host.innerHTML).toMatchSnapshot();
});
```

7. To close off the test, add this step – it performs a check for
    accessibility:

```
test("should demonstrate no issues with
accessibility", async () => {
```

```
const render = () => AvatarHTML;
const result = render();

const results = await axe(result, {
  rules: {
    region: { enabled: false },
  },
});

  expect(results).toHaveNoViolations();
  });
});
```

8. Last but by no means least, we need to add two more commands to the `package.json` – crack that file open, then add this code immediately before the `test:breadcrumbs` command:

```
"test:avatar": "vitest
--dir=src/lib/components/avatar",
"coverage:avatar": "vitest run --coverage --dir=src/
lib/components/avatar --coverage.all=false",
```

Both lines should be on one line each, not wrapped around in your editor.

9. Save and close the file. Switch to your Node.js terminal session, ensuring the working folder is still set to the project area.

10. At the prompt, enter npm run test and press Enter – if all is well, we should see our tests pass without issue.

11. Next, switch to a Node.js terminal session and change the working folder to our project area.

12. At the prompt, enter `git add .` and press Enter to pull all of our files together, ready for committal.

13. Next, enter `git commit -m "Addition of tests for Avatar component"` to create a commit and press Enter.

14. Finally, enter `git push` to upload all the changes to our repo. Assuming you set up Netlify earlier, this will kick in and rebuild the library with the new changes.

Excellent – assuming all went as planned, we now have a new Avatar component that we've written based on the original created in React and that we've plumbed into our Storybook instance.

By now, most of what you've seen will seem somewhat familiar, particularly as we've created over 15 components for our library! That said, it's still good to review what we've created, so let's pause and dig into the code in more detail.

Understanding the Changes Made

Although the last exercise was quite lengthy, most of it covers steps we've seen before – it may have been for different components, but that doesn't matter: reusing the same principles makes life much easier! So, what did we achieve in this latest addition to our library?

We began by creating a story for our instance of Storybook – we imported a set of functions from Storybook, along with the documentation file and our component. At the same time, we added the now-familiar <Meta> tag tag to tell Storybook where to place the new component in our setup. You will notice that I've used the React Components location; this is purely to keep any new additions separate from the original components, at least for now!

Next, we added various stories to our Story file – all four follow the same format as others. We call the component and pass in different values for the src, status, and statusSize arguments. We then finished the first part of this demo by committing all of the changes thus far into our repository before previewing the changes on the Netlify site.

We're not quite finished yet, though – there is still one more addition: a test! We need to add a test file to our existing collection to show we have at least basic test coverage for this component.

Adding this test was straightforward – we created a test spec file before importing Vitest (as we did for other components) and the Avatar component. We then added the describe block, starting with setting some prop values to pass to our component, before creating the first assertion to test that the component renders without issue.

We then added more assertions to cover a scenario where the avatar shows a busy status, an assertion to get a visual snapshot, and one to check for accessibility; once we saved the test, we ran it to confirm a successful pass before uploading all changes to our GitHub repository. Before we move on, though, I want to call out one small but important point: the location of our Avatar image. You will notice that we put it into the public folder at the top, but there is no reference in the URL path within our component. What gives?

Well, this is down to the power of Svelte – it is clever enough to know that the public folder is really for static images, so we will treat this as if it were the root of any website. It means that even though we used / in the URL path for our avatar image, it translates to the public folder – Svelte links to it during the build process.

If we had used a relative URL to this folder, as one might have expected to do so, then you would get this warning in the console log: ...files in the public directory are served at the root path. Instead of /public/avatar. png, use /avatar.png.

Okay – let's crack on. At the start of this chapter, I mentioned two words, key to where we go from here – they were "what next"? As I am sure you will appreciate, we can go in any direction we want, although much of that will be determined by your project needs!

As part of answering that bigger question at the top of this chapter, I want to explore one topic more and see what we could or should do. We've created a set of valuable components, but what about theming them? Could we add a theme capability – should we?

Adding a Theme Manager

These are all great questions and sensible ones at face value. After all, it would be good to provide components that follow a consistent format regarding properties such as color, padding, or fonts.

However, as you will soon see, there is more to this than it seems. Before we get to that, let's consider some of the questions we could ask to help determine what theme support could look like for our library.

Determining the Approach

Setting the approach is so critical – after all, we're creating components that we can reuse; how should we add a capability to theme them as well? It sounds like a reasonable premise...but as is often the case, there is more to this story than initially seems! The more I dug into this, the more I found something of a sting in this tale – before we get into that, let's have a look at some of the questions we need to ask to create a theme:

- Should it be an existing package or combined with one or more components? We can create one theme component but use Vite's power to bundle it with different components as we see fit.

- Should we design and build our own theme manager (and theme) or attempt to build in support for themes based on packages such as Tailwind?

- Do we only provide our themes, or can we offer the capability to create a custom theme provided by whoever uses our components?

- Do we use CSS and/or JavaScript to handle overriding our styles? What about the styles we have implemented in each component already?

- What colors would we use? Not everyone will want to use our choice of colors...so is it even practical to choose them?

...and it's that last question that got me thinking: Should we even add a theme manager, at least for now? Let's assume that, for the moment, we will start adding something and look at one possible option before we explore why theme support may not be so helpful for our library.

Implementing the Changes

For this next demo, I've simplified code from a Svelte REPL playground demo I found online to remove some toggling functionality so it only renders one theme.

I will treat this demo as a proof of concept, so I will host it in Storybook but in a separate section outside the core library and use a folder structure that differs from the original version. It won't matter, as what we're doing is a proof of concept; if we were to go ahead with this change, we would need to tweak the naming to make it more consistent with our core library components.

The original code for this demo can be found at `https://svelte.dev/repl/7c8a6f2f0dff4f82a998bbff608c890a?version=3.59.2`.

DEMO – ADDING THEME MANAGER SUPPORT

To set up the proof of concept, follow these steps:

1. First, we need to create the folder structure for our proof of concept – for this, create a folder called themes under `\src\lib`.

2. Inside this folder, create two subfolders – one called `Button` and the other called `Button-Themed`.

3. With the folder structure in place, we can now start adding code – open a new file, then add this block, saving it as `Button.js` in the `\src\lib\themes\Button` folder:

```
<svelte:options customElement = "garnet-button" />
<button class="bg-primary">Checkout</button>
```

4. Next, we need to create the theme manager support component – for this, open a new file and then add this code:

```
<script>
   export let primary = '255, 0, 0';
   export let smallBorder = '2px';
</script>

<div style={
   `--theme-primary: ${primary};` +
   `--theme-small-border: ${smallBorder};`
}>
```

```
  <slot/>
</div>

<style>
  :global(h1) {
    color: rgb(var(--theme-primary));
    border: var(--theme-small-border) solid black;
  }
  :global(.bg-primary) {
    background-color: rgba(var(--theme-primary), .2);
  }
</style>
```

5. Save the file as Theme.js in the \src\lib\themes folder.
   With that component now in place, we can begin to use it – we
   will do so in a Storybook decorator file. Open a new document
   in your editor, then add this code:

```
<script>
  import Theme from '../Theme.svelte'

  let theme;
  theme = {primary: '0, 255, 0', smallBorder: '4px'};
</script>

<div>
  <Theme {...theme}>
    <slot />
  </Theme>
</div>
```

6. Save the file as ButtonDecorator.svelte in the \src\
   lib\themes\Button-Themed folder.

7. We're almost done with the code – there are two more files
    to add! The next one is for Storybook support – this follows a
    similar format to others we've created earlier in the book. Crack
    open a new file, then add this code, starting with defining some
    imports and two constants:

```
import Button from "../Button/Button.svelte";
import ButtonDecorator from "./ButtonDecorator.svelte";
import { BADGE } from "storybook-addon-badges";

const BADGES = {
  ...BADGE,
  ALPHA: "Alpha",
};

const meta = {
  title: "Garnet UI Library Themed/Button",
  decorators: [() => ButtonDecorator],
  parameters: {
    badges: [],
  },
};
```

8. Next up comes the default fallback template for Storybook:

```
export default {
  title: "Garnet UI Library Themed/Button",
  component: Button,
  ...meta,
};
```

9. We end with the base variant and parameters block to display
    an Alpha badge and code used:

```
export const Default = (args) => ({
  Component: Button,
```

```
    props: {
      ...args,
    },
  });

  Default.parameters = {
    badges: [BADGES.ALPHA],
    docs: { source: { type: "code" } },
  };
```

10. Last but by no means least, we need a copy of the
    documentation file for this component – go ahead and extract
    a copy of Docs.mdx from the code download for this book and
    drop it into the \src\lib\themes\Button-Themed folder.

11. Save and close everything. Revert to a Node.js terminal
    session, then make sure the working folder is set to our Garnet
    project area.

12. At the prompt, enter npm run storybook and press Enter – if all
    is well, we should see our Button proof of concept displayed
    when browsing to http://localhost:6006 and clicking
    Garnet UI Themed Library ➤ Button ➤ Default (Figure 12-2).

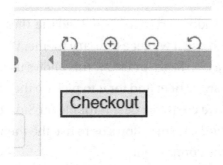

Figure 12-2. *Preview of the themed button in Storybook*

Phew – for a simple demo, there were a lot of changes! Admittedly, some of these are similar to what we've done before, so we'd expect to have to add something similar for any new components we create. That said, this demo highlights some critical points about how we might add theme support, so let's take a moment to explore them in more detail.

Understanding What We Changed

When I started to research the updates for this edition of this book, one of the topics I wanted to cover was theme support – at face value, it looked like a sensible addition to the library. However, the more I delved into the code changes, the more it became less attractive as an option!

Even though we created a proof of concept, we've had to make what looks like a fair few changes in this last demo – it has raised the question of whether this is the right thing to do (and I'll come back to this in a moment). For now, though, let's consider the changes we had to make. We began by setting up a new folder structure so that it didn't conflict with the core components (at least for now).

We then moved on to creating a simple Button component – I was keen to keep this part as a proof of concept, so creating something quick and dirty outside of the core folders means we can do things without getting in the way of our library.

Next came the trickier part – we assembled the `Theme.js` file, which includes the styling to use if we set a `primary` theme. We can see it using CSS variables, such as `--theme-primary`; this allows us to pass in values from props into our style sheet and for it to pick up the changes. To show off using the theme, we created a decorator file for Storybook called `ButtonDecorator.svelte`. This allows us to use the theme in Storybook without modifying the component.

To finish, we added a Storybook file for the new component – this shows off the Default variant of the button, currently set to show a (less than ideal) shade of green. Granted, it's not consistent with our current theme color, but hey – this is a proof of concept!

"And Now to Answer That Question…"

Yes, indeed – it's time to come back to that so-called sting of why adding theme support may not be such a useful idea. Let me explain what I mean.

When it comes to adding features, I'm sure you will agree that we can always add them as a *technical* exercise, but doing so may not necessarily be the right thing to do. In this case, while researching the code for this edition of the book, it got me thinking about whether adding theme support would be sensible for our library:

- What is a theme? It's just providing properties such as font-size or color, so would this be set at a component level or (more likely) at the site level?

- How do we deal with overriding existing properties? The option we created had used :global, which potentially would be needed but is likely to create issues around styling specificity.

- When creating a theme, it's too easy to become opinionated about what a theme should look like or offer – is this right? People may use the components, but they could be put off if they present an issue that requires extra code to circumvent.

- Remember how I touched on whether we should use $$restprops in our components or make sure our components offer the right props explicitly? The previous comment about what a theme is ties into this – we can use $$restprops to tell Svelte to accept any props not expressly provided, but this can lead to poor optimization, as Svelte doesn't know what to expect. Instead, it would be better to offer explicit props, including any we might otherwise include in a theme.

- At a basic level, a theme is just providing properties such as font-size or color – do we need a theme manager for this, or would a simpler option be to make sure that the component offers the right props instead?

There is one overriding question that trumps all of the above – do we need to invent the wheel? While researching for this book, I came across many examples of how developers had written theme components, such as the one we've used in this chapter.

However, it seems (at least for now) that no one has written anything about theme manager support for *web components* – therein lies the difference: Does this mean it's not possible, or is it even needed? Remember that this component library is designed to work with other frameworks and Svelte, so would adding theme support work anyway? I think it would be much better to focus on providing components that work reliably and consistently across different frameworks and let those using them deal with theming – they will know what they need. If required, we can tweak properties to suit if they need to change!

Summary

All good things must come to an end sometime...

Although I can't proclaim to know who said these wise words, their meaning is very true – sadly, we have indeed come to the end of our adventure with Svelte Web Components! We've covered a lot over the last few pages of this book, so let's take a moment to review what we have learned.

We began this chapter with a look at reviewing the site – we learned that it's essential to have that final check over our content to ensure we don't let any (at least apparent) mistakes fall through into production. At the same time, we understood that this step acts as a way to sign off the content – we can treat it as confirmation that development has finished and we're ready to move our code into production.

Next up, we then talked about setting a road map – I highlighted the importance of basing this around two critical decisions: what you want to see in it as the library author and what it might be used for if working in a corporate environment. We then started converting what would be our next component – this time, we based it on one written initially in React while learning that understanding the component's functionality is a better way to translate it into an equivalent in Svelte than simply doing a "lift and shift."

We then finished by exploring a proof of concept for adding a theme manager to our library. We worked through some example code before discussing how, even though it might be a nice feature to have, there are several reasons why it may not be the right thing to implement in a web components library.

Phew – we have come to the end of our adventure! I've had a great time building and writing this book – it's had its ups and downs while highlighting that Svelte is still a relatively new technology with a few quirks. But hey – all frameworks create their little quirks over time; it's just a case of learning how to get around them to achieve your desired result. I hope you've enjoyed the content and found something helpful, as much as I have, and that you can put it to good use in your future projects.

Index

A

Accessibility, 262, 295
  chrome extension, 299–303
  expectations, 298, 299
  experiment, 296–298
  testing, 295
Accordion, 90, 96, 256, 261, 293
Accordion component
  adding with Storybook, 91–94
  code reviewing, 95
  creation, 85–90
  JSON file, 90
  unitary components, 90
AccordionItem, 87, 90, 91
Accordion.stories.js, 94
Accordion.svelte, 87, 90
ActiveTabValue, 120, 123, 124
Alarm component
  code breaking, 212, 213
  creation, 206–212
  default story, 216
  Storybook addition, 213–216
  variants, 216–219
AlarmHTML property, 314
Alert component
  basic styling, 141–146
  building, 135–140

codes, 149, 150
components to
    Storybook, 142–145
icons, 134
reality, 140
statement, 141
variants, 145–150
AlertHTML, 308
Animation components, 195
  alarm component, 206–219
  cubic-bezier-based, 195
  progress bar, 196–206
  switch component, 220–229
App.svelte app, 277
App.svelte file, 275
argTypes, 43, 70, 103, 116, 144, 171,
    249, 251
aria-label attribute, 313
aria-labelledby attribute, 313
autofocus, 316
Avatar components, 366
  code, 371, 372
  creation, 367–371
  documentation file, 380
  public folder, 381
  scenario, 381
  Storybook, 372–380

Printed in the United States
by Baker & Taylor Publisher Services

Printed in the United States
by Baker & Taylor Publisher Services